Transformative Language Learning and Teaching

Transformative learning has been widely used in the field of adult education for over 20 years and yet until recently has received little attention in the field of world languages. Drawing on best practices and the research of distinguished international world language experts, this volume provides theoretical and classroom-tested models of transformative education in world languages in major university, state, and governmental programs. Chapters outline theoretical frameworks and detail successful models from cutting-edge programs in a wide range of languages, with plenty of examples included to make the theory accessible to readers not yet familiar with the concepts. Classroom teachers, program administrators, and faculty developers at every level of instruction will find support for their courses. With its innovative approach to the teaching and learning of languages, this volume is a seminal text in transformative language learning that will stimulate discussions and innovation in the language field for years to come.

Betty Lou Leaver is former Provost of the Defense Language Institute Foreign Language Center (DLIFLC), where her programs earned the American Association of University Administrators' 2016 Khaladjan International Award for Innovation in Higher Education. Author or editor of 20 books, including *Developing Professional-Level Language Proficiency (2004),* Leaver provides workshops for the US Embassy Speaker program, served as DLIFLC liaison to the North Atlantic Treaty Organization (NATO) Bureau of International Language Cooperation, and has administered programs for the National Aeronautics and Space Administration's (NASA's) International Space Station, New York Institute of Technology (NYIT) in Jordan, and the U.S. Foreign Service Institute.

Dan E. Davidson, Director of the American Councils Research Center (ARC) and Emeritus Professor of Russian at Bryn Mawr College, has written extensively on Russian corpus linguistics and the impact of immersion learning on the linguistic and cultural development of second language learners. In 2015, he was appointed to the Commission on Languages, American Academy of Arts and Sciences, is a member of the Russian and Ukrainian Academies of Education, and Vice- President of the International Association of Teachers of Russian (MAPRIAL).

Christine Campbell is President of Campbell Language Consultants and Professor Emerita of the DLIFLC, where she was Associate Provost. She is former President of the American Association of the Teachers of Spanish and Portuguese (AATSP) and recipient of its 2020 Distinguished Leadership Award. Named a Distinguished Alumna by Purdue University in 1994, she served as Chair of the AATSP Task Force Committee, which oversaw the revision of the World Readiness Standards in Spanish.

Transformative Language Learning and Teaching

Edited by

Betty Lou Leaver

Provost, Defense Language Institute Foreign Language Center (retired)

Dan E. Davidson

American Councils for International Education
Emeritus Professor, Bryn Mawr College

Christine Campbell

Emeritus Professor, Defense Language Institute Foreign Language Center

CAMBRIDGE
UNIVERSITY PRESS

CAMBRIDGE
UNIVERSITY PRESS

University Printing House, Cambridge CB2 8BS, United Kingdom

One Liberty Plaza, 20th Floor, New York, NY 10006, USA

477 Williamstown Road, Port Melbourne, VIC 3207, Australia

314–321, 3rd Floor, Plot 3, Splendor Forum, Jasola District Centre,
New Delhi – 110025, India

79 Anson Road, #06-04/06, Singapore 079906

Cambridge University Press is part of the University of Cambridge.

It furthers the University's mission by disseminating knowledge in the pursuit of education,
learning, and research at the highest international levels of excellence.

www.cambridge.org
Information on this title: www.cambridge.org/9781108836098
DOI: 10.1017/9781108870788

© Cambridge University Press 2021

First published 2021

A catalogue record for this publication is available from the British Library.

Library of Congress Cataloging-in-Publication Data

NAMES: Leaver, Betty Lou, editor. | Davidson, Dan E. editor. | Campbell,
 Christine, 1952- editor.
TITLE: Transformative language learning and teaching / [edited by] Betty
 Lou Leaver, Dan E. Davidson, Christine Campbell.
DESCRIPTION: New York : Cambridge University Press, 2020. | Includes
 bibliographical references and index.
IDENTIFIERS: LCCN 2020030983 (print) | LCCN 2020030984 (ebook) | ISBN
 9781108836098 (hardback) | ISBN 9781108799348 (paperback) | ISBN
 9781108870788 (ebook)
SUBJECTS: LCSH: Language and languages--Study and teaching (Adult
 education) | Language and languages--Study and teaching--Foreign
 speakers. | Language teachers--Training of. | Transformative learning.
CLASSIFICATION: LCC P51 .T73 2020 (print) | LCC P51 (ebook) | DDC
 418.0071--dc23
LC record available at https://lccn.loc.gov/2020030983
LC ebook record available at https://lccn.loc.gov/2020030984

ISBN 978-1-108-83609-8 Hardback
ISBN 978-1-108-79934-8 Paperback

Contents

Figures

Tables

Contributors

Christine Campbell (PhD, Purdue University) is President of Campbell Language Consultants, having worked in a variety of positions at the DLIFLC before retiring as Associate Provost. In her last position there, she headed a directorate that practiced transformative teaching and learning. She has been a member of several editorial boards and has provided service to the profession as President of the American Association of the Teachers of Spanish and Portuguese and as Chair of the Task Force Committee, whose purpose is to revise the World Readiness Standards in Spanish. She was also Director of Test Development for the National Spanish Examinations and a member of the Board of Governors of the UC Consortium for Language Learning and Teaching. She received the Civilian of the Year Award for the Ninth Region from the Association of the United States Army in 1996 and was named Distinguished Alumna by Purdue University in 1994.

Stéphane Charitos (PhD, University of North Carolina at Chapel Hill) is Director of the Language Resource Center at Columbia University. He has given papers and published in areas as diverse as sixteenth- and twentieth-century French and francophone literature, cultural and film studies, modern Greek studies, and critical theory, and on issues related to technology, globalization, and language education. He is the Principal Investigator on the Shared Course Initiative, a project funded by the Mellon Foundation to teach less commonly taught languages collaboratively among Columbia, Cornell, and Yale universities.

Emilie Cleret (MA, Sorbonne Université, Paris) is Head of the English Department within the *Enseignement militaire supérieur* (French Higher Military Education). She designs the English courses for the *École de guerre* (French War College) and for the *Centre des hautes études militaires* (higher command and staff course). She implemented transformative pedagogy in the French War College in 2016 and published an article about this transformation, "Transformation at the learner, teacher, and instruction levels: One teacher's story at the French War College," in *Dialog on Language Instruction* in 2017.

Ray Clifford (PhD, University of Minnesota) has held positions as Associate Dean of the College of Humanities at Brigham Young University (BYU), Director of the BYU Center for Language Studies, and Chancellor of the

DLIFLC. He designed the tests and research that first empirically validated the major proficiency scales for reading and listening, and has published extensively on foreign language teaching and testing. He has served as president of the American Council on the Teaching of Foreign Languages, president of the National Federation of Modern Language Teachers Associations, and chair of the NATO Bureau for International Language Coordination, where he continues to serve as senior advisor. The Fédération Internationale des Professeurs de Langues Vivant (FIPLV), an official partner nongovernment organization (NGO) with the United Nations Educational, Scientific, and Cultural Organization (UNESCO), presented him with the FIPLV International Award, and he was awarded the Vice President of the United States National Performance Review "Hammer Award" for reinventing government.

Jérôme Collin (PhD candidate, Sorbonne Université, Paris) is Head of the French Department in the French War College. He also teaches French to foreign officers in the Center for Advanced Military Studies. He is currently writing his dissertation with Professor Philippe Monneret at the Sorbonne University in Paris on the contribution of teaching grammar prototypes to progress in acquiring the four competencies. He is simultaneously studying semiotics at Sorbonne University's Graduate School of Social Sciences and has coauthored a book on visual semiotics with J. M. Floch, *A reading of Rublev's Trinity* (2009).

Andrew R. Corin (PhD, UCLA) is Professor Emeritus at the DLIFLC, where his most recent position was Associate Provost and Director of the Office of Standardization and Academic Excellence. He served previously as Dean of Resident Education and Dean of Educational Support Services in the Directorate of Continuing Education (DLIFLC's directorate for advanced courses, distance learning, and nonresident education). Previous positions included: Adjunct Associate Professor of Slavic Languages and Literatures, UCLA; Research Officer with the International Criminal Tribunal for the Former Yugoslavia; and Assistant Professor of Russian and Linguistics at Pomona College. He is the author of numerous publications and presentations in Slavic linguistics, philology and cultural history, foreign language instruction, and the investigation of violations of international humanitarian law.

Cori Crane (PhD, Georgetown University) is Associate Professor of Practice in the Department of Germanic Languages and Literature at Duke University. Her research interests closely align to her curriculum development and teacher mentoring work, with recent and current projects located in the areas of graduate student-teacher education, literacy-based instruction, reflective teaching and learning, and transformative learning. She is coeditor (with Carl Niekerk) of *Approaches to Ali and Nino: Love, identity, and transcultural conflict* (Camden House, 2017) and coauthor (with Heidi Hamilton and Abigail Bartoshesky) of *Doing foreign language: Bringing Concordia Language Villages to language classrooms* (Prentice Hall, 2005). Her publications have appeared in *L2 Journal, Die Unterrichtspraxis/Teaching German, Profession, The Language Educator*, and various American Association of University Supervisors, Coordinators, and Directors of Language Programs (AAUSC) volumes. Her publications relate to transformative learning, a focus on structured reflection, and the value of disorienting dilemmas in language instruction.

Dan E. Davidson (PhD, Harvard University) is Director of the American Councils Research Center, President Emeritus of American Councils for International Education (Washington, DC), and Emeritus Professor of Russian and Second Language Acquisition, Myra T. Cooley Lectureship, Bryn Mawr College. His 68 authored/coauthored scholarly articles focus primarily on Russian, second language acquisition, and international education development, including "Assessing language proficiency and intercultural development in the overseas immersion context," in Evans-Romaine and Murphy (eds.), *Exploring the U.S. Language Flagship program* (Multilingual Matters, 2016). In 2015, he was appointed to the Commission on Languages, American Academy of Arts and Sciences, and is an elected member of the Russian Academy of Education and the Ukrainian Academy of Pedagogical Sciences, Vice-President of the International Association of Teachers of Russian (MAPRIAL), and past Chair of the College Board World Languages Advisory Committee, the Joint National Committee for Languages, and the Alliance for International Education Exchange.

Karen Evans-Romaine (PhD, University of Michigan) is Professor of Russian in the Department of German, Nordic, & Slavic, University of Wisconsin–Madison (UW-Madison), and Director of the UW-Madison Russian Flagship program. She served as Director of the Middlebury College Kathryn Wasserman Davis School of Russian and of the Ohio University Spring Quarter in Moscow program. Her research focuses on Russian literature, particularly intersections between literature and music, and Russian language pedagogy. She is: coauthor, together with Richard Robin and Galina Shatalina, of the two-volume introductory Russian textbook *Golosa* (*Voices*, Pearson); coeditor, with Dianna Murphy, of *Exploring the US Language Flagship program: Professional competence in a second language by graduation* (Multilingual Matters); and coeditor, with Tatiana Smorodinskaya and Helena Goscilo, of the Routledge *Encyclopedia of contemporary Russian culture*. She has taught

Russian language and culture at all levels, Russian literature in Russian and English, and Slavic language pedagogy.

Amer Farraj (MS, California State University at Monterey Bay) is an independent scholar and teacher of Arabic for US government programs. Prior to working in this position, he served as the Department Chair of Arabic in the School of Resident Education, Directorate of Continuing Education (CE), DLIFLC, specializing in advanced levels of Arabic language proficiency through the development of near-native skills. He also worked as an Arabic instructor in the Distance Learning Division of CE at DLIFLC.

Donald C. Fischer, Jr. (PhD, University of New Mexico), Professor Emeritus and retired Provost at the Defense Language Institute, teaches in the Master of Instructional Science and Technology program at the California State University at Monterey Bay. He has also served as University of New Mexico Project Manager for the National Telecommunications and Information Agency Hispanic Educational Telecommunications System, Northern New Mexico Network for Rural Education, the Star Schools Navajo Education Technology Consortium projects, and as Executive Director of Albuquerque's cable access Teach and Learn Network. Prior to that, he served as Commandant of the DLIFLC and as a logistics management officer in the United States Army, retiring as a colonel.

Ted Fleming (EdD, Teachers College, Columbia University) is Adjunct Associate Professor of Adult Education at Teachers College, New York, where he studied with Mezirow as his tutor. He also worked with Paulo Freire in Boston. He is External Advisor to the Greek Municipality of Larissa's UNESCO-funded Learning City project. He received the Jack Mezirow Theory of Transformative Learning Award for "original contribution to the theory of learning," writing on Axel Honneth, and delivered the first Mezirow Memorial Lecture at Columbia University in 2016. He is a retired senior academic and Head of Adult Education Department at Maynooth University, Ireland. He is a member of the International Expert Panel advising the Irish government's Further Education and Training Authority (SOLAS) on including student voice in adult education services. Recent books include, with Kokkos and Finnegan, *European perspectives on transformation theory* (Palgrave, 2019) and, with Murphy, *Habermas, critical theory and education* (Routledge, 2012).

Sally Rice Fox (MA, California State University at San Marcos) recently retired as Coordinator of the San Diego County Office of Education, where she specialized in integrated and designated English language development

(ELD), dual language immersion, and world languages. Prior to that, she was the Lead English Learner Resource Teacher for La Mesa-Spring Valley, where she became a certified trainer for Project GLAD® (Guided Language Acquisition Design). She began her career in education as a Spanish–English bilingual 3rd grade teacher in Imperial Beach, CA. She served on the Board of the California Association for Bilingual Education and has published articles for the National Association for Bilingual Education, Dual Language Education New Mexico, and a Mandarin resources website. She recently served as a cochair of the World Languages Standards Advisory Committee for the California Department of Education.

Nadra Garas (MPA, American University in Cairo) is Director of Institutional Research and Chief of Survey Research at American Councils for International Education. She is the principal author of the *K-16 national foreign language enrollment survey* (2017) and coauthor of academic publications on survey design, research methods, and case-study and quantitative analysis. She conducts research on language learning and intercultural development, assessments, and survey design and survey research methods. She has coauthored articles on language acquisition, intercultural development, and survey methods. She is responsible for coordinating and conducting research, program evaluations, large-scale data collection, and research grants held by American councils. Garas is an Intercultural Development Inventory (IDI)-qualified administrator and works extensively on IDI-related data analysis.

Thomas Jesús Garza (EdD, Harvard University) is UT Regents' and University Distinguished Teaching Associate Professor of Slavic and Eurasian Studies at the University of Texas at Austin. He is also Director of the Texas Language Center. He teaches, conducts research, and publishes on Russian language and culture, foreign language pedagogy, and comparative cultures. His research has been published in journals including *Foreign Language Annals*, *Russian Language Journal*, *Modern Language Journal*, and *Slavic and East European Journal*, and he has authored several Russian and English as a second language (ESL) textbooks, and contributed chapters to numerous compilations. He has led, and continues to lead, study abroad programs to Russia since 1981 under the auspices of the American Council of Teachers of Russian, of which he is current president. During his 28-year tenure at the University of Texas, he served as department chair for six years and director of a Title VI National Resource Center (NRC) for eight.

Jason Goulah (PhD, State University of New York, Buffalo) is Professor of Bilingual-Bicultural Education and Director of the Institute for Daisaku Ikeda

Studies in Education at DePaul University in Chicago, IL, as well as Executive Advisor at the Ikeda Center for Peace, Learning and Dialogue in Cambridge, MA. At DePaul, he also directs programs in bilingual-bicultural education, world language education, and value-creating education for global citizenship. He is a former high school teacher of Japanese, ESL, and Russian as foreign and heritage languages, and has conducted curriculum and professional development for Chicago Public Schools, New York City Schools, and other school districts. His books include, among others, *Daisaku Ikeda, Language and education*, which received the 2015 American Educational Studies Association (AESA) Critics Choice Book Award, *Makiguchi Tsunesaburo in the context of language, identity and education*, and *TESOL and sustainability*. He received the 2009 Northeast Conference on Teaching Foreign Language (NECTFL) Stephen A. Freeman Award for his work on transformative language learning.

Stacey Margarita Johnson (EdD, University of Memphis) is Assistant Director of the Center for Teaching and Senior Lecturer in the Department of Spanish and Portuguese at Vanderbilt University. She is also the Editor of *Spanish and Portuguese Review* and producer of the podcast "We teach languages." Stacey's research focuses on classroom practices, hybrid/blended instruction, professional development, and adult learning. She is the author of *Hybrid language teaching in practice: Perceptions, reactions, and results*, coauthored with Berta Carrasco (2015), and *Adult learning in the language classroom* (2015), a monograph that explores transformative learning through language study. She is currently working on a coedited collection entitled *How we take action: Social justice in a K-16 language classroom* with Kelly Davidson and L. J. Randolph and a coauthored book on problem-based language learning with Claire Knowles.

Erin Kearney (PhD, University of Pennsylvania) is Associate Professor of Foreign and Second Language Education at the State University of New York at Buffalo, where she works with novice language teachers and future applied linguists. Her work, ranging from preschool settings to K-12 schools and university-level classrooms, appears in the *Modern Language Journal*, *Language Awareness*, *Foreign Language Annals*, the *Journal of Second Language Writing*, and a book to be published with Multilingual Matters, *Intercultural learning in modern language education: Expanding meaning-making potentials*. She has received research funding three times through the American Council on the Teaching of Foreign Languages (ACTFL) research priorities program, has served on the ACTFL Board of Directors, and is an active advocate at state and national levels for world languages education.

Jeff King (EdD, University of North Texas) is the Executive Director of the Center for Excellence in Transformative Teaching and Learning at the University of Central Oklahoma (UCO). Concurrently, he is directing a $7.8 million Title III Strengthening Institution Programs grant for a student transformative learning record and leading the Transformative Learning International Collaborative, a group of 16 (and growing) institutions around the world interested in target language (TL) instructional practice and the development of graduates motivated and equipped to contribute to the social good. Prior to his position at UCO, he served as Director of the Koehler Center for Teaching Excellence at Texas Christian University. In all, he has 27 years in faculty professional development in higher education, with a focus on learning-centered pedagogy/andragogy (including transformative learning), the authentic assessment of learning outcomes, high-impact practices, the assessment of teaching effectiveness, and related topics.

Deborah J. Kramlich (PhD, European School of Culture and Theology) is a Visiting Postdoctoral Research Associate at Payap University and an English teacher at the Christliche Deutsche Schule, both in Chiang Mai, Thailand. Additionally, she lectures on intercultural communication, as well as educational theories and instructional design, and consults with schools and non-profits to implement principles of transformative learning in their curriculum and instruction. She has written a curriculum on academic reading and intercultural adjustment for the Europäische Fernhochschule Hamburg and taught English in four countries, ranging from primary school to university. Her PhD research focused on teachers fostering and facilitating transformative learning through their person and practice in European theological schools.

Cornelius (Neil) C. Kubler (PhD, Cornell University) is Stanfield Professor of Asian Studies at Williams College and Distinguished Research Fellow in the Institute for Advanced Studies in Humanities and Social Sciences at Shaanxi Normal University. Previously, he served as Mandarin, Cantonese, and Japanese Language Training Supervisor and Chair of the Department of Asian & African Languages at the Foreign Service Institute, US Department of State. Additionally, for six years, he was Director of the advanced Chinese field school in Taipei. He served from 2014 to 2016 as American Co-Director of the Hopkins-Nanjing Center and has directed intensive Chinese language training programs in the USA, China, and Taiwan. Author or coauthor of 31 books and over 60 articles on Chinese language pedagogy and linguistics, he has trained hundreds of Chinese and Japanese language instructors in the USA, Asia, and Europe.

Betty Lou Leaver (PhD, Pushkin Institute, Moscow) is Director of the Literary Center of San Juan Bautista. She previously served as Provost, Associate Provost, and Dean at the DLIFLC. She established the language program for the International Space Station (NASA), and served as a language training supervisor at the Foreign Service Institute, curriculum developer for the Federal Foreign Language Training Lab. She was Dean at the New York Institute of Technology in Jordan, President of the American Global Studies Institute, Co-Director of the Center for the Advancement of Distinguished Language Proficiency at San Diego State University, and Founding Director of the Center for the Languages of the Central Asian Region at Indiana University. She has published 21 books and more than 100 articles. Her transformative education efforts at DLIFLC received the 2015 Nikolai Khardajian Award for Innovation in International Education by the American Association of University Administrators.

Maria D. Lekic (PhD, University of Pennsylvania) is Academic Director of the Russian Overseas Flagship, American Councils for International Education (Washington, DC), and retired Associate Professor of Russian, University of Maryland, College Park. Dr. Lekic is author or coauthor of several research studies concerned with the assessment of language and cultural proficiency at the advanced levels, principal designer of the Russian Overseas Flagship "Level 3 curriculum," and coauthor of several widely used textbooks of Russian, including the two-volume video-based *Live from Russia!* (Kendall/Hunt). She is a recipient of the A. S. Pushkin Medal for distinguished service to the study and teaching of Russian.

David Little (DEd, National University of Ireland) retired in 2008 as Associate Professor of Applied Linguistics and Head of the School of Linguistic, Speech and Communication Sciences at Trinity College Dublin. He has published extensively on the theory and practice of learner autonomy in L2 education, the management of linguistic diversity in schools and classrooms, and the use of the *Common European Framework of Reference for Languages* to support the design of L2 curricula, teaching, and assessment. From 1998 to 2010, he played a leading role in the development and implementation of the Council of Europe's European Language Portfolio at national and European levels. From 2000 to 2008, he was non-stipendiary Director of Integrate Ireland Language and Training, which was funded by the Irish government to support the teaching of English to adult refugees and immigrant children and adolescents.

Mary Ann Lyman-Hager (PhD, University of Idaho) is Professor Emerita of European Studies and French at San Diego State University (SDSU), where she directed a national Language Resource Center. She served on the editorial boards of *Foreign Language Annals*, *CALICO Journal*, and *Language Learning and Technology*, the Executive Board of *CALICO*. She served on the SDSU Research Foundation Advisory Board and is currently on the Alumni Board of Directors of Cornell College. She is the author of numerous articles in the field of language acquisition and technology. She was a program reviewer for many colleges and universities, as well as on dissertation committees, both nationally and internationally. She was awarded the outstanding faculty award (Monty) for the College of Arts and Letters at San Diego State in 2016 and the Hal Wingard Lifetime Achievement Award by the California Language Teachers' Association in 2017.

Dianna Murphy (PhD, Ohio State University) is Director of the Language Institute at UW-Madison. She is also Associate Director of the UW-Madison Russian Flagship, Executive Director of the Korean Flagship, and a core member of the PhD Program in Second Language Acquisition. Murphy's research has been published in the *ADFL Bulletin*, *Foreign Language Annals*, *Frontiers: The Interdisciplinary Journal of Study Abroad*, the *Modern Language Journal*, and the *Russian Language Journal*. Her publications also include the 2016 coedited volume (with Karen Evans-Romaine), *Exploring the U.S. Language Flagship program: Professional competence in a second language by graduation* (Multilingual Matters), and the 2014 coauthored *Modern Language Journal* monograph (with Sally Magnan and Narek Sahakyan) *Goals of collegiate learners and the standards for foreign language learning*, based on a survey of over 16,000 US postsecondary foreign language students.

Martha Nyikos (PhD, Purdue University) is Coordinator of World Languages & ESL Teacher Education at Indiana University in Bloomington, Indiana. Trilingual in Hungarian, German, and English, she has taught elementary and high school German and ESL and is the academic-year pedagogical coordinator for Bridges: Children, Language, World, a joint Title VI community outreach program for children without access to learning world languages. She has served on the editorial board of the *Modern Language Journal* and the Indiana State Standards Committee. Since 2001, she has taught strategies-based instruction for CARLA's summer institute, University of Minnesota, and has received three federal-funded STARTALK grants to train teachers of less commonly taught languages. The focus of her current research is on oral language development in young dual-language learners and on parental support of heritage language maintenance. Coupled with her research on teacher agency, she provides teacher professional development internationally.

Rebecca L. Oxford (PhD, University of North Carolina) is Professor Emerita and Distinguished Scholar-Teacher, University of Maryland, and now teaches as an adjunct professor at the University of Alabama at Birmingham. A Lifetime Achievement Award stated, "Oxford's research changed the way the world teaches languages." She has published extensively, including 14 books and many articles focused on: strategic, self-regulated language learning; transformative education; peace education and peacebuilding in language learning; spiritual paradigms for research; language learning motivation; and methods for language teaching. She coedits two book series: *Spirituality, Religion, and Education* (Palgrave/Springer) and *Transforming Education for the Future* (Information Age Publishing). Earlier, she edited the *Tapestry* book series (Heinle/Cengage), containing 69 innovative ESL/English as a foreign language (EFL) textbooks with versions for North America, the Middle East, and the Far East. She was a Fulbright Specialist in Costa Rica, held honorary positions at two Chinese universities, and has presented her work in 45 countries.

Shannon Salyer (PhD, University of Tennessee) is the National Program Manager of the Armed Services Vocational Aptitude Battery (ASVAB) Career Exploration Program and Department of Defense Language Testing in the Defense Manpower Data Center's Office of People Analytics. Prior to that, she worked as a senior research scientist for the DLIFLC. Additionally, she has taught courses in psychology at Pfeiffer University and the University of Tennessee.

Farid Saydee (PhD in Education, Claremont Graduate University & San Diego State University Joint Program) is the Founder/President of Language Mentors International, where he provides educational consultancy services to institutions of higher education throughout the nation. He has served for over ten years at the Language Acquisition Resource Center (LARC), SDSU, as Associate Director and Director of Instruction. In addition, he is an ACTFL mentor, quality assurance analyst, and proficiency tester/rater (ACTFL Assessment of Performance toward Proficiency in Language [AAPPL], Oral Proficiency Interview [OPI], Oral Proficiency Test by Computer [OPIC], Writing Proficiency Test [WPT]). His areas of focus are curriculum and instruction as related to second language acquisition and transformative learning. He has published several scholarly articles and is the principal author or coauthor of three textbooks in Pashto and two in Dari.

Michael J. Sosulski (PhD, University of Chicago) is Provost and Professor of German at Wofford College in Spartanburg, SC. Prior to assuming this role, he taught at Kalamazoo College in Southwest Michigan and Pacific Lutheran

University (Tacoma, WA). His scholarly interests range from the teaching and learning of German as a foreign language to performance studies, and include in-depth explorations of early modern German theatrical traditions (*Theatre and nation in eighteenth-century Germany* [Ashgate Press, 2007]), as well as the transculturation of American hip-hop music in German-speaking Europe. His article "From Broadway to Berlin: Transformative learning through German hip-hop" (*Die Unterrichtspraxis/Teaching German*, 46[1], Spring 2013) was awarded Best Article in *UP* for that year. He has taught courses that cover all aspects of German language acquisition, as well as German theatre and film.

Nelleke Van Deusen-Scholl (PhD, University of Florida) is Associate Dean of Yale College, Director of the Center for Language Study, and Adjunct Professor of Linguistics at Yale University. Her research interests focus on applied linguistics, sociolinguistics, heritage language learning, and technology-enhanced language teaching and learning. She is coeditor, with Nina Spada, of the book series *Language Learning and Language Teaching* (John Benjamins). Current publications include an edited book, *Second and foreign language education* (Volume 4 of the *Encyclopedia of language and education*, with Stephen May), and coauthored chapters with Stéphane Charitos: "Engaging the city: Language, space, and identity in urban environments" (AAUSC Volume 2017) and "The shared course initiative: Curricular collaboration across institutions" (AAUSC Volume 2016). Her most recent publication is "Heritage language education in a distance environment: Creating a community of practice" in the volume *Connecting across languages and cultures. A heritage language festschrift in honor of Olga Kagan*.

Foreword

As I read these chapters, various memories came back to me. As a child, my grandmother lived in our house. She was my babysitter for five years until I went to school. I remember learning the prayers she taught me in German, her mother tongue; mine was English. *"Vater unser in Himmel"* echoes through the decades. God was German. The Grimm Brothers Fairy Tales and their Hansel and Gretel are strong memories. In the 1950s, the words opened another world, a world of imaginings, of stories, of people, and of family, at a time when Europe had not recovered from the German experience. With these words, a storied soul was formed. All the narratives were true, packed with values, ideologies, and mythologies. So vividly were the stories told that these may have been my first trips abroad. Language was at least informative and probably formative. These words forged relationships of care and recognition, and of curiosity. It was a biographical glue holding together a young identity and family with stories and interesting people and places. I might now even call it soul work. Later, my third language was Irish, the dominant language of school until university. Cicero was translated into Irish, not English. I remember in university not knowing the English words for sodium nitrate and other terms in chemistry and physics. Language, like travel, could broaden or narrow the mind! However, I always thought of other places and peoples as interesting and worth exploring.

Frames of reference seem to be constructed in these biographical and linguistic ways. One's biographical story gets transformed in transformative language learning and teaching.

Frames of reference that are constructed in an individual's life history are also embedded in a society and culture with values, histories, feeling, and ideologies. Academics or language students and scholars undertake research, develop teaching methods, create zones of proximal development, build abstract theories, read Freire, Mezirow, and Paul Tillich, and do all in the service of shifting the paradigm of teaching and learning. I have a sense that positing biographical experiences as over and against theoretical work is probably a false dichotomy. The relationship between theory and practice, thinking and doing, as well as teaching and learning, are reconfigured by Freire as *praxis*. They are also reconfigured by Dewey. This scholarly collection also locates language learning not only in the personal, the individual, and, as I suggest, the biographical, but also in the social, the historical, and the cultural domains. The social and personal collide in language teaching and learning.

Transformative learning is a structural shift in the basic premises of thought and action, and in how we make meaning. The authors in this collection bring other friends to the discussion, including Vygotsky, O'Sullivan, Rogers, and Dewey. All help to redefine learning in ways that make connections that we do not normally make. Everything is connected.

Language learning and teaching in universities has been located in faculties of humanities. If language studies are a search for meanings or for translated words, then that may be appropriate; however, in this work, a case is made for language studies as a social science. Many of the chapters are located in the context of real-world problems where everything is connected, and connected knowing is the stuff of language learning. This is not just so that social problems may be expressed and translated into different words, but so that they can be understood more thoroughly as they are located in social, economic, and political contexts and embedded in language. The climate change debate or working with refugees are good examples of how a transformative vision of language learning and teaching may be better understood. Language learning is presented as fostering citizenship in a global community of activists and thinkers determined to make the world a better place for all. In a world of translation apps, there is more at stake now. We will not "Google translate" our way forward out of these challenges.

Charlemagne (d. 814) is credited with saying that "to have a second language is to have a second soul," and Dirkx, a named ally in this collection, has defined transformative learning as soul work. Transformative language learning and teaching may be soul work and may be an antidote to misunderstandings and misrecognitions that define our age and that undermine self, society, and most likely the planet.

Ted Fleming

Teachers College Columbia University, New York

Acknowledgments

The editors wish to thank all of those who have made the completion of this book possible. First, foremost, and forever, we are indebted to Cambridge University Press for its willingness to take on a project that is so focused on the future of foreign language learning and teaching (not the past or even the present). We especially thank Rebecca Taylor, Acquisitions Editor at Cambridge University Press, who thoroughly understood our intent and the significance of our content, and became our strongest advocate. Her unfailing support was critical to seeing this volume through. In addition, her assistant, Isabel Collins, has held our hand through every technical step of this project, and we very much appreciate her assistance.

Likewise, we much appreciate the contribution of Carl Leaver in lending his professional graphics and typesetting skills to ensure that all figures and illustrative material submitted in support of the various chapters of this book met professional standards. His work ensured consistency and provided welcome assistance to chapter authors.

We consider it proper to acknowledge the theoretical contributions of related fields and inspiration for this volume that have come from the pioneering work of Mezirow (e.g., 1981, 1996), Fleming (e.g., 2008; Fleming et al., 2019), Cranton (e.g., 1994, 2001), and Dirkx (e.g., 1997, 2012) in adult education, Miller and Seller (1985) in curriculum and instruction, and Rogers (e.g., 1969/1986) in psychology. These influences have inspired colleagues in our field to apply transformative education concepts to their classrooms and, in this volume, to share them with the greater foreign language education field.

Several colleagues served as readers as we were pulling together the various chapters in this book, and we are very grateful to them for their insights and for catching leaps in logic, infelicitous expressions, and even typographical errors. Their efforts have helped considerably in producing a well-considered manuscript. We thank Dr. Steven Sacco and Dr. Masako Boureston for their assiduousness in reading every single chapter and providing highly helpful feedback. Others who provided feedback on a few too many chapters include Dr. Valery Belyanin, Youssef Carpenter, Dr. Patrick McAloon, Irene Krasner, Dr. Robert Lucius (USMC, Ret.), and Dr. Scott McGinnis. Their assistance is highly appreciated.

Likewise, three blind reviewers provided feedback to Cambridge University Press that we incorporated into the final version of this book. Their insights were invaluable.

Finally, we thank Dr. Michael Nugent, Defense Language and National Security Education Office, for his encouragement at key stages in the development of this volume and of our efforts in compiling it. His own work in building and promoting the National Flagship programs has been critical to the advancement of foreign language policies and practices over the past two decades.

Abbreviations

AAUSC	American Association of University Supervisors, Coordinators, and Directors of Language Programs
ACTFL	American Council on the Teaching of Foreign Languages
AI	artificial intelligence
B2	independent user
BILC	Bureau of International Language Cooperation (a NATO activity)
C1/C2	proficient user
CAEP	Council for the Accreditation of Educator Preparation
CAEP/ACTFL	Council for the Accreditation of Educator Preparation/ American Council on the Teaching of Foreign Languages
CA	culminating activity
CAL	Center for Applied Linguistics
CBI	content-based instruction
CEFR	Common European Framework of Reference (in Languages)
CEFRL	Common European Framework of Reference in Languages
CLS	Center for Language Study
CLT	communicative language teaching; also refers to communicative approaches
DLIFLC	Defense Language Institute Foreign Language Center
DLNSEO	Defense Language and National Security Education Office
DLPT	Defense Language Proficiency Test
DO	developmental orientation
EdG	École de Guerre
EFL	English as a foreign language
ESL	English as a second language
FL	foreign language
FLED	foreign language education
FSI	Foreign Service Institute
IDI	Intercultural Development Inventory
ILR	Interagency Language Roundtable
L1	first language/native language
L2	second language/target language
LARC	Language Acquisition Resource Center
LMS	learning management system

LOTE	languages other than English
NATO	North Atlantic Treaty Organization
NFLRC	National Foreign Language Resource Center
NSEP	National Security Education Program
OACD	open architecture curricular design
OECD	Organization for Economic Cooperation and Development
OG	orientation gap
OPI	Oral Proficiency Interview
PBL	project-based learning
PO	perceived orientation
ProM	project modules for language and culture learning
PTC	performance training cycle
SBI	scenario-based instruction
SDSU	San Diego State University
SLA	second language acquisition
STLR	student transformative learning record
TBI	task-based instruction
TESOL	teaching English to speakers of other languages
TL	target language
TLLT	transformative language learning and teaching
TP	transformative pedagogy
UCO	University of Central Oklahoma
USG	United States government
VALUE	Valid Assessment of Learning in Undergraduate Education
ZPD	zone of proximal development

1

Introduction

Betty Lou Leaver, Dan E. Davidson, and Christine Campbell

Transformative Language Learning and Teaching presents a new philosophy of
education for world language instruction intended for those with a commitment
to the preparation of linguistically and biculturally competent language users
who are ready to take ownership of their learning. Unlike in the field of adult
education, where transformative education has been recognized for more than
two decades, the application of transformative principles to the study and
teaching of world languages has received relatively little attention. It is the
absence of a comprehensive discussion of transformative education[1] within the
language field that has provided the impetus for the present volume.

The contributors to this collection address the existing gap in the literature by
drawing on their scholarly work and professional experience, supported, where
possible, by available empirical data. In some cases, authors report remarkable
levels of success in making use of the principles of transformative education in
their teaching practice. In other cases, they share the challenges and varying
degrees of success that they have encountered along the way. If the language
field is to make sense of transformative language learning and teaching (TLLT)
and benefit from its potential, the broad-ranging and frank discussion of the
positions, applications, and results presented in this volume will be essential.

The chapters that follow explore various strands of TLLT, some clearly
emergent or transitional, as reflected in current practice. How these strands will
become interwoven in the future is, as yet, undetermined and, to a great extent,
unpredictable. For that reason, the editors have endeavored to be comprehensive
in approaching TLLT.

1.1 General Content of the Volume

This volume offers an overview of TLLT in language programs at the current
moment. While some levels of education, for example, adult learning, certain
institutions, for example, government programs, and certain fields like overseas

---

[1] In this volume, "transformative learning" and "transformative teaching" are used
interchangeably, with "transformative education" sometimes serving as an umbrella term.

immersion (see Davidson et al., this volume) have moved into TLLT more rapidly than others, the editors have assiduously sought to include representation from a broad range of educational and proficiency levels, noting that contrary to popular misconception, TLLT is not limited to adults or to learners at the higher proficiency levels.

Thus, the volume addresses all levels of language education from pre-K through graduate school, adult learning, and teacher education in world languages, dual language immersion, English as a second language (ESL) and bilingual education. Due to the newness of the topic, substantial attention is devoted to a discussion of the principles of transformative education as applied to language and cultural acquisition, including TLLT-influenced or TLLT-based curricular and program designs, learner autonomy, cultural learning, teacher professional development, assessment, education beyond the classroom, and study abroad. This volume also includes a wide range of languages from a number of language families.

Although one cannot speak about a singular approach for transformative programs, as previously noted, common features of transformative programs are often readily identifiable. Crucial to the successful incorporation of TLLT components has been an open, accepting, and creative faculty, since curricula alone cannot create change. All educational reform ultimately begins with the classroom teacher. Common features of TLLT as currently being implemented in a variety of educational settings and reflected in the chapters in this volume include the following:[2]

- Materials and daily communications are authentic and unadapted, beginning at the earliest levels of instruction.
- The classroom is immersive. Immersion in-country reflects the typical life of the native speaker of the same age to the extent practicable.
- Personal transformation involves cognitive, emotional, and cultural shifts occurring within the individual, that is, developing self-awareness, resolving disorienting dilemmas, identifying cognitive distortions, managing emotions, and integrating two (or more) cultures on their own terms.
- Highly individualized programs are informed by learning styles and strategies and the "invisible classroom" emanating from inherent personality variables.

---

[2] These principles are not immutable rules, but examples of common features observed across the wide variety of programs in this volume. For example, Fleming, Kokkos, and Finnegan (2019) point out significant differences in transformative learning in adult education between American expressions of transformative education, which encompass not only critical reflection, but also spiritual sensibilities, and European expressions, which reflect humanism and critical social traditions.

- Open architecture curricular design (OACD) (a term taken from a parallel concept in computer design that allows for interchangeable parts) supports increasingly textbook-free classrooms as learners develop greater proficiency and teachers modify syllabi corresponding to learners' changing needs.
- The grading system uses formative assessments and feedback, with occasional summative assessments (projects, presentations, contracted assignments, and portfolios), that integrate outcome and process, instead of separating them.
- Programs empower learners to take charge of their own learning.
- Program design and supervisors empower teachers to take charge of their own classrooms as advisors, mentors, coaches, planners, and strategists (Leaver et al., 2019).

Classrooms in TLLT often take on new shapes as flexible group organization with swiveling chairs and activities outside the classroom make for generally more fluid workspaces. The classroom is less *the* location of learning and more just one *auxiliary* location of learning, where scenario-based instruction takes learners into real-life experiences or simulations.

Given the need in TLLT for assuring appropriate levels of learner autonomy, the changing needs and interests of successive groups of learners, and the predominance of standardized testing measures across the modern language fields, transformative course planners and instructors are challenged to think differently about the learning process and the curricular tools available to them for ensuring greater levels of learner ownership over the learning process.

1.2 Structure of the Volume

This volume contains seven parts: Theoretical Framework; TLLT Applications in Government Programs; TLLT Applications in University Programs; TLLT in Immersion Programs; TLLT and the Learner; TLLT and Faculty Development; and TLLT and Assessment.

1.2.1 Theoretical Framework (Part I)

Part I (Chapters 2–4) explores theories of TLLT as applied to the three major subfields of language education: world language education,[3] second language education, and bilingual education. These studies examine existing and potential linkages between widely accepted communicative teaching methods and

---

[3] Terms used for this field include *foreign language education* and *L2*. We have chosen to use the term currently preferred by the American Council on the Teaching of Foreign Languages.

transformative principles and practices. The collection does not seek to present a fixed, overarching framework for TLLT. By its nature, TLLT avoids rigidity, focusing on the personal, the idiosyncratic, and the particular needs of groupings of learners, and understanding that transformation cannot be mandated or guaranteed by fixed protocols. Through learner involvement in the learning process and flexibility in curricular experiences, TLLT prompts and allows for transformation to occur. Predicting how and when transformation will occur for any given learner in any given program is imprecise at best, being a product not only of the individual nature of transformation, but also of the current early stage of TLLT development in the language education world. This volume points out the work of early adopters, who, for the past decade or longer, have shaped TLLT programs within their institutions, where TLLT principles such as open architecture course design, discussed in detail by Campbell (this volume), Corin (this volume), and Leaver (1989), have been implemented. For the most part, it should be noted that the Russian and German fields have led the way in TLLT (see Crane & Sosulski, this volume; see also Krasner, 2018; Leaver, 2018).

Leaver describes a series of paradigm shifts in the teaching of world languages that began in the 1970s and 1980s with replacing structural methods, focused on translation and accuracy, with what has been labeled *communicative approaches*, focused on using language for transaction. Increasingly, the teaching of world languages has taken on the characteristics of transformation, pulling from the fields of psychology, sociology, and adult education.

Oxford draws upon neurobiological research and dynamic systems theory, among other disciplines, to establish several linkages between Mezirow's cognitive-analytic approach to transformative learning and Dirkx's emotional-integrative approach. Cognition and emotion are different aspects of a unitary cortical phenomenon. Transformative learning can be both cognitive and imaginative; it can be collaborative and individually based; and it can include depth psychology alongside a more practical reflective approach.

Finally, Goulah explores the multilingual turn in transformative education in the collectivist vocabulary of the Buddhist-influenced writings of Ikeda and O'Sullivan. Inner transformation toward what Ikeda (2010a) calls the "greater self" occurs most completely through dialogic meaning-making, according to Goulah, and a resulting heightened awareness of the other, rooted in the principle of the oneness of all life and the natural environment.

1.2.2 TLLT Applications in Government Programs (Part II)

Part II (Chapters 5–7) focuses on the curriculum, classroom learning, and role of the teacher as experienced in government language programs, both US and European. Government institutions have served as incubators for TLLT because of their relative wealth of resources, recurrent program cycles, relatively large numbers of participants, and strong emphasis on accountability, all helpful in researching the results of large and small curricular interventions.

Campbell provides a detailed overview of the concept of OACD. She addresses the challenges of its introduction and implementation by means of two case studies from a large-scale government language training institution.

Corin's study goes on to describe a TLLT-informed, OACD-based high-impact course template, produced by the author and his colleagues for use across various languages and proficiency levels within the same institution. In this case, the institution is the Defense Language Institute Foreign Language Center but the template would be applicable to non-government immersive-learning environments as well.

The final study in this section, by Cleret, describes the introduction and adaptation of TLLT principles within an entirely different institutional and national culture: an officer-level English language training program within the French War College, heretofore dominated by a traditional, grammar-translation teaching model. Cleret shares the challenges and successes of converting from a traditional model to a TLLT program.

1.2.3 TLLT Applications in University Programs (Part III)

Part III (Chapters 8–11) presents multiple examples of how the principles and key practices of transformative learning can be incorporated into existing university courses and programs. Johnson describes the effective use of accessible authentic cultural materials and critical reflection activities (oral and written) within existing language courses as a means of encouraging students to question their own cultural assumptions and integrate the perspectives of members of the L2 community under study.

Van Deusen-Scholl and Charitos make use of project-based learning and fieldwork research models to link the classroom directly with local multilingual and multicultural communities in order to engage students personally and critically with the social and historical spaces in which languages are used today. By comparison, Garza's chapter demonstrates the power and potential of virtual communities to stimulate cultural transformations among world language learners associated with successful study abroad, in this case, students of Russian at the University of Texas (Austin), where direct access to the L2 community is not available to the large majority of his language students.

Finally, Evans-Romaine and Murphy describe the range of academic, residential, and social learning environments, both face-to-face and virtual contexts, available within the domestic Russian Flagship program, seven of which are discussed in terms of transformative learning principles. The authors stress the importance of fostering student engagement and student agency, skills that will be critical for their success in the Russian Overseas Flagship academic-year capstone program in Kazakhstan and future careers as global professionals.

1.2.4 TLLT in Immersion Programs (Part IV)

Participant and teacher reports of "transformative experiences" in the context of study abroad learning pre-date the concept of transformative education and continue to occupy a prominent place in much of today's study abroad literature. Lessons learned from successful study abroad experiences have, in turn, informed domestic classroom teaching and vice versa, building a closed-loop feedback system that has improved both classroom and extramural programs and helped to move them in transformative directions. Part IV (Chapters 12–15) focuses on this transformative symbiosis between learning and experience.

Davidson, Garas, and Lekic examine the affordances of intercultural development during the year-long overseas Russian Flagship program at Al-Farabi Kazakh National University in Almaty. As the strongest example available in L2 in terms of long-term qualitative and quantitative data, this study takes up overseas where Evans-Romaine and Murphy's chapter leaves off in the USA, and shares examples of student reflections on disorienting dilemmas and the emergence of a more ethno-relativist and empathetic stance toward cultural differences.

Farraj looks at programs that prepare learners for study abroad experiences while in US-based government Arabic-language classrooms and then move into teacher-supported in-country experiences that focus on local community engagement and service learning, the result being documented increased proficiency, an enhanced understanding of underlying social phenomena, and changes of the native speaker in the native speaker's country through the development of work-based relationships. Likewise, Collin describes changed perceptions and deeper cultural understanding – and acceptance – of the French culture by officers from other countries studying in an immersion environment at the French War College.

Part IV ends with one of the most innovative emerging trends in K-12 education. Lyman-Hager, Fox, and Saydee examine the introduction and early-stage educational impact of Dual Language Immersion within the San Diego Public School System from a TLLT vantage point, reporting the role of TLLT in achieving necessary levels of teacher reorientation and the successes of the model, as measured by its subsequent expansion within the state of California. While K-12 learners, given their age and maturational levels, generally lack the experience with (and, some might argue, the capacity for) self-regulation, critical reflection, and learner autonomy essential to the Mezirowan formulation of transformative education, Bloom (1956) argued that children as young as age five are capable of employing higher-order thinking skills, a significant component of transformative learning, and an increasing number of K-12 teachers and teacher educators have found ways of bringing transformative learning to the elementary school level in subjects other than language (Heddy & Sinatra, 2013; Pugh et al., 2010).[4] However, one wonders whether the resolution of the deeper disorienting dilemmas created by cross-cultural encounters, especially at pre-bilingual levels of proficiency, might require a greater cognitive sophistication than can generally be expected from younger children. Carefully implemented and researched programs like the dual-language programs in San Diego therefore have the potential to inform the TLLT and K-12 fields in important ways.

1.2.5 TLLT and the Learner (Part V)

Part V (Chapters 16–20) presents the more salient learner attributes addressed in the current pedagogical literature. Authors focus on learner autonomy, learner self-efficacy, and the interplay of cognition, affect, and transformation.

Kramlich's learners are like study abroad students to some extent in that they experience the disorienting dilemmas that come from immersion experiences. However, as migrants, their "immersions" are long-term, if not lifelong, which evokes another level of response to the disorienting dilemmas experienced by those entering and embracing foreign cultures. Kramlich presents the dilemmas and suggests ways in which an aware classroom teacher can help resolve them.

Fischer uses the latest technology to promote transformative experiences. The applications he describes are effective for distance-learning programs, classroom supplementation, and independent learning. He suggests that technology can provide infrastructure and scaffolding to support transformation in learning and teaching, particularly in bringing the distant world close and opening windows (and doors) to other cultures in ways likely to create a desire for a better understanding of the culture associated with the language being studied.

Kearney further enters into the mind of the individual learner with two studies that reveal learners' meaning-making repertoires, the disorienting dilemmas that arise in learning languages and encountering new meaning-making resources, and the ways in which the classroom environment and teacher can shape a learner's perspective transformation and semiotic empowerment.

---

[4] Girod and Wong (2002, p. 211) cite one such example in which a 4th-grader, after completing a transformatively taught unit on rocks, said "I think about rocks differently than I did before."

Moving beyond meaning-making to learner understanding of and controlling the mechanisms of meaning-making and meaning-imparting, Little summarizes the origins and theoretical underpinnings of the exercise of reflective agency as a transformative conception of language learner autonomy, and describes the learning dynamic, classroom procedures, and learning outcomes to which it gives rise, with reference to teenage Danish learners of EFL and immigrant English language learners (ELLs) attending an Irish primary school.

Finally, Salyer and Leaver delve into the cognitive and affective domain, and the strategies that appear – or do not – as learners are presented with disorienting dilemmas. Their chapter illustrates various forms of cognitive distortion and affective dissonance, and suggests ways in which teachers can assist learners in remediating them as they struggle with changing perceptions arising from their attempts to resolve disorienting dilemmas.

1.2.6 TLLT and Faculty Development (Part VI)

To move into a transformative mode of instruction, faculty must have a strong belief and trust in transformative learning and the tools to deploy it in their classrooms or distance-learning and study abroad programs. While some teachers intuitively develop such tools on their own, in the experience of the editors and contributors to this volume, most teachers benefit from faculty development and the sharing of the tools. Part VI describes two programs (different languages) that seek to provide such development for teachers.

Nyikos uses features of constructivist and social cognitive theory to help preservice teachers discover, unpack, critically analyze, and share core beliefs regarding cognitive and affective dimensions of their ongoing language learning and teaching. By closely scrutinizing critical reflection as a tool for reaching transformation, she notes the process and difficulty of shifting paradigms, the strong hold of habit, the hidden classroom, and the factors that intervene.

Similarly, Kubler uses transformative aspects of teacher education to train preservice instructors of Chinese and Japanese. He also notes the difficulty of creating/accepting paradigm change, particularly in teachers who come from traditional teaching environments in China and Japan.

1.2.7 TLLT and Assessment (Part VII)

While the formative and summative assessment of linguistic and communicative skills enjoy a rich tradition in many parts of the world, there is a growing understanding among educators of the limitations of most test instruments to capture (let alone measure) the full range of critical thinking skills, cross-cultural understanding, and empathetic and socio-pragmatic skill sets that world language learners may acquire in the course of their studies. Authors contributing to Part VII (Chapters 23–25) look at testing models, self-assessment rubrics, and grading mechanisms that incorporate an assessment of transformation itself.

Beginning with the need for learner reflection and assessment in the classroom, Crane and Sosulski provide a review of best practices and guidelines for developing assessment tools that can help world language instructors identify and understand moments of perspective-shifting among their students, as well as the crucial skills that underlie the ability to transform one's meaning perspective: structured reflection, questioning strategies, narratives, and evaluation rubrics.

Clifford, who has done much to promote and refine proficiency testing, suggests that the proficiency tests currently in use are insufficient for measuring progress in transformative classrooms and suggests a new model, depending on the distance of transfer (perspective change) – whether it is "near" (less of a change) or "far" (more of a change, i.e., a greater step toward bilingualism/ biculturalism).

Finally, King shares a grading rubric for programs based on the University of Central Oklahoma's approach to transformative education, which is now in use in multiple universities in a number of countries. While originally developed for learning in general, the grading rubric provides language teachers in TLLT programs with a useful matrix that has been tested and found to be successful.

1.3 Intended Audience

With this volume, the editors and chapter authors hope to promote reflection about the next generation of pedagogical models. It is designed for new and seasoned teachers, as well as for program directors, teacher educators, and decision-makers at any educational level and in any language.

1.4 Resources

This volume contains a comprehensive reference list. Given that a compendium of works about transformative education and language learning does not exist, the editors hope that unifying chapter references will create a rich resource for anyone exploring TLLT.

PART I

Theoretical Framework

Transformative Language Learning and Teaching

The Next Paradigm Shift and Its Historical Context

Betty Lou Leaver

Many world language methodologists agree with Kumaravadivelu (2003) that the field has entered a post-method era.[1] The methods still visible in the rearview mirror are the communicative approaches, which are very much alive in many schools and universities. Lying ahead is the marginally mapped territory of transformative language learning and teaching (TLLT), a manifestation of larger changes already under way in the dominant transactive education philosophy of world language learning: in the twenty-first century, our society is viewing the importance of language and cultural competence for all citizens in a different way than in the twentieth century (American Academy of Arts & Sciences, 2017).[2]

Kuhn (1962)[3] describes a paradigm shift as a fundamental change in the concepts and accepted practices of a scientific discipline, signaling not evolution, but a revolution, in the field. In the past century, the proposition that the development of communicative competence underlay language acquisition sparked the development of successive and often overlapping waves of language teaching methods and schools, from direct method and the natural approach, to more recent communicative approaches such as task-based language teaching and content-based instruction (Bateman & Lago, n.d.), all focused essentially on the same goal: proficiency across skills within the framework of the *World-readiness standards for learning languages* (The National Standards

---

[1] This article reflects the current situation of terms in free variation: language learning, world language learning, the older foreign language education (FLED), and languages other than English (LOTE).

[2] Some second language (L2) teachers started to implement aspects of TLLT in their classrooms at least two decades before the paradigm acquired a label. In many cases, their more holistic/non-Cartesian, learner-oriented, and socially mediated approaches were not understood, not accepted, and/or resisted by peers and administrators who insisted on textbook-based learning, most often laboring under the influence of dualistic thinking (Descartes, 1668/2013) Slowly, though, their practices are being seen as necessary for transformative learning.

[3] While Kuhn is generally the philosopher credited with the term "*paradigm shift*," the concept dates from Kant (1781), who proposed the concept of revolutions in ways of thinking (*Revolution der Denkungsart*) in *Critique of pure reason.*

Collaborative Board, 2019).[4] These methods have generally been referred to as the "*communicative approach(es)*" or "*communicative language teaching*" (CLT).

CLT represented a comprehensive break with the past – a Kuhnian revolution against the earlier grammar-translation method – and was labeled by some as "the new paradigm" (Jacobs & Farrell, 2003).[5] Today, TLLT represents a break with CLT.

True paradigm shifts are revolutionary in the sense that they mark a deliberate break with the approaches and methods that preceded them. The transition may also reflect significant social or political changes impinging on the prevailing educational philosophy.

2.1 Changing Educational Philosophies: Comparing Three Paradigms

Educational philosophies inform academic goals and motivate the selection of materials, activities, and control over the learning process, while advancing a defined set of teaching and learning beliefs and practices. Since the mid-twentieth century, foreign language education (FLED) has experienced three distinct educational philosophies: transmission, transaction, and transformation (Leaver & Granoien, 2000). Table 2.1 describes the educational philosophies of *transmission*, *transaction*, and *transformation*, and how they have shaped the teaching of languages over time.

2.2 The Old Paradigm: Transmission Approaches to World Language Education

Nearly all teachers have experienced the transmission approach to FLED, if not in their own teaching practice, then as learners in transmission programs that expected learners to memorize vocabulary and know many things about the

---

[4] The *World-Readiness Standards for Learning Languages* (The National Standards Collaborative Board, 2019) present five areas (the 5 Cs) for teaching and assessment: communication, cultures, connections, comparisons, and communities.

[5] Beyond CLT, the term "*new paradigm*" has been applied at various times to new concepts in language education, such as, more recently, the focus on translingual and transcultural competence, an orientation toward pragmatics (Canagarajah, 2014), and multiliteracy, which has been defined, in turn, as a multi-modal (representations of language in voice, drawing, etc.) approach (Guo & Feng, 2015), deep text analysis (Menke & Paesani, 2019), a multi-genre curriculum design (Warner & Dupuy, 2018), and teaching that is inclusive of linguistic, communicative, cultural, and technological diversity (The New London Group, 1996).

Table 2.1 Comparative educational philosophies

	Transmission	Transaction	Transformation
Goal	To know	To do/be able to do	To become
Information flow	Teacher to learner	Teacher to learner, learner to learner	Multidirectional and beyond the classroom
Roles	Teacher leads, learner responds	Teacher facilitates, learners (inter)act	Teacher as counselor, learners as clients
Progress check	Summative tests	Performance, prochievement, & proficiency tests, projects	Self-assessments, diagnostic & formative assessments
Cognition	Rote memory, reproduction	Recognition, schemata, associative memory, higher-order thinking	Critical thinking, creative thinking, reframing, awareness
Methods	Grammar translation, mastery learning	Communicative approaches, task-based instruction, content-based instruction	Learner-centered, scenario-based instruction, open architecture curricular design
Activities	Translation, fill-ins, matching, factual Q&A, grammar exercises	Projects, tasks, focus on form	Analysis & evaluation, exploration, comparison, research projects
Materials	Textbooks, teacher-prepared handouts	Textbooks, teacher supplements, authentic materials	Authentic materials, authentic people, authentic situations
Outcome	Right answers	Proficiency	Personal change

Source: Adapted from Leaver and Granoien (2000).

language: words, grammar rules, current events, and cultural history. Testing was objective and focused on knowing the one right answer, typically elicited by fill-ins, factual questions, matching activities, translations (single word or long texts), true–false statements, and multiple-choice tests. In transmission programs, the teacher acted as a "sage on the stage" and was expected to be a fount of knowledge. Teachers would spend hours preparing activity sheets that learners would complete in a fraction of the time that it took to prepare them. Textbooks, as well as teachers, presented predigested information to learners, transmitting essential elements of knowledge.

2.3 A New Paradigm: Transactive Approaches to World Language Education

The move from transactive to transformative approaches to language learning and teaching pulled learners from their seats and onto center stage, while the teacher became the "guide on the side." Acquisition of knowledge was replaced with skill development, or the ability to use the language to do things, for example, to make transactions. Activities included role plays of real-life activities. Tasks replaced exercises and teachers' time was economized: a teacher could develop a task in a few minutes that might take learners up to an hour to complete. Tests required examinees to complete a task, not to reproduce a rule, and learners might have to work with an authentic reading that they had not seen before as part of checking whether they had adequately developed reading strategies. Higher-order thinking skills[6] were reintroduced into the foreign language (FL) classroom; learners learned to use the language while analyzing situations, synthesizing information into new products, and evaluating/making judgments about all manner of things. A reliance on associative memory and the development of schemata replaced pure rote learning. The teaching of grammar as a set of rules was replaced with focusing learners' attention on form as they encountered it (Doughty & Williams, 1998). Project-based learning, collaborative work among learners, and the completion of specific research tasks supported the integration of all four skills. Project presentations contributed to the development of speaking skills; projects also served as a form of testing, using rubrics for scoring. Favored methods evolved during the development of this paradigm, such as communicative approaches: task-based instruction, learner-centered instruction, project-based instruction, and content-based instruction. Textbooks incorporated communicative activities, taught functions and notions, and introduced excerpts from mass media. As CLT spread, authentic materials increased in popularity.

2.4 A Next (Emerging) Paradigm: TLLT

TLLT, in its essence, causes the learner to change in some way – thinking, behavior, acceptance of the other, values, mindset, and/or emotion. Undergirding transformative activities are the influences of three twentieth-century scholars in education and human development: Jack Mezirow, an American professor of adult education (himself influenced by Brazilian educator Paolo Freire[7] and

---

[6] Analysis, synthesis, and evaluation (Bloom, 1956).
[7] In *Pedagogy of the Oppressed*, Freire (1970) argued for using the real-life experiences of learners in instruction.

German philosopher Juergen Habermas[8]); Lev Vygotsky, a Russian psychologist and educational theorist; and Carl Rogers, an American psychologist. All contributed to the shape of TLLT.

Mezirow taught adult education at Columbia University, where he developed a learning theory positing that a reflection–change–action process underlay the learning success of adult women re-entering university studies. In his theory, education must result in change stemming from encountering disorienting dilemmas that shake learners' belief systems and cause them to reflect, dissect, and analyze. He enumerated coping with a disorienting dilemma as the first of ten phases[9] to transforming cognitively (see Kearney, this volume; Oxford, this volume), emotionally (see Dirkx, 2009; see also Oxford, this volume), and spiritually (see Dirkx, 2009; see also Goulah, this volume). Language learners can point to one disorienting dilemma after another from study abroad experiences (see Davidson et al., this volume; see also Savicki et al., 2008), interaction with native speakers (see Farraj, this volume), participation in the social and religious life of émigré communities (see Leaver, 1989), or even in observation of culture from afar. A simple case in point might be dealing with the high context of the Arabic language in which "yes" can often mean "no," depending upon context and speaker intent – a very difficult concept for American learners to understand on an intellectual level, let alone being able to operate within such parameters in society. In fact, this yes–no lack of differentiation might even strike the American learner as morally wrong – at least until the fundamental change required for transformation and development of biculturalism takes place. Study abroad experience, which is critical to the development of advanced language proficiency, heightens the possibility of encountering disorienting dilemmas and presents them in starker contrast – here can be found the intersection of Mezirow's theory of transformation as informed by Freire (the integration of experience into learning) and Habermas (the ability to reason through these dilemmas).

The zone of proximal development (ZPD) (Vygotsky, 1930, 1934/1986) has influenced both transaction and transformation. Attuning lessons to what a learner can do now, will be ready to do soon (ZPD), and is far from ready to

---

[8] Habermas (1962, 1971, 1989) supported the ability of man to rationalize and rationally communicate; although his work was more politically enriched, it fertilized Mezirow's ground in the education sphere.

[9] The ten phases include: (1) disorienting dilemma; (2) self-examination with emotions; (3) critical assessment of assumptions; (4) recognition of discontent; (5) exploration of options; (6) planning actions; (7) acquisition of needed knowledge and skills; (8) rehearsing new roles; (9) building competence and self-confidence in new roles; and (10) a reintegration into one's life with changed perspective.

do makes a critical difference in the speed of an individual learner's progress toward bilingualism. TLLT requires not only a deep understanding of each learner's ZPD, but also a consistent application of this understanding through an open architecture curriculum design (OACD) that promotes a flexible syllabus, based on: selecting curricular materials in accordance with individual learner interest and need (see Campbell, this volume; see also Krasner, 2018; Leaver & Campbell, 2020); formative assessment that takes into account learning styles and strategy use, as well as specific levels of language development (Cohen, 2014); the concept of the learner as a client (Mahatmya et al., 2014); and the frequent use of contracts for setting course goals (Ismail & Yusof, 2012; Knowles, 1986), with the teacher acting as mentor, rather than as a director.

Rogers (1986) is often overlooked by TLLT educators, who do not realize that their instinctive tendency to assist learners in reframing their ideas, perceptions, and understandings when encountering a cross-cultural disorienting dilemma emanates from the generally pervasive influence that Rogers had on psychology of the 1970s and 1980s – both clinical and, by extension, educational. Pre-dating Mezirow's work on frames of reference (changes in habits of the mind or in points of view),[10] Rogers's concept of learner as client is reminiscent of the psychologist's approach to mentoring. In transformative classrooms, learners have a say in the content of the course and in the activities of the classroom, and when that classroom takes place in a foreign country, much reframing is needed rapidly. In transformative programs, the role of the teacher morphs into that of a counselor or guide, helping learners to: (1) identify learning needs and interests; (2) redraw their maps, keeping in mind that the map is a representation, not the territory itself (Ehrman & Dörnyei, 1998); (3) understand themselves and others, as well as the influence of their ego boundaries, that is, the thick or thin psychological/emotional "membranes" that either keep out or let in the other (Hartmann, 1991); and (4) pull apart their cognitive distortions (see Salyer & Leaver, this volume). This focus indeed changes class content. Traditional content is often pre-planned but the teacher cannot pre-plan who ends up in the classroom as learners. Therefore, a move toward the flexible content that characterizes OACD programs is likely inevitable.

The influence of Mezirow, Vygotsky, and Rogers led to the development of transformative classrooms with shared characteristics not previously seen in transactive or transmissive classes. These characteristics include:

- a goal of producing bilingual/bicultural people through transformations fostered by language learning experiences (see Davidson et al., this volume);

---

[10] Mezirow (2000) suggests two kinds of reframing: objective and selective. The first requires critical analysis of the other. The second requires critical analysis of the self.

- a multidirectional information flow among autonomous learners and teacher-coaches, who lead learners to self-awareness, cultural awareness, an understanding that the map is not the territory, and subsequent reframing of perspective or situation;
- OACD classrooms with flexible syllabi adapted to learner need and unique to each individual class (see Campbell, this volume);
- reliance on authentic materials, people, and situation-based instruction (see Corin, this volume; Garza, this volume), not on textbooks; and
- activities that cause learners to encounter disorienting dilemmas and use critical thinking, reflection, analysis, and research to understand them (see Crane & Sosulski, this volume; Davidson et al., this volume; Johnson, this volume; Kearney, this volume).

In specific terms, the TLLT learner might interview local immigrants (or in a study abroad program, a co-worker, supervisor in a local internship, or other students at their university) about culturally based issues, analyze the responses, and (if there is a means or justification to do so) undertake a project as a result that contributes to an improvement of some sort, such as creating a case study based on the issue, writing a series of editorials, participating in a citizens' discussion group, preparing an article for a newspaper or magazine, proposing a change to the local city council, undertaking community service, or providing one-on-one support to émigrés. Similarly, learners might interview local native speakers for a class-produced television show, lead local tours in the foreign language, or, extramurally, participate in musical groups with immigrants (Leaver, 2018). At least for now, these types of TLLT activities differ in important ways from contemporary aspects of transformative learning in adult education: whereas transformative adult education often focuses on creating change in society, TLLT seeks to understand and create a synthesis with the other society. That is particularly true for both leading TLLT English classes and local language study in places like China, where, ultimately, "productive bilingualism" (Gao, 2014) results from the interdependence of the first language and acquired language(s) (Wang, 2018; Zheng & Gao, 2017).

Some educators point out that some aspects of TLLT have been used in communicative classrooms for years. While this is technically true, TLLT pushes these teaching practices beyond transactional expectations, and, as a result, transformative instructional adaptation makes TLLT classrooms quite different from communicative classrooms. For example, both transactive classrooms and TLLT promote learner autonomy; however, TLLT grants a greater level of ownership to the learner over the learning process, including assisting in defining the syllabus and the choice of authentic materials for learning. Likewise, the level of attention focused on awareness and the appreciation of cultural differences within foreign language study differs between communicative and TLLT programs. TLLT programs note cultural and linguistic differences, large and small, not as disembodied curiosities or abstractions to be learned (or memorized), but as manifestations of a different experience of the world, of one's place in it, and of how things work (or of how to get things done). TLLT challenges learners to look for meanings in the speech, behaviors, and practices of others that may differ from their own established cultural assumptions and expectations, to reflect on these differences, and to understand how their own views of the world are culturally embedded as well.

On the other hand, frequent summative testing is not common in transformative courses, where the focus is on individual growth, the measurements for which may be both cognitive and attitudinal, objective and subjective, and as much determined by the learner and the peers in the target culture/community as by the teacher (see Davidson et al., this volume; King, this volume; see also King, 2017). The ultimate success of a learner in a transformative program is readily visible to the learner and teacher, as is the extent to which the learner has developed the skills and mindset to operate effectively and appropriately within the bilingual/bicultural reality, which is often best delineated by occasional formative assessment.

In a very early example of TLLT – the Russian "internship" program for American diplomats at the Foreign Service Institute (FSI) in the 1980s – learners worked with Russian immigrants for one afternoon a week, helping these immigrants assimilate into American culture (Leaver, 1989). As part of this service-learning component of the FSI Russian curriculum, both the immigrants and the learners encountered disorienting dilemmas that challenged both groups and led to changes, some of which were accomplished jointly. Concurrently, in 1984, the FSI launched the advanced Russian course with the goal of taking learners linguistically and culturally to near-native levels of proficiency in six months of intensive study (30 hours a week) – and succeeded with every learner for the next six years. That program relied upon a contract between learners and instructors regarding the choice of topics to be studied and the learning activities to be used, taking into account the learners' future work assignments, learning styles, current strengths and deficiencies in the language, and opportunities in the Washington DC area for making target-language presentations to émigré communities and participating in émigré professional and social activities.

Similarly, in the 1990s, the training of American astronauts and Russian cosmonauts for their assignments to the International Space Station included two-hour weekly simulations of a crisis onboard the station, which the learners had to work through first in English and then in Russian without faculty help. Simulations included both cross-linguistic and cross-cultural difficulties. The space-traveler learners provided realistic situations for simulations to their earthbound instructors. Faculty developed post-simulation language training to help learners assess their experiences and gain new, needed skills. Together, the teachers and learners developed plans for improving their preparation linguistically and, as a binational team, to handle any such problems if they were ever to encounter them onboard the station (Leaver & Bilstein, 2000). In this case, more Mezirow phases dominated the training than would be evident in the case of the FSI diplomatic training, for example, self-assessment of competence in a bilingual/bicultural simulation, identifying dissatisfactions, exploring new roles, and developing self-confidence, among others. Since training took place in both the USA and Russia, learners from both countries had opportunities to confront and resolve disorienting dilemmas – and, even beyond language and culture, to move toward a synthesis in scientific understandings, interpersonal relations, and the smooth working of a binational team.

2.5 Concluding Observation

A paradigm shift presumes an initial slow change, with some precocious programs leading the way. For example, Table 2.1 shows a historical transition from transmission to transaction to transformation. By the same token, aspects of transformative learning have most likely infused foreign language-focused study abroad from the earliest days of these programs. With time, the shift expands by fits and starts until it reaches a tipping point.

As TLLT spreads among language programs, a safe prediction might reflect a gradual move toward the now more standard Mezirowan description and then, over a longer period of time, a move onward by some into the spheres of transformative learning that go beyond pure cognition and beyond TLLT as described in this volume, and into various permutations of the affective domain, and/or embracing spirituality, defined as the quest for life meaning and self-awareness (Pierce, 2013) or more literally (Anderson, 2014). Others may choose to delve into deeper cognitive processing (Ehrman, 1996), focus on greater personal and global relevancy (O'Sullivan, 1999), or (less likely in the L2 field but possible) become involved in promoting social change (Kroth & Cranton, 2014) or the interconnectedness of the immaterial, natural, and geopolitical spheres (Goulah, 2006). The beginning of a paradigm shift tells us very little of the nature of the fully mature paradigm other than to know that it *will* "transform" the current paradigm.

DISCUSSION QUESTIONS

1. Select four to five language textbooks and determine what educational philosophy they reflect based on the table of contents, activities, and manner in which language (grammar and vocabulary) is treated. If a particular activity can be considered as reflecting both transactive and transformative philosophy, such as the use of authentic materials, identify to which it truly belongs (and defend that identification).
2. Interview one to two teachers who use TLLT. Ask them why they chose TLLT, what challenges they have encountered, and what they have found to be the benefits.
3. Read Kuhn's work on paradigm shifts. Determine how TLLT meets the definition of a paradigm shift (or does not). Can you identify any other paradigm shifts in language education? Do you think there can be simultaneous paradigm shifts? What do you think has caused these shifts?

3

Shaking the Foundations

Transformative Learning in the Field of Teaching English to Speakers of Other Languages

Rebecca L. Oxford

In this chapter, Paul Tillich's (1948, 2012) image of "the shaking of the foundations" is used to describe transformative learning in the field of teaching English to speakers of other languages (TESOL).[1] This foundation-shaking can occur for learners of English as a second language (ESL) or English as a foreign language (EFL), as well as for future teachers of ESL and EFL.

The first section of the present study concerns Jack Mezirow's cognitive-analytic approach, constituting the "first wave" of transformative learning. John Dirkx's emotional-integrative approach, in the "second wave" of transformative learning, is presented in the second section. It would be difficult to find any two transformative learning approaches more dissimilar, at least superficially. The third section points to neurobiological research, psychological research, and complexity theory, which together support the interweaving of the cognitive and emotional strands of transformative learning. This means that Mezirow's and Dirkx's approaches are not as opposite as they might at first seem.

The integration of either approach to actual teaching practice in ESL or EFL necessarily places heavy language demands on the learner. Only those ESL or EFL students with strong English proficiency can currently benefit; however, this limitation is likely to recede as new curriculum designs are developed. Adaptations of both approaches in ESL/EFL teacher education are discussed in the first and second sections.

3.1 Mezirow's Cognitive-Analytic Approach

The *cognitive-analytic approach* to individual transformative learning is represented by the influential work of Mezirow. In this approach, transformative

---

[1] Paul Tillich (1948, 2012) employed the phrase "the shaking of the foundations" to refer to a profound transformation in religious thinking and contemporary life. *The Shaking of the Foundations* (Tillich, 1948, 2012), one of his many books, contains 22 sermons drawing on copious cultural and historical sources, from the ancient Greeks to Marx. The collection reveals Tillich's concept of God as the "Ground of Being" and many other insights that were revolutionary at the time. For the current chapter, the main importance of Tillich's book lies in the title's powerful imagery.

learning involves a number of rational phases in the process of altering "taken-for-granted" (unexamined) cognitive frames of reference, also known as "perspectives" or "meaning schemes." These phases help individuals' perspectives to become more reflectively discriminating and thus more capable of generating meaningful beliefs to guide actions.

Mezirow began his work on transformative learning while studying women's re-entry programs at community colleges. The earliest version of his transformative learning theory (Mezirow, 1978b) included a nonsequential set of phases, not all of which needed to be experienced, starting with a disorienting dilemma and ending with integrating a new perspective into one's life. This process was called "perspective transformation." Baumgartner (2012) noted that for Mezirow's approach at the time, as well as later, making a decision to take action was more crucial than taking action.

In the 1980s, Mezirow expanded and refined his theory of perspective transformation and referred to perspectives as "meaning schemes." He borrowed ideas from German philosopher and sociologist Habermas about cognitive interests or domains for learning: technical learning, which Mezirow called "instrumental learning," based on hypothetico-deductive reasoning; practical or dialogic learning, which occurs through consensus-seeking discussions; and emancipatory learning or critical self-awareness, which ultimately leads to perspective transformation (Baumgartner, 2012; Mezirow, 1981). Mezirow expanded the number of elements/phases several times, yet he indicated that perspective transformation could occur through sudden insights or through multiple transitions of assumptions. He also asserted that people could transformatively learn through various kinds of reflection.

Mezirow noted that ten phases in the perspective transformation process included experiencing a disorienting dilemma; examining one's own assumptions; critically assessing the assumptions; recognizing dissatisfaction and its sources; exploring alternatives (i.e., new role options); planning a course of action; acquiring new knowledge; trying out new roles; building competence; and integrating the new perspective into one's life. The early assumption of randomness or nonsequentiality of Mezirow's phases was seemingly belied by his various revisions, which involved moving the phases around in ways that seemed to emphasize a potentially underlying sequence.

As Baumgartner explained, Mezirow's work was criticized for (1) portraying a unitary identity rather than recognizing an individual's multiple identities; (2) being overly rational and cognitive; (3) largely ignoring emotions (though Mezirow did mention anxiety); and (4) paying little attention to intuition, nonconscious learning, the imagination, and the collective unconscious. In response, Mezirow admitted that some of these factors could be important to transformative learning, though his approach remained strongly cognitive and rational (Baumgartner, 2012).

The approach was also criticized for being totally oriented toward transforming the individual, as portrayed in abstract, decontextualized ways. Critics argued that Mezirow did not take into account how contextualized social forces (e.g., ideology, race, class, gender, and power) affect the individual or vice versa (Baumgartner, 2012). In short, Mezirow's approach is not a critical theory in the sociopolitical sense, though it included participants' critical reflection (Mezirow, 1998). His response (Mezirow, 2006) to this criticism was that his theory was not intended to be political; rather, it could be a "foundation for learning how to take social action" (Baumgartner, 2012, p. 110). I do not think Mezirow's transformative learning theory needed to be a thoroughgoing critical theory of social transformation, but his seeming disconnection from the immediate social context seems odd, especially given what was going on while he was developing his theory – wars, anti-war protests, race riots, burned cities, poverty marches, waves of feminism, and other social movements.

Not to put too fine a point on it, Mezirow seemed surprisingly blind to the possibility that people from collectivist cultures could embody autonomy. He asserted (Mezirow, 1978b) that people in individualist, autonomy-emphasizing societies can transform their perspectives but people in collectivist cultures – which, though Mezirow did not mention it, constitute the world's majority – are hampered from perspective transformation due to their collectivist belief systems. Critical theorists in the TESOL area deflated the idea that autonomy is only an individualistic matter and can only or primarily exist in individualistic cultures (Esch, 1996; Pennycook, 2001). These critical theorists indicated that collectivist autonomies exist, just as do individualist autonomies, with the former involving collaborative rather than individual decision-making. Given that collectivist autonomies exist, then collectivist forms of perspective transformation must also exist. Fortunately, Freire (1970, 2018) was fully engaged in strengthening collectivist autonomy, as witnessed by his classic work *The Pedagogy of the Oppressed.*[2] In that book, he described the oppressed group, aided by teachers as mentors and cultural workers, taking responsibility for their own social liberation via praxis (i.e., action linked with values), conscientization (i.e., consciousness aimed at self-empowerment or autonomy), dialogue, and social engagement, all aiming at literacy and equality.

Despite criticisms, Mezirow's approach has had many replication studies and is attractive to numerous researchers and teachers. The approach garnered very positive responses in an informal, narrative study (Oxford, n.d.) of several

---

[2] Calleja (2014) contends that Freire (1970, 2018), whose orientation was so different from Mezirow's, was an influence on Mezirow's early thinking (see also Freire, 1975, 1993a, 1993b, 1998a, 1998b; Freire & Freire, 1994, 1997). For more on critical theory and transformative learning, see Brookfield (2000, 2005, 2012).

graduate classes of future ESL/EFL teachers who had read about Mezirow's phases in the course "Teaching ESL and EFL to Adults." These prospective teachers used Mezirow's approach in a simplified form to analyze and discuss the individual disorienting dilemmas that they were facing or had faced. These participants were particularly drawn to the disorienting dilemmas; each person had a story that needed to be told. Expressing the dilemmas allowed the participants to state and critically analyze their assumptions, their roles, and their possible new roles. Participants applied as many of the phases as they deemed relevant in order to explore their perspectives systematically. Some hardy souls followed the process all the way through the phases of making an action plan and gaining new knowledge on the way to integrating the new perspective. When offered the opportunity, certain future teachers also chose to interview former or current ESL or EFL learners, who primarily hailed from Germany, Mexico, and a few Central American countries, using Mezirow's phases as a helpful interview template. In quite different activities, the soon-to-be teachers also engaged with Dirkx's approach, which deals mainly with less rational factors.

3.2 Dirkx's Emotional-Integrative Approach

Dirkx's approach to individual transformative learning could be described as *emotional-integrative*. It is strongly influenced by depth psychology, especially the work of Carl Jung (1964, 1969). This approach has been extensively used to foster transformative learning in small groups (see Boyd, 1991; Boyd & Dirkx, 1991; Dirkx, 1997, 2001, 2008a, 2008b, 2012; Dirkx et al., 2006). Depth psychology "emphasizes relational, emotional, and largely unconscious issues associated with development of the individual, interpersonal interactions, and social development" (Dirkx, 2012, p. 117; see also Jung, 1964, 1969). Dirkx explained ego consciousness, the personal unconscious, the transpersonal (collective) unconscious, and individuation in Jungian theory and transformative learning. Individuation is the process of becoming a unified, integrated, unique person. Jungian theory is complex in its emphasis on the multiple, interactive aspects of our unconscious selves, which contain universal, cultural, and personal memories, images, myths, and symbols, and which include fluid masculine and feminine elements. Individuation means slowly unifying all these disparate pieces and bringing the conscious and the unconscious closer together.

For Dirkx, emotions are the "messengers of the soul," so he emphasized "emotional soul work" as the basis of transformative learning. His approach is often called the "imaginal method," which involves imaginatively elaborating the meaning of emotions in human lives, rather than dissecting emotions with reason (Dirkx, 2001). Soul can be awakened, nurtured, and expressed in the classroom and even in cooperative online settings. The subject matter and readings of assigned texts can sometimes spark dynamic discussion and engagement. Submerged emotions, images, and symbols often come to the surface. The facilitator helps the students to debrief by asking them to consider what was emotionally meaningful to them and why. This debriefing is done in four parts: (1) paying attention to and describing an emotion-laden image that has arisen from the unconscious and identifying the context, people, and relationships involved in the image; (2) associating current experiences (e.g., in group work) with similar past experiences in which the emotion-bearing image arose, thus getting at the private myth; (3) amplifying the image, that is, making use of popular culture, literature, and mythology to expand the meaning of the original image from the personal to the transpersonal, thus tapping the collective myth; and (4) animating or personifying the image and then interacting with it. The fourth element involves a two-way communication (a written dialogue or an "empty-chair" role play) between the person and the personified image, which tends to reveal more of itself and its meaning.

Using a Jungian framework, Dirkx's approach moves from the personal to the collective, including cultural aspects. Although Dirkx's writings so far have not shown him to be a critical theorist, and though the imaginal method focuses on the growth of the individual, this growth occurs in the social context, that is, the small group, larger cultural groups, and the collective unconscious. The imaginal method's openness to culture and to language relate well to the ideas of Kramsch (1993), who explained that since language is social practice, culture is at the very heart of language teaching and learning.

Given that Dirkx's transformative learning is emotional soul work, it is understandable that the classroom might be seen as a spiritual or sacred space. Stevick (1990), who described his own "sacramental," caring, emotionally deep approach to language teaching and learning (see also Arnold & Murphey, 2013; Kristjánsson, 2015), would have had a friend in Dirkx. Other concepts and processes that could correlate well with Dirkx's imaginal method are mindful, empathic listening (Oxford, in press); contemplative inquiry (Zajonc, 2006); deep education and radical amazement in creation spirituality (Oxford, 2016a); and pedagogy of the heart (Culham et al., 2018). Merriam and Bierema (2014) noted that connections to self, to others, to the world, and to a higher being are central to spirituality in adult education.

As mentioned earlier, part of Oxford's informal, narrative study concerned Mezirow's transformative phases. In the study's second part, future teachers in graduate classes on "Teaching ESL and EFL to Adults" and "Teaching ESL Reading and Writing" participated in learning activities involving intuition, images, and emotions. The professor led such activities before she had read Dirkx's work. Upon reading it, she recognized Dirkx as a comrade and became even more purposeful in her practice of engaging participants' intuitive, emotional, and spiritual depths during special moments in class. As the professor shared objects, song lyrics, imagistic poems (e.g., by Rumi, Hafiz, and Dickinson), and photographs of nature and people, participants let their unconscious emotions and images arise and, in reflective discussion, linked them to past experiences and to their hopes for teaching. Participants led self-created activities involving a hopeful Native American myth ("the wolf of love"), a video of Martin Luther King, Jr., a Hemingway story, a Holocaust story told by a Jewish student, meditative music played by a professional violist in the class, a metaphorical video of children led to their deaths by a menacing toy store, and much more. Participants expressed both joy and concern about situations in society and the environment. They described anxiety, sorrow, and collective guilt about the Holocaust and the caste system in India. A participant from the elite Brahmin caste in India described grief and empathy for Dalits, formerly called "Untouchables," and another participant from India quietly, but without shame, revealed herself to be a descendant of Dalits. Images, emotions, and insights revealed private myths, which participants expanded by calling on collective myths in additional literature and in fantasy and adventure films. Only the fourth part of the Dirkx's debriefing (i.e., interacting with images via writing or empty-chair role play) was omitted because of time constraints.

These fluid processes occurred at various times and were integrated into more structured lessons involving teaching demonstrations, analytic reports, debates, and online games. The adapted imaginal method had many advantages: it bonded participants to each other; it freed emotions and intuitions in positive ways; it fostered rich creativity that led to exciting and successful ESL and EFL teaching; and it developed more empathic, more confident teachers who were better able to deal with their emotions, others' emotions, and diverse cultures. Possible disadvantages are as follows. First, the instructional processes that Dirkx described were not always straightforward. This was understandable because many of his works focused on the philosophy of transformative learning, not specific instructional steps, and because much of the imaginal approach is spontaneous, though it has a general shape. Second, some educational systems or teachers might be averse to using activities that are intuitive, emotional, or spiritual. Third, if a rigid curriculum were in force, the fluidity of the imaginal method would be difficult to integrate into that curriculum.

3.3 Shall the Twain Ever Meet?

On the surface, Mezirow's and Dirkx's dramatically different approaches, based respectively on cognition and emotion, might lead to a judgment that "never the twain shall meet." However, convincing reasons for rejecting a putative split between cognition and emotion are available from neurological research, psychological research on problem solving and peak experiences, and complexity theory.[3]

3.3.1 Cognition and Emotion in Neurobiology

The human brain is emotional (Le Doux, 1998), as well as cognitive. As noted by Lewis (2005, p. 194): "[C]ognition and emotion were never two distinct systems at all.… [A] neuroscientific analysis finds them to be different aspects of a unitary phenomenon in which interpretation and relevance emerge together." Emotions can be divided into two subsystems (MacIntyre, 2002; Oxford, 2016b): (1) a subcortical, amygdala-based, primitive, automatic system, including joy, sadness, disgust, anger, fear, and other basic emotions; and (2) a more "cognitive" system in the cerebral cortex that allows experiencing and regulating emotion through conscious reflection.

3.3.2 Cognition and Emotion in Problem Solving and Peak Experiences

Emotions and cognition help us understand complicated things and solve complex problems. When engaged in moral dilemmas, we experience automatic or "gut-level" responses, emotions, and intuitions (Gibbs, 2010; Greene, 2009; Haidt, 2008). The dilemma's nature determines whether emotion or logical reasoning predominates. "Personally involving dilemmas" stimulate brain areas associated with emotion, while "impersonal dilemmas" stimulate reason-focused brain areas (Sigelman & Rider, 2012, p. 444).

Peak experiences likewise link emotion and cognition. Maslow (1970, 1971) described peak experiences as the transient but powerful moments of self-actualization, joy, excitement, ego transcendence, timelessness, empathy, and creativity that most people have. In his view, a peak experience is an epiphany: "a great and mystical experience, a religious experience if you wish – an illumination, a revelation, an insight … [leading to] 'the cognition of being' … almost, you could say, a technology of happiness" (Maslow, 1971, p. 169, emphasis added).

---

[3] See also views on emotion from social psychology, social constructivism, social constructionism, cognitive linguistics, and critical poststructuralism (Oxford, 2015), as well as linkages between emotion and metacognition (Oxford, 1996). Cognitive psychologist Piaget (1981) also discussed the unity of cognition and affect.

3.3.3 Cognition and Emotion in Complexity Theory

Complexity theory, also called "dynamic systems theory," focuses on relationships among complex systems or multiple components of a complex system. Emotion and cognition are complex systems that closely and necessarily interact. Their relationship is mutually influential, organic, holistic, nonlinear (sometimes having unpredictably disproportionate outcomes), emergent (meaning that patterns emerge from the interconnections of systems), and dynamic (changeable, fluctuating). For more about complexity theory in TESOL, see Oxford, (2018).

3.3.4 Yes, the Twain Shall Meet

"No one theoretical perspective needs to mean others are excluded. That is, transformative learning can be both cognitive and imaginative; it can be collaborative and individually based; it can include depth psychology alongside a more practical reflective approach. Dreams and reflections need not compete with each other" (Lawrence & Cranton, 2009, p. 316; see also Cranton & Taylor, 2012). Taylor (1998) cautioned that not all students are inclined toward transformative learning, but if elements from Mezirow's cognitive-analytical approach and Dirkx's emotional-integrative approach were carefully selected and creatively interwoven, many ESL and EFL students, as well as future language teachers, would probably be eager to experience transformative learning.

Cognition and emotion are necessary to each other. Both Mezirow's and Dirkx's approaches, if slightly enhanced and adjusted, could honor emotion and cognition, and neither approach would lose its unique flavor. For instance, the disorienting dilemma and the other phases in Mezirow's approach naturally stir up emotions, and participants could name and discuss these emotions, thus making perspective transformation optimally meaningful. Dirkx's imaginal method is infused with emotions, images, and intuitions, and when reflection on these phenomena occurs during reading, writing, and oral discussion, cognition clearly happens. Thereby, the twain (emotion and cognition) interact more easily and more overtly, while the general emphases of the two transformative learning approaches are maintained. With that, the shaking of the foundations becomes more powerful and more meaningful.

DISCUSSION QUESTIONS

1. List at least five main differences between the transformative learning approaches of Jack Mezirow and John Dirkx. Considering these differences,

with which of these two approaches do you feel most comfortable? Give several reasons for preferring that approach.

2. What would your ideal transformative learning model contain? Given that the approaches of Dirkx and Mezirow are so different, would it be possible to select or adapt elements from the two approaches to help create your ideal transformative learning model? If yes, list the elements that you would select or adapt and explain your reasons. If no, provide at least three reasons why not.

3. Look carefully at other forms and applications of transformative learning in this volume and in other sources on transformative learning. Which forms and applications seem more oriented toward cognition, which seem more oriented toward emotion, and which seem to have a balance between the two? What, if anything, does the complexity perspective tell you that might help you answer this question?

4

Transformative Learning at the Multilingual Turn

Toward an East–West Perspective of Selfhood

Jason Goulah

As transformative learning theory is increasingly applied to the fields of bilingual and second and world language education (e.g., Arce, 2000; Cummins, 2019; Foster, 1997; McClinton, 2005; Osterling & Webb, 2009; Sun, 2013; Zheng & Gao, 2017), these fields must consider what version of "transformative learning" they should embrace, and why. Emerging from the discipline of adult education, transformative learning theory comes in multiple varieties, with each highlighting different aspects of perspectival and behavioral transformations among teachers and learners.

This chapter argues that given the radical changes in the world's climate and biosphere (Bonneuil & Fressoz, 2015; USGCRP, 2018), and their impact on language learners and on the changing nature of language, culture, literacies, and semiotics (Goulah, 2012, 2017; Goulah & Katunich, 2020; Pennycook, 2004, 2017), the language field is well advised to look specifically to the transformative learning theories of Daisaku Ikeda (1991–2011, 2010a, 2010b) and Edmund O'Sullivan (1999, 2002, 2008; see also O'Sullivan & Taylor, 2004; O'Sullivan et al., 2002). Their versions of transformative learning place importance on the existential crises of climate change, casting the external environment as a reflection of individuals' inner lives. They argue that any ameliorative changes in the biosphere will only come from transformed individual and cultural practices born from a profound transformation of the spiritual, social, and ecological self. This chapter concludes, then, that as the fields of bilingual and second and world language education cohere into the *multilingual turn* (Conteh & Meier, 2014; May, 2014), the existential crises of climate change demand that these fields enact an even greater paradigm shift by engaging climate as the integrating focus of language and culture learning and instruction. Ikeda and O'Sullivan provide an important East–West, *bi-/multicultural* foundation for such transformative language learning.

4.1 Which Version of Transformative Learning Theory?

The transformative learning field itself has yet to agree on a single definition or leading perspective shared across disciplines (Taylor & Cranton, 2012). However, much of the extant literature concerning transformative learning in general, and relative to language education in particular, draws mainly on theories espoused in Jack Mezirow's (1978b) adult-centered psychological phases of transformation, Paulo Freire's (1978) perspective of *conscientização* (or *conscientization*), and Lev Vygotsky's (1997) cultural-historical theory.

Due to space constraints, readers are referred to Oxford's chapter for a treatment of Mezirow's (2012) perspective and Taylor and Cranton (2012) for explanations of Freirean influences in transformative learning. These three frameworks are important in their own right and indeed for transformative learning theory; however, the perspective taken in this chapter is in agreement with Oxford's critiques of Mezirow's version, particularly that its deliberately apolitical and solely psychological-cognitive dimensions are limiting, especially for the field of language education, which is completely entangled in the sociopolitical, the ethnoracial, the socio-emotional, and the spiritual (e.g., García & Wei, 2014; Miller, 2017; Pennycook, 2004, 2017; Platero & Drager, 2015; Rosa & Flores, 2017; Smith & Osborn, 2007). It has likewise been argued that language education is also completely entangled in the biospherically ecological and in the new materialisms of the Anthropocene (or *"Age of Man"*) (Goulah & Katunich, 2020; Küchler, 2017; MacPherson, 2003, 2010; Maffi, 2001; Nettle & Romaine, 2000; Pennycook, 2004, 2017; Stibbe, 2015). However, as these entanglements have found comparatively less purchase in the language education literature, this chapter focuses on them because versions of transformative learning – particularly those of Ikeda (1991–2011, 2010a, 2010b) and O'Sullivan (1999, 2002, 2008; O'Sullivan & Taylor, 2004; O'Sullivan et al., 2002) – provide important pathways for examining them as the field of language education moves into the Anthropocene.[1]

With regard to Freire, his work does not reflect transformative learning in the same sense that Mezirow or O'Sullivan, for example, explicitly label their work *transformative learning*. While Freire's (1970) roots in adult education position him well within the transformative learning discourse, and his work informs part of O'Sullivan's approach to transformative learning (addressed later), his focus on the economic and political dimensions of liberation can be limiting and prescriptive. Indeed, Freirean theory has informed much of language education theorizing in the form of critical pedagogy and critical applied linguistics, which have already had major impacts in illuminating the socioeconomic, power, and ethnoracial dimensions of language, culture, and language education; however, as Pennycook (2001) illustrates, Freirean critical

---

[1] For early investigations of this entanglement in related fields, see Pennycook (2017) in critical applied linguistics, Fløttum (2017) in communications, Cronin (2016) in translation theory, and Stibbe (2015) in ecolinguistics.

pedagogy and critical applied linguistics tend to veer away from maintaining a truly critical stance in any meaningful way.

With regard to Vygotsky, my own early applications of transformative learning drew on Vygotskian (Vygotsky, 1997) notions of the subjective "*sense*" (*смысл; smysl*) of language rather than its "*meaning*" (*значение; znachenie*) in the development of learners' transformed perspectives and understanding of *deep culture* (Goulah, 2006).[2] I continue to rely on Vygotsky's approaches of sociodialogic learning but, strictly speaking, would not call his theories "transformative learning." Vygotsky's cultural-historical theory may help us to conceptualize or effectuate transformative learning but it is not transformative learning *per se*.

Moreover, while the ideas of Mezirow and Freire have been used to address ecological crises (Diducka et al., 2012; Jones, 2010), neither engages transformation relative to environmental ethics, biospheric degradation, ecojustice, or global warming. None attends to the nature of transformation necessary for addressing the existential crises of the Anthropocene. None addresses the spiritual, cultural, and onto-epistemological fabric beyond mental perspectives that inform transformations in one's ecological and climatic worldview and behavior. As Hathaway (2011, p. 282) states: "[w]hile transformative learning theory has traditionally focused on 'perspective transformation' ... shifting to an ecological worldview is particularly challenging due to the depths of the transformation required and the entrenched cultural dynamics that perpetuate the status quo."

Here, one might look to John Dirkx's (e.g., 1997) perspectives of transformative learning, which *do* explicitly engage the spiritual and the emotional – transformative learning as nurturing the learner's "soul." Together with Jessica Kovan, Dirkx also examined the transformative learning dimensions of environmental activists, finding that "their lives are characterized by struggles that represent a profound form of learning, involving recognition and understanding of one's work as a calling or vocation as well as exemplifying the kind of transformative learning reflected in Jung's concept of individuation" (Kovan & Dirkx, 2003, p. 99). However, whereas Dirkx's scholarship has

---

[2] Deep culture constitutes an abstract worldview based on culture embedded in language and existing beyond the "surface culture" that, in language education, is often reduced to "foods, fairs, folklore, and statistical facts" (Kramsch, cited in Hinkel, 1999, p. 5). Goodman (2002, p. 187) argued that "both transformative learning and cultures of peace have to do with changes primarily in the deep culture. This is not to say that changes in the other levels [of culture] are not sought or are seen not to matter, but rather that it is the deep culture that is primary." For a full discussion of transformative learning relative to language education and "deep culture," see Goulah (2006).

examined aspects of environmental activists' transformed perspectives, Ikeda's and O'Sullivan's approaches are more centrally located in the socio-ecological and eco-spiritual dimensions of human transformation. Moreover, whereas Mezirow, Freire, and Vygotsky implicitly and explicitly view transformation in individual terms, Ikeda's and O'Sullivan's perspectives view the individual's inner transformation as entirely contingent on and interdependent with the external in a two-way vector of influence. Rather than self-actualization, their perspectives are couched in transformation as both social self-actualization and ecological self-actualization, or what I call transformation through socio-ecological and eco-spiritual self-actualization.

4.2 Toward a Socio-Ecological and Eco-Spiritual Transformation in Language Education

Stein-Smith (2016) posits that in an interconnected world, the multilingual turn is essential for effectively addressing complex global issues. This is because it fosters a "global personal cultural identity," enhances "effective communication … and cultural understanding," and develops "global citizenship values" (Stein-Smith, 2016, p. 2254). One of the many complex global issues that she cites for multilingualism and language education to engage in is meeting the United Nations (2015) Sustainable Development Goals (SDGs). She is not alone. In 2016, the Study Group on Language and the United Nations cooperated with the Center for Applied Linguistics, the Center for Research and Documentation on World Language Problems, and other organizations to host a 2016 symposium on language and the linguistic implications of the SDGs. Likewise, also in 2016, TESOL Italy hosted an international conference on sustainable development for scholars, teachers, and practitioners from multiple professional disciplines to engage TESOL and sustainability holistically, where environmental, cultural, economic, and social concerns intersect. In 2017, the annual conference of the American Association of Applied Linguistics included a session on language and biospheric sustainability (Katunich et al., 2017).

Toward this end, the field of language education requires a form of transformative learning that allows it to foster an "eco-ethical consciousness" (Goulah, 2017; Martusewicz et al., 2011), or what O'Sullivan and Taylor (2004) called an "ecological consciousness" through transformative learning. Such consciousness is similar to Palmer's (2019) important notion of *ideological clarity for critical consciousness* in language education, which endeavors to cultivate learners' capacities to "reflectively discern the differences in power and privilege rooted in social relationships that structure inequalities and shape the material conditions of our lives," "to recognize one's role in these dynamics," and "to act to change them." Such ideological clarity for critical consciousness is, Palmer asserts, a means for multilingual learners to "read the world to change it" in a Freirean sense. However, one aspect of material conditions that Palmer does not note are the current climatic-biospheric conditions and the intersection of these with language learners (Bowers, 2001, 2012; Goulah, 2017; Kelly, 2009; MacPherson, 2003, 2010; Maffi, 2001; Miller; Nettle & Romaine, 2000). This chapter encourages such exploration through the transformative learning perspectives of Ikeda and O'Sullivan.

4.3 O'Sullivan, Ikeda, and Transformative Language Education

Seemingly unaware of each other, Ikeda in the East (Japan) and O'Sullivan in the West (Canada) both highlight the need for, in O'Sullivan's (2002) phrasing, a transformed cosmology (i.e., worldview), the development of ecological selfhood, enhanced spirituality, and an understanding of cultural and socioeconomic quality-of-life issues (see also O'Sullivan & Taylor, 2004; O'Sullivan et al., 2002). The cultivation of these aspects, O'Sullivan (2002, p. 3; see also Hathaway, 2011, p. 284) maintains, requires personal experience of:

> a deep, structural shift in basic premises of thought, feelings, and actions. It is a shift of consciousness that dramatically and irreversibly alters our way of being in the world that impacts our relationship with other human beings and the greater Earth community, including understanding of relations of power in interlocking structures of class, race and gender; our body awareness, our visions of alternative approaches to living; and our sense of possibilities for social justice and peace and personal joy.

According to Markos and McWhinney (2004, p. 76), with the arrival of O'Sullivan's work, transformative learning theory progressed from its "initial cognitive, rationale focus," inspired by the work of Jack Mezirow, "to appropriately include aspects of the sensory, intuitive, emotional, experiential, and spiritual in a more holistic, ecological approach to the individual's path of transformation." Within this more inclusive and expansive, ecological and holistic sense, O'Sullivan (1999, p. 2) considers the "fundamental educational task of our times [to be] to make the choice for a sustainable planetary habitat of interdependent life forms over and against the dysfunctional calling of the global competitive marketplace." To achieve this, O'Sullivan (1999, p. 4) positions inner and outer transformation "within a broad cultural context."

For Ikeda (2003), the aforementioned four aspects in O'Sullivan's framework can be understood through 共生 (kyōsei), Ikeda's ethic of "creative coexistence," which he defines as "the ethos that seeks to bring harmony from conflict, unity from rupture, that is based more on 'us' than 'me.' It signals a spirit that seeks to encourage mutual flourishing and mutually supportive relationships among humans and between humans and nature" (Ikeda, 2003, p. 6). This ethic is enacted through what he considers global or planetary citizenship, namely, by cultivating:

- the wisdom to perceive the interconnectedness of all life and living;
- the courage not to fear or deny difference but to respect and strive to understand people of different cultures and to grow from encounters with them; and
- the compassion to maintain an imaginative empathy that reaches beyond one's immediate surroundings and extends to those suffering in distant places. (Ikeda, 2010b, pp. 112–113)

Ikeda adds that the all-encompassing interrelatedness – what is akin to ecological selfhood in O'Sullivan's formation – forms the core of his Buddhist framework and provides the eco-spiritual basis for the concrete realization of the qualities of wisdom, courage, and compassion. The continual enhancement of such wisdom, courage, and compassion is not only the indication of continual human becoming in an ecological web; it is also a full awakening to the true reality of the interdependent causality of human life, in this life, as we are.

As the wisdom, courage, and compassion that Ikeda envisages interlink environmental, ecological, and climatic issues with poverty, human and animal rights, health, food security, peace, and other global issues, their manifestation requires "a fundamental rethinking of our way of life – as individuals, as societies and in terms of human civilization itself" (Ikeda, 2010b, p. 39). In the realm of schooling, Ikeda (2003, p. 14) proposes enhanced critical literacy development and the need for 人間教育 (ningen kyōiku), literally "human education," as a new form of education that "encourages creative coexistence with the natural environment and which fosters a culture of peace." Part and parcel with ningen kyōiku, Ikeda (2010b, p. 39) also advocates for education for sustainable development, with the following three goals in mind:

- To learn and deepen awareness of environmental issues.
- To reflect on our modes of living, renewing these toward sustainability.
- To empower people to take concrete action to resolve the challenges we face.

Ikeda (1991–2011) calls such self-directed empowerment 創価 (sōka), or "value creation," which is the unlimited capacity to create meaning from one's learning and life's realities – meaning that serves oneself and others through truly contributive living (see also Makiguchi, 1981–1988, vols. 5 and 6). The three goals in Ikeda's framework align with O'Sullivan's (1999) three goals of educating to "critique, survive, and create possibilities in" the complexifying Anthropocenic moment. Furthermore, the wisdom that Ikeda refers to here is echoed by Hathaway and Brazilian eco-liberation theologian Leonardo Boff in their call for the "wisdom needed to understand the nature of the global [ecological and climatic] crisis, imagine new ways of working for transformation, and guide us toward a vision of sanity" (Hathaway, 2011, pp. 282–283; see also Hathaway & Boff, 2009).

In the final analysis, the transformative learning propounded by O'Sullivan and Ikeda is socio-ecological and eco-spiritual. It is globally inclusive, drawing from Eastern and Western religious and philosophical traditions, and calls for the conscious cultivation of ecological selfhood and transformed cultural practices for individuals, societies, and civilizations. It seeks to enact what Ikeda (2019) calls the need for "proactive and contagious change," that is, an inner transformation in what O'Sullivan (1999) calls the "deep interiority" of each individual. Ikeda (1991–2011) terms this process 人間革命 (ningen kakumei), or "human revolution." It warrants noting that although Ikeda does not use the specific label of "transformative learning," his Eastern educational perspective is fundamentally one of profound inner transformation (Stearns, 2018; Urbain, 2010). Like O'Sullivan, Ikeda (2007, p. 51) maintains that "When we change, the world changes. The key to all change is our inner transformation – a change in our hearts and minds. This is human revolution. We all have the power to change. When we realize this truth, we bring forth that power anywhere, anytime, and in any situation."

4.4 Conclusion

Unlike for Mezirow, Freire, and Vygotsky, the transformative learning approaches of Ikeda (1991–2011) and O'Sullivan (1999) cohere around the role of education in fostering socio-ecological and eco-spiritual perspectives that can lead us as individuals and as a civilization to grasp our mutual interdependence with the environment and our communities, and to fundamentally transform ourselves for the betterment of ourselves, our societies, and the planet. This process represents ecological selfhood in the richest sense. Whether engaging standards-based climate science and spirituality with English-learning religious refugees in the USA, or war and environmental sustainability with socioeconomically diverse learners in a Japanese immersion program abroad, or spirituality relative to adolescents' study of Japanese language, pop culture, and ecology in a working-class public high school, among other examples, I have repeatedly demonstrated that such an inner transformation for the sake of external transformation is possible in bilingual and second and world language education (Goulah, 2007, 2011, 2017; Goulah & Katunich, 2020).

Taken together, the approaches of Ikeda and O'Sullivan converge in addressing the complexity of the human condition in a climatically interdependent world. For Ikeda and O'Sullivan, inner transformation toward what Ikeda (2010a) calls the "greater self" occurs most completely through dialogic meaning-making, whereby such transformation is an intentional and continual self-mastery that requires the release of the lesser self "caught up in the snares of egoism" and the development of the greater self that is actualized in causality and is spatio-temporally infinite (Ikeda, 2010a, p. 175). Based on the principle of the oneness of life and environment, this greater self can be understood simply as one that fully identifies and empathizes with others' suffering, and is therefore driven to relieve it. As I have indicated elsewhere, this transformed greater self:

> is an open, expansive character amplified by empathy that extends not only to other people but to all life and living, and thus to the natural environment. It is a self rooted in respect for the dignity of all life— including one's own—and the wisdom to perceive the inextricable interdependence of that life. In the context of language and culture education, this greater self of one's full humanity emerges wholly only through persistent "immersion in the ocean of language and dialogue fed by the springs of cultural tradition" (Ikeda, 2010a, p. 203). (Goulah, 2017, p. 95)

DISCUSSION QUESTIONS

1. This chapter offers a theoretical perspective of transformative language education for socio-ecological and eco-spiritual selfhood. Where and how in the language and culture education curriculum might this perspective be enacted in instructional practice, lesson planning, and student engagement?
2. What do these enactments look like across the grade span, from the elementary through adult levels, and how can and should we assess whether such transformations have occurred?

PART II

Transformative Language Learning and Teaching Applications in Government Programs

5

Open Architecture Curricular Design

A Fundamental Principle of Transformative Language Learning and Teaching

Christine Campbell

The term "open architecture curricular design" (OACD) was introduced by Leaver in 2015[1] at the Defense Language Institute Foreign Language Center (DLIFLC) in conjunction with an institute-wide initiative to raise the proficiency of graduates of the basic course. The official goal was to ensure that 80 percent of the graduates attain Interagency Language Roundtable[2] (ILR) Level 2+ in Listening Comprehension and Reading Comprehension by 2022.[3] OACD is a fundamental principle of transformative language learning and teaching (TLLT), the broader educational approach that Leaver proposed to implement to support the new initiative to achieve higher levels of proficiency (Leaver & Campbell, 2020). The primary goals of TLLT are personal transformation that results in bilingual and bicultural competence and learner autonomy.

This chapter reports specifically on the results of the application of OACD within a number of learning contexts at DLIFLC, beginning with an overview of its history, tenets, and common features, followed by a brief description of two actual case studies of its implementation.

5.1 **History**

In education, Dewey (1938/1997), Freire (1998a, 1998b, 1998c), and Rogers (1969/1986), among others, have described how learning empowers the individual. Dewey elucidated the role of personal change in learning, and Freire elucidated the individual nature of learning and the role of personal experience in it. Rogers saw learning as a uniquely individual, self-regulated process facilitated by a mentor.

---

[1]   The practices associated with an open architecture curricular design significantly pre-date the use of the term (Clifford, 1988). The evolution of the practices is described later in this chapter.

[2]   The ILR Language Skill Level Descriptions, which delineate levels of proficiency using a scale from 0 through 5, informed the development of the ACTFL Proficiency Guidelines scale from Novice Low through Distinguished. For more information, see www.govtilr.org and www.actfl.org/publications/guidelines-and-manuals/actfl.

[3]   In the chapter, level references will be to both the ILR and the ACTFL scales at the start, then only to the former (cf. ILR/ACTFL).

In the 1980s and 1990s, theorists and practitioners in the field of language learning began to recognize and address more directly the needs of the individual learner. In 1984, in the "Introduction" to the path-breaking *Teaching for proficiency, the organizing principle*, Higgs (1984) underscored the imperative to tailor lesson plans and activities to the needs of learners. Nunan (1988, 1997a, 1997b, 2006a, 2006b) discussed negotiating aspects of the curriculum with learners and accommodating learner needs by varying tasks to learner levels, while Oxford (1990, 2017) examined the learning strategies employed by learners. Dabbs and Leaver (2019) and Ehrman and Dörnyei (1998) explored the relationship between language learning success and Jungian personality types (Jung, 1921), and Ehrman and Leaver (2002) studied the cognitive styles associated with language learning. Ehrman, Leaver, and Oxford (2003) identified the complex relationships among learning styles, learning strategies, and successful second language acquisition, while Dörnyei (2005) proposed insightful ways of understanding motivation in language learning, expanding on the pioneering work of Gardner and Lambert (1972) on the integrative-instrumental model of motivation, as well as the research on learner self-efficacy of Bandura (1977). These and other studies have contributed to an ongoing dialogue among specialists and practitioners concerning individual learner differences, which has influenced OACD and TLLT more generally.

With its stress on systematic tailoring to individual learner needs, OACD was a key feature of the TLLT program in Russian at the Foreign Service Institute in Washington DC in the 1980s, where the goal of the advanced language course (informally called the "50/50 model"), was ILR 4/4 (ACTFL Distinguished) in Listening Comprehension and Reading Comprehension. There, a theme-based syllabus, versus a textbook, served as the curricular framework and learners chose themes to examine, research, write about, and present throughout the course. An important part of the course was community-based service learning, in this case, with the Russian-speaking émigré community of the Washington DC area (Leaver, 1989). Leaver brought OACD to the Czech and Russian basic courses at DLIFLC during 1989–1993 and later, in 2006, introduced it into the intermediate and advanced courses at the DLIFLC Continuing Education Directorate (CE), where post-program proficiency scores have consistently outpaced those of previous years (Leaver & Campbell, 2015). In 2015, Leaver borrowed the term "open architecture" from the world of technology, where it applies to "a type of computer architecture or software architecture that is designed to make adding, upgrading, and swapping components easy.... For example, the IBM PC and Apple IIe have an open architecture supporting plug-in cards, whereas the Apple IIc and Amiga 500 computers have a closed architecture" (Wikipedia, "open architecture," August 2016).

5.2 Tenets

To understand OACD and its applications more specifically, it is critical to be aware of their role within TLLT. OACD is one of a number of fundamental principles of TLLT (listed in detail in the Introduction), which include: authentic and unadapted materials early on in the instruction; an immersive environment in the learning space; personal transformation; highly individualized programs[4] (Dabbs & Leaver, 2019); a focus on formative assessments in the grading system; and OACD – a framework that encourages teacher–learner negotiation through the use of a theme-based syllabus (versus a textbook), generally beginning at Levels 1+/Intermediate High and above, though there is evidence of the successful introduction of OACD at much lower levels (Clifford, 1988; Duri, 1992), depending on factors such as teacher and learner readiness. OACD and the other TLLT principles operate within a context that is grounded in the national standards (The National Standards Collaborative Board, 2019) and is content-based and learner-centered.

OACD is a flexible model where teachers are empowered to change activities and tasks according to learner needs, specifically their learning styles, and strategy repertoire (level of fossilization, interests, and ZPD [Vygotsky, 1978/2013]). While language learning professionals have been especially conscious of the necessity of adapting to individual learner needs since the 1980s, in many cases, the tailoring has not been systematic and teachers have not directly and consistently solicited input from the learners themselves on the curriculum, that is, what activities are meaningful, which materials are engaging, and so on. OACD promotes teacher–learner collaboration – or negotiation (Nunan, 1988, 1997a, 1997b, 2006a, 2006b) – on aspects of the curriculum. Here, the two parties contribute to the drafting and revising of the curriculum. The role of the teacher evolves from facilitator of learning to advisor/mentor/coach: a "learning counselor/concierge and curator of content" (DiRienzo, 2015) who provides valuable support, for example, resources, to learners as they do short- and long-term projects, both individually and in pairs and groups.

The project-based instruction (PBI) literature (Carreira & Chik, 2017) indicates that themes, topics, and sub-topics dealing with real-world problems motivate learners. Such material can be used with learners at lower proficiency levels, such

---

[4] The term "invisible classroom" as applied to the language learning environment was first used by Ehrman and Dörnyei (1998) to indicate the interplay of individual differences, especially personality types, and interpersonal dynamics that covertly shape inter-student relationships, resulting in a functional or dysfunctional classroom. Understanding and modifying instructional activities to meet learners' individual needs includes, to a large extent, teaching the invisible classroom.

as Level 1. For example, it is possible to adapt a Level 3 societal topic such as ethnic discrimination for the Level 1 learner by identifying and expanding on a survival-level sub-topic such as comparing food and dress in the target language culture and the native language culture, where the teacher can then mentor learners as they reflect, even at the younger ages and in their limited language, on cultural difference, respect for other cultures, and lack of respect for other cultures, that is, ethnic discrimination in the broadest sense. An excellent example of how PBI works at the K-6 grade level is available at TEDx (Martin, 2016), where 4th grade learners collaborate in groups on projects that involve solving actual, real-life problems: one group prepares a presentation to present to a local water board on a water problem in the community; another builds a website for a business; another readies a demonstration about a business prototype.

In OACD, a textbook guides teachers through Level 1/Intermediate Low and Intermediate Mid to ensure standardization in the learning and acquisition of basic linguistic features, such as structure and vocabulary. Generally beginning at Level 1+/Intermediate High and above, but occasionally at lower levels, depending on teacher and learner readiness, there is no textbook, but rather a theme-based syllabus orienting teachers as they construct what Kumaravadivelu (2003, pp. 33, 39, 40) terms "personal theories of practice," applying macrostrategies such as maximizing learning opportunities, facilitating negotiated interaction, promoting learner autonomy, contextualizing linguistic input, and integrating language skills. To enrich teacher "theories of practice," ACTFL recently compiled a list of recommended "high-leverage teaching practices" (Glisan & Donato, 2017) for incorporation into unit and daily lesson plans:

- facilitating target language comprehensibility;
- building a classroom discourse community;
- guiding learners to interpret and discuss authentic texts;
- focusing on cultural products, practices, and perspectives in a dialogic context;
- focusing on form in a dialogic context through PACE;[5] and
- providing oral corrective feedback to improve learner performance.

---

[5] "The high-leverage teaching practice that has been chosen for focus on form is a Dialogic Story-Based Approach called PACE [Presenting; Attention; Co-Constructing; Extending] (Adair-Hauck & Donato, 2016). This approach reconciles the polarized views of deductive and inductive approaches. It allows teachers and students to work together to build understandings of form as they are encountered in meaningful texts. The approach invites the learner to experience meaning through an engaging, coherently organized text and then construct concepts about target language structures through discussion and dialogue with the teacher" (Glisan & Donato, 2017, pp. 94–95).

OACD, macrostrategies, and high-leverage teaching practices equip teachers to set up optimal learning conditions that facilitate the attainment of higher levels of proficiency. The combination of (1) a theme-based syllabus at Levels 1+/Intermediate High and above and (2) formative assessments frees learners from an over-concentration on test preparation so they can focus on learning the language and enhances teachers' creativity in lesson preparation as they are not restricted by test content.

5.3 Typical OACD Common Features at the 1+ Level and Above

OACD teachers exhibit common features, such as:

- use of authentic materials from day one;
- deliberate, continual use of the target language;
- learner delivery of content;
- project/scenario-based instruction;
- development and use of higher-order thinking skills;
- use of formative assessments;
- integration of both formal and colloquial language;
- integration of non-standard language;
- incorporation of collaborative learning, such as group presentations and projects based on learner research;
- use of a wider variety of listening and reading genres across the full spectrum of social media platforms, such as Instagram, Twitter, WhatsApp, possibly Facebook, LinkedIn, blogs, and so on (Campbell & Sarac, 2017);
- systematic defossilization;[6]
- focus on stylistics, including use of register;
- focus on discourse analysis;
- incorporation of *super-authentic* (Cohen, 2015) language – language spoken by two or more people with ambient noise, grammatical mistakes, fillers, and so on; and
- top-down and bottom-up processing of high-level presentations on topical domains such as politics, economics, and history by guest speakers.

---

[6] Ehrman (2002) describes five types of fossilization that must be defossilized in order to reach the highest levels of proficiency, generally methodically (systematically), with teacher assistance, ongoing diagnostic/formative assessment, and extensive practice: functional (continued use of incorrect or limited linguistic forms); instructor-fostered (habit of overly compliant teachers adapting to learners' errors); domain (narrow language use); affective (continued dependence upon a teacher); and strategic (not moving beyond compensation strategies that work well at lower levels to metacognitive strategies that are required at higher levels).

5.4 Actualizing OACD in the Learning Space: Two Case Studies

5.4.1 Case 1: A Short-Term Intensive Course for the Level 1+/Intermediate-High Learner of Korean

Lyu (2018) – the teacher for the course described here – discusses how to use well-designed oral discussion as a technique for improving listening and reading comprehension, delineating a language course based entirely on this technique. The learners are Level 1+ military linguists in CE at DLIFLC who participate in the four- to six-week intensive course six hours per day of class, five days per week, where the goal is to increase proficiency by half a level in the two targeted skills, as well as speaking. OACD is influenced by Nation and Newton's (2009, p. 5) conditions for learning through meaning-focused output:

- The learners write and talk about things that are largely familiar to them;
- The learners' main goal is to convey their message to someone else;
- Only a small proportion of the language they need to use is not familiar to them;
- The learners can use communication strategies, dictionaries, or previous input to make up for gaps in their productive knowledge; and
- There are plenty of opportunities to produce.

Regarding the first and third items, Lyu clarifies that learners must have background knowledge of the discussion theme and specific topic, as well as adequate linguistic knowledge to express themselves, for the activity to be successful.

No textbook is distributed, just authentic materials. Practicing OACD, teacher and learners negotiate the discussion themes, specific topics, and activities, regularly modifying them in response to input from both parties. Each class centers on one discussion topic. Homework materials, which are differentiated based on proficiency level, focus on the next topic for class discussion in order to provide learners with background knowledge for the discussion. During class, learners orally present their summaries and participate in a variety of discussion formats. Regarding results, Lyu reports that of 23 learners in six courses during the years 2015 to 2017, 19 (83 percent) increased proficiency by at least half a level in listening and reading comprehension in the Defense Language Proficiency Test (DLPT).

5.4.2 Case 2: A Long-Term Intensive Course for the Beginning Learner of Egyptian Arabic

Jones (personal communication, February 15, 2018) – the teacher of the course described here for learners with no prior knowledge of either Egyptian Arabic or Modern Standard Arabic – affirms that OACD facilitates the use of authentic materials from day one within a content-based instructional environment. Regarding its application in the Egyptian Arabic basic course at DLIFLC, she reports:

> With OA[CD], the voice of learners is heard and their interests taken into consideration. When learners are asked by the teacher to take responsibility for their own learning, their intrinsic motivation increases as they research areas of interest and prepare content for delivery. When the teacher is empowered to take responsibility for her/his teaching,[7] s/he can work with learners to negotiate aspects of the curriculum throughout the entire course.

Jones has observed that learners at Level 1 are more attentive when working with authentic than with textbook materials. While authentic materials render instruction more relevant because their provenance is real life, to be most effective, they must be used with a variety of other curricular features, such as those listed earlier.

Due to the speed, pragmatics, and discourse types in authentic listening materials such as documentaries, soap operas, songs, and films, teachers usually need to apply scaffolding techniques (Donato, 1994; Mitchell & Myles, 2004; Vygotsky, 1978/2013) to help learners cope with the new information because, during initial classes, much vocabulary is unknown, structural knowledge is minimal, and difficulty understanding vocabulary delivered orally is to be expected. Gradually, teachers can introduce fragments of the authentic material in phases, where grammatical features, semantics, phonological issues, and cultural and social background information are addressed as they emerge (Van Lier, 1996). Teachers can further support learners by ensuring that they have had instruction in language learning strategies such as inferencing from context, risk taking, circumlocution, and so on, and are methodically applying them in their learning.

Jones emphasizes that each stage in OACD, regardless of level, requires clear learning objectives and expected outcomes in alignment with level-appropriate activities primarily assessed through formative assessments. Regarding course evaluation, learners and teacher are offered multiple opportunities throughout the course to reflect on the curriculum through formal and informal oral and written surveys.

Course results attest to the merits of OACD. The proficiency scores from one Egyptian basic course in 2018 composed of five learners and two teachers exceeded the planned 2022 goal: 80 percent achieved Level 2+ and above in

---

[7] Historically, teaching teams in the basic course at DLIFLC have used a prescribed textbook, which teachers have been expected to adapt to learner needs, and standardized teaching practices based on the latest trends in language learning.

listening comprehension; 100 percent achieved Level 2+ and above in reading comprehension; 80 percent achieved Level 2 in speaking.

5.5 Conclusion

In today's dynamic learning space, where learners expect and take advantage of opportunities to learn at all hours of the day, language professionals are called to explore and continually experiment with new and different curricular models as we search for better ways to facilitate, and support, learning. Educators, such as the many referenced in this volume, have successfully implemented TLLT and its principles, such as OACD. Institutions like the University of Hawaii at Manoa, in its Korean Language Flagship Program (Cheon, 2018), and the French War College, in its English and French Language Departments (see Cleret, this volume; Collin, this volume), are exploring its application. Some teachers, such as Rebecca Aubrey (2019 ACTFL National Language Teacher of the Year), have opted to create their own materials in collaboration with learners, rather than use a textbook, engaging in what she terms "free-range learning" (Aubrey, 2019). The history of strong proficiency results demonstrated across multiple languages in the context of CE at DLIFLC over the past seven years, those in the Russian Program at the Foreign Service Institute in the 1980s, and those in the Egyptian Arabic basic course at DLIFLC recently are indicative of OACD's merits. With its emphasis on systematic tailoring to learner needs, the constant solicitation of input on aspects of the curriculum from the learners themselves, the use of a theme-based syllabus rather than a textbook at Level 1+/Intermediate High and above, and the implementation of formative assessments as the primary source of feedback to improve the learning and teaching process, OACD can contribute to more effective learning.

DISCUSSION QUESTIONS

1. What are the curricular challenges facing you in your teaching? Are they connected with:
   - uncertainty about what curricular design to select;
   - lack of time to research options;
   - obstacles to change by school/university administration;
   - curricular designs imposed by school/university administration; and/or
   - uncertainty about what assessments to use?
2. Research existing curricular designs. What are the similarities and differences across the designs? Devise a contrastive analysis chart and present it to an audience.

6

Foreign Language Learning Efficiency

Transformative Learning in an Outcomes-Based Environment

Andrew R. Corin

This chapter describes the experience of planning and implementing one form of open architecture curricular design (OACD) (see Campbell, this volume) within a specific transformative language learning environment (Leaver & Campbell, 2020) to meet two requirements that arose during 2012–2014 at the Defense Language Institute Foreign Language Center (DLIFLC). It also describes a confluence of pressures that motivated both the requirement and form of response. These are circumstances replicated ever more frequently in foreign language education/training (FLED) as practitioners must respond simultaneously to increasingly stringent demands for accountability and our ever more complex understanding of effective FLED practices.

The initial requirement was to improve outcomes for "post-Defense Language Proficiency Test (post-DLPT)" cohorts. These are short (typically four- to eight-week) ad hoc courses for students who, at the conclusion of the program, initially fail to achieve Basic Course graduation requirements: ILR 2/2/1+ (listening/reading/speaking) on the DLPT and Oral Proficiency Interview (OPI). The second, beginning 2013, responded to the impending elimination of DLIFLC's 6- to 12-month resident intermediate and advanced (int/adv) programs, replacing them with courses roughly three to four months in length but with analogous objectives (minimum .5 ILR level increase per skill: 2 > 2+ through 3+ > 4).

In both instances, it was necessary to design a form of curriculum applicable across the range of languages offered at DLIFLC. Moreover, it was imperative that courses could be brought online rapidly, initially within days for post-DLPT inputs, and weeks or months in the case of intermediate (objective 2+) and advanced (objective 3 or higher) courses, regardless of instructors' previous experience with such curricula.

The approach clearly could not be based on textbooks, yet it had to satisfy complex planning requirements to achieve required outcomes in such limited time frames. The response was to design what was essentially a template that encapsulated the desiderata for a high-impact short course but could be "populated" with content or modified on short notice. Course planners were not required to adhere to the template, but it provided a simple and effective planning tool that was adopted for many of the courses. This approach incorporated scenario-based and content-based instruction with fully integrated activities in a modular curricular design (SBI-CBI). Since a traditional linear scope-and-sequence approach with articulation of content between successive chapters was not feasible, SBI-CBI relied instead on "vertical spiraling" (defined later).

The immediate purpose of this approach was to enable rapid proficiency growth for learners with a broad range of incoming proficiency levels within unusually short time frames. However, SBI-CBI also implemented central components of transformative language learning (enumerated by Campbell, this volume); indeed, it depended upon them for success. SBI-CBI placed students in situations in which they must seek, internalize, integrate, and exploit information and ideas from a variety of authentic target language (TL) cultural sources to construct open-ended responses to intellectually demanding needs defined by the scenario. In this process, they experienced incompatibilities with existing perspectives up to and including disorienting dilemmas (Mezirow, 1991). Resolution of such "perspective clashes" required the engagement of critical and higher-order thinking, which is a key academic desideratum, and promoted growth toward the cross-cultural awareness and competencies required for professional-level and distinguished-level foreign language (FL) proficiency (ILR 3–4).

6.1 The Current FLED Environment: Tension among Competing Requirements

Two critical features generate primary challenges for FLED today and were felt acutely at DLIFLC during the period of SBI-CBI development. One is the ever-expanding spectrum of dimensions, principles, and practices believed to contribute to effective FL learning. The second consists of two linked components: a *law of rising expectations* and the increasing emphasis on *accountability for learning outcomes*. The challenge is to achieve accountability in satisfying rising expectations in an environment in which resources for FL learning remain static and periodically under threat. In the DLIFLC context, this challenge could only be met by integrating the greatly expanded range of factors now thought to affect learning – already a tall order – in a way that allowed for rapid deployment and easy adaptability.

The complexity of current FLED practices can be illustrated by the evolution that has occurred since the audiolingual method's reliance on practice repetition as a component of a practice- and drill-based approach within a behavioristic framework of second language acquisition. Today, FLED understands and applies practice/repetition within a more complex framework that includes emphases on contextualization, authentic materials, immersive learning, learner empowerment and autonomy, developing and engaging critical thinking and higher-order thinking skills. TL is used to meet real or simulated needs, and the range of contexts and modalities of TL exposure and utilization is maximized. Promoting transformative growth as a key factor in attaining the cross-cultural competencies characteristic of upper-range proficiency adds yet another layer of complexity. Numerous other parameters relate to individual learner differences, including biographical background, personality, habitual learning strategies, preferred sensory channels, meta-cognitive awareness, and motivational profiles (Dörnyei et al., 2015; Ehrman et al., 2003; Oxford, 2017). Others take cognizance of the dynamics, both overt and covert (i.e., the "hidden classroom"), within learner cohorts (Ehrman & Dörnyei, 1998; see also Salyer & Leaver, this volume). Multiple considerations relate to the efficient utilization of time, including optimizing (as opposed to maximizing) overall hours devoted to language study, in-class and out-of-class activities (e.g., "flipped classrooms"), in-class versus in-country experiences, and the integration of FL learning with other topics. Obviously, these components of our current framework go far beyond practice repetition, but all bear on its application and illustrate the complexity inherent in FL study and teaching today.

This complexity suggests a need for curricular planning that is not only principled, but also intricate. However, the exploitation of learner and cohort variation, the attainment of transformative objectives, the ever-evolving TL environment, and a requirement for rapid implementation militate against the use of static or "prepackaged" courses in favor of OACD.

The second crucial characteristic of the twenty-first-century FLED environment is the widespread emphasis on the quantification of language acquisition through proficiency and performance-based scales (e.g., ILR, ACTFL, CEFR). In concert with more articulated and evidence-based accreditation requirements for defining and tracking overall program performance based on measured student learning outcomes (ACCJC, 2014),[1] this generates internal and external pressures to ensure that learners achieve specified proficiency or performance levels.

The need for professional-level and, in some contexts, distinguished-level linguistic and cultural competencies (ILR 3–4) has been well documented within business and government (both civilian and military) communities over the past two decades – levels of knowledge, skills, and cultural understanding rarely encountered among university, military school, or service academy

[1] The Accrediting Commission for Community and Junior Colleges of the Western Association of Schools and Colleges (ACCJC) is the accrediting agency for DLIFLC.

graduates in previous decades.[2] In response to these heightened demands, notable results have been achieved through the integrated exploitation of FLED best practices.[3] Moreover, some programs now have learning outcome objectives at or approaching professional level. DLIFLC recently increased its Basic Course student learning objectives from ILR 2/2/1+ to 2+/2+/2 (DLIFLC, 2017, 2018).[4] The federally supported Language Flagship core program seeks to produce graduates possessing ILR 3 proficiency (DLNSEO, 2018, p. 20). Sacco (2014) discusses a similar development among international business programs in the USA and Europe.

The outcomes-based environment thus impels course designers toward a concept of *efficiency of FL learning*. It is no longer sufficient to ensure that learning is taking place (i.e., that a program is *effective*); it is essential that the program also be *efficient*, enabling learners to achieve ambitious final learning outcomes within constrained time and other resource limitations. Moreover, learning at this pace must be sustainable for the instructional team, and replicable from cohort to cohort.

6.2 SBI-CBI as a Response to the Challenge

In order to achieve learning efficiency, course developers must confront the natural tension that exists between two aspects of the current FLED framework as described earlier. On one side is the demand for built-in curricular structure to ensure the incorporation of numerous academic desiderata. On the other is the need for curricular flexibility to enable diagnostic-based instruction with ongoing formative assessment, learner empowerment and autonomy, and (in the case of DLIFLC's post-DLPT and shortened int/adv courses) the rapid implementation of mission-responsive solutions. Course structure should thus allow for significant in-course modification in response to emerging needs and learning opportunities without disruption or learner confusion. The course should also allow for updating between consecutive iterations to incorporate

---

[2] Department of Defense (2005) and Inspection: United States Department of State and the Broadcasting Board of Governors, Office of the Inspector General (2013) show advocacy for cadres with ILR Level 3 and 4 proficiency, respectively. Sacco (2014) explores the profound significance of upper-range TL proficiency in international business.

[3] Corin (1997) illustrates an earlier DLIFLC example. More recently, DLIFLC int/adv courses have commonly produced Level 3+/4 outcomes. The Language Flagship programs commonly produce graduates with superior proficiency (DLNSEO, 2018).

[4] As of the time of writing, the minimum graduation requirement remains 2/2/1+, with the objective of achieving 2+/2+/2 for 76 percent of graduates by 2024.

lessons learned, respond to current target culture developments, and incorporate new ideas, all without time-consuming course revision.

The "template" developed for the post-DLPT and shortened int/adv courses has the following central components in common. First, it is *scenario-based and content-based*. These approaches are well suited to an open architecture and modular curriculum, the engagement of critical thinking and higher-order thinking skills, as well as integrating activities over the course of a day, week, or longer, and serving a focus for learning activities.

Second, it is *modular* in the sense of Stryker and Leaver (1997, p. 180), that is, organized into "self-contained units of study and independent of one another and could be presented in any sequence." Modular organization entails abandoning or de-emphasizing traditional linear scope and sequence (i.e., the sequenced introduction of specific language elements and functions) as a principle of unit sequencing and organization in favor of "vertical spiraling."[5] This implements Tarone's (2017) admonition (paraphrased from my notes): "Don't be so worried about what your students *can't* do. They very likely can, just not as well at first. Don't place a glass ceiling over them by limiting the tasks that you allow them to attempt." Vertical spiraling is simply the repeated application throughout a course, module, day, or hour of series of tasks of increasing demand based on authentic sources, preferably in an immersive (TL-only) environment.[6] Each task/activity is itself organized as a performance training cycle (PTC),[7] and modules are designed to maximize the number of these series of PTCs of increasing complexity during a module, day, or even hour. The goal is to achieve an upward spiral of performance at every task level (see Figure 6.1), rather than an upward gradation of exposure to, and proficiency in, ever higher-level tasks and text types over the course of a term (see Figure 6.2).

Performance may be rudimentary in early PTCs but improves over successive cycles. Vertical spiraling corrects the mismatch within traditional scope-and-sequence approaches between the progressively increasing time needed to achieve ever higher levels of proficiency (the "inverted pyramid") and time-on-task with ever higher-level task and text types (a non-inverted pyramid

---

[5] Vertical spiraling need not eliminate all elements of sequencing. Dababneh (2018) considers one crucial element of a successful modular curriculum to be a progression of ever more cognitively challenging topics over successive modules. This serves to make SBI-CBI more accessible for learners with limited incoming knowledge and proficiencies, as well as for those accustomed to more structured and sequenced learning.

[6] Corin (1997) provides an early discussion with different terminology.

[7] A PTC is simply a sequence of work-up, performance, and debrief/feedback with troubleshooting.

- **Activity Cycle**
  - Argumentation
  - Narration
  - Description
  - Naming

- **Upward progression of:**
  - Demand
  - Performance

- **Upward Spiral over Course:**

Figure 6.1 Vertical spiraling. This figure illustrates re-cycling an upward progression of task types utilizing authentic sources, yielding an upward progression of performance. The terms *naming*, *description*, *narration*, and *argumentation* are chosen arbitrarily as indexical for classes of activities characteristic of proficiencies at ILR Levels 0+, 1, 2, and 3. Thus, *naming* refers to text/task types that learners can often deal with effectively at ILR level 0+ and so on.

- **Activity Progression**
  - Argumentation
  - Narration
  - Description
  - Naming

- **Upward Progression of:**
  - Text Type
  - Task Type

- **Upward Progression over Course:**

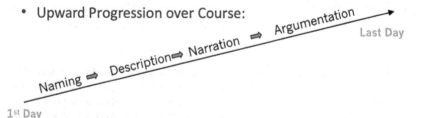

Figure 6.2 Linear scope and sequence. This figure illustrates a linear scope-and-sequence approach based on a gradual upward progression of text and task types.

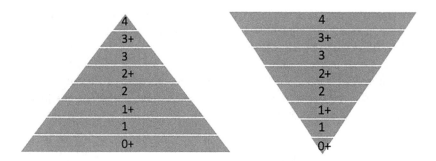

Time-on-Task at Text   Time Needed to Achieve
and Task Level   Proficiency Level

Figure 6.3 Time allocation. This figure illustrates time allocation under linear scope and sequence: inverted pyramid of time-to-next-proficiency-level mated to non-inverted pyramid of time-on-task at each text/task level. Numbers (0+ – 4) refer to ILR proficiency levels.

[see Figure 6.3]). Modules are also easier to bring online or modify than units based on linear scope and sequence, as the need to artificially limit text and task types (as well as specific vocabulary, phraseology, and language functions) at earlier stages and to articulate between preceding and following units is eliminated. For post-DLPT cohorts and shortened int/adv courses, modules intended for use over the course of a single week were favored. Modules of this length allow for rapid design and implementation, ease of adaptation/ modification, and maintaining learner energy, while providing sufficient opportunity for students to develop significant performance skills for an end-of-module scenario.

Activities within the module are *fully integrated*. A key integrating component is the culminating activity (CA), a final scenario that provides an organizing principle for the module. All module activities build the knowledge and skill base needed to perform the CA. All activities are also mutually integrated as participants explore various dimensions or sub-topics contributing to the CA; each activity reinforces or deepens learning from every other sub-topic. Learners are also integrated with one another by ensuring that, at each stage of work, each participant depends upon the inputs of every other participant, thus ensuring a cooperative approach, heightened motivation, and focused attention from all students. For this reason, the CA should itself consist of multiple stages to ensure that students pay critical attention while others present during the first stage. Integration is further achieved through an initial negotiating process, agreeing on sub-topics, possibly breaking into teams to focus on different perspectives, and allowing students to take ownership of the process and mentally map out the learning lying ahead of them. Intermediate topical scope is a final critical requirement for full integration. The module topic must be broad enough to support inquiry into multiple sub-topics contributing to the CA but sufficiently constrained to ensure that sub-topics are sufficiently linked so as to be mutually informing.

6.3 Sample SBI-CBI Module

The following outline of a week-long module on humanitarian aid to North Korea has been used for demonstration and professional development purposes at DLIFLC; a reduced version has been used in DLIFLC's Korean Basic Course program.[8] Its structure is analogous to week-long modules employed for post-DLPT and int/adv courses in a variety of languages.

In this module, students are cast as members of a working group of a fictitious Korea-based USA–South Korean Joint Committee on North Korea, whose Board of Directors (BoD) will soon meet with visiting American policy makers. As their CA, the "working group" will prepare and deliver recommendations to the BoD regarding policies that the Committee should advocate in regard to humanitarian aid to North Korea.

Following the introduction and planning session, each day is devoted to research on one sub-topic. These may include: (1) North Korea's humanitarian situation; (2) South Korean political and humanitarian policies toward North Korea; (3) the Six-Party Talks and international humanitarian policies toward North Korea; and (4) recent developments in North and South Korea.

The CA consists of multiple segments. During the first, the working group debates the pros and cons of alternative policies; in the second, they negotiate, draft, and present a consensus based on the debate outcome. As a reflective follow-up, individual participants may compose an op-ed piece, taking advantage of all preceding activities. Over the course of the module, students complete as many vertically spiraled PTCs as time permits to gradually develop their presentation skills for the CA.

Among the numerous week-long modules designed and selected for implementation were modules entitled "The Waters of Iran" (drawing together physical geography, climate change, geopolitical, strategic, and open waters perspectives) for the post-DLPT and int/adv Persian Farsi program),[9] "Sustaining

---

[8]   The full module design was authored by Dr. Mina Lee.

[9]   This module, designed by Dr. Parandeh Kia, utilized a portfolio approach for its CA.

Gains in Poverty Reduction and Human Development in the Levantine Region" (including topics of unemployment, desertification, illiteracy, political instability) for the Levantine Arabic conversion program,[10] and many others. Under a linear scope-and-sequence approach, these topics would most likely be considered inappropriate for students in the post-DLPT context.[11]

6.4 Results and Lessons Learned

SBI-CBI was initially developed to meet the need for improved post-DLPT outcomes. While the operational pace prevented the systematic comparison of results to those from other approaches, available data indicated that SBI-CBI outcomes were superior overall to those of the traditional programs for these languages. For example, data from six post-DLPT Persian Farsi cohorts administered by the Directorate of Continuing Education between December 2011 and October 2012 are indicative.[12] Of 22 students for whom incoming and outgoing DLPT scores were available, 19 achieved at least a half-level improvement in listening or reading (speaking was not measured). Nine achieved a full-level improvement in at least one skill. Four achieved a 1.5-level increase in one skill, and one achieved a 2-level increase (ILR 1 > ILR 3) in listening. In end-of-program questionnaires, most students indicated satisfaction with the method. Informal reporting from int/adv program chairs indicates that most have continued to employ SBI-CBI or variations thereof.

As with any new approach, SBI-CBI experienced growing pains. These pertained primarily to the post-DLPT experience as the int/adv instructor corps had more extensive experience with the components of this approach: SBI, CBI, TL-only instruction, modular design, and so on. One challenge was an understandable level of exhaustion and disappointment of students assigned to the post-DLPT course after failing to achieve graduation requirements on the DLPT/OPI. Another was "culture shock" due to students' insufficient previous experience learning through analogous methods. Most adjusted successfully to the new environment but several concrete steps were defined for mitigation. One was an initial low-stress week during which students read English texts on area-studies topics to create schemata for employment during SBI-CBI. Another was strategically situated "sheltered time" (English allowed) before or after immersive study to troubleshoot difficulties that resisted resolution during the immersive phase.

---

[10] This module was designed by Dr. Reem Dababneh.

[11] Dababneh (2018) provides further examples from the Arabic int/adv program.

[12] The Continuing Education faculty began applying an analogous methodology to post-DLPT cohorts prior to the formalized development of the "template."

6.5 **Conclusion**

Contributions of SBI-CBI to OACD and transformative language learning and teaching (TLLT) include vertical spiraling as a path to proficiency growth that maximizes learner autonomy and learner empowerment, time-on-task with higher-level text/task types, reliance on authentic sources in an immersive environment at earlier stages of learning, and the integration of activities. In the vertical spiraling environment, performance levels achieved depend on participants' incoming proficiency levels. What is expected is a gradual enhancement of performance from PTC to PTC and from module to module. For this reason, an ancillary benefit of the approach is its capacity to accommodate multilevel cohorts of students with diverse needs. Finally, DLIFLC's 2012–2014 experience with students having at least ILR 1 proficiency indicates the likely benefit of introducing aspects of OACD and TLLT into earlier stages of training to prepare students to assume a greater role in managing their language learning and as preparation for their studies at more advanced levels.

DISCUSSION QUESTIONS

1. What strategies might you employ to enable multilevel cohorts of students to function effectively and cooperatively in a TL-only, scenario-based learning environment so that all benefit?
2. Are there other instructional and curricular models, including those included in this volume, that have similarities to what is here termed "vertical spiraling"? How do these various models differ in their approaches to increasing learners' engagement with higher-level tasks and unmodified authentic texts?
3. How would you differentiate between scenario-based and project-based instruction in regard to both their process and their effect? Interview two or more instructors and consider whether they share common conceptions about these approaches.

7

The Challenges of Implementing Transformative Pedagogy

Emilie Cleret

This chapter examines the transition of the English-language program for French military officers at the French War College (École de Guerre) over two years from traditional grammar-translation teaching to a transformative philosophy of education that embraces transformative pedagogy (TP) and open architecture.

This academy is located in Paris, opposite the Eiffel Tower, within a heritage monument called the École Militaire. It was founded in 1751 by King Louis XV and it embraces a long-standing military tradition.

The École de Guerre is currently training what many have called the 9/11 generation – those who took on a military career just after the terrorist attacks. This is a generation of combat-proven officers with extensive field experience on land, at sea, and in the air in the Middle East, Mali, the Sahel, Afghanistan, and Iraq.

Every year, about 180 French senior officers join the École de Guerre for a one-year course after selection through a competitive exam. They come from the army, the navy, the air force, the gendarmerie, and military directorates, and have about 15 years of operational and command experience. They are future leaders of the French forces. In addition, 70 foreign officers from 60 countries join the cohort every September. The main objective of the course is to help these officers move away from a tactical level of command to become decision-makers at operational and strategic levels.

A team of 18 teachers from English-speaking countries deliver the English program to the French officers once they have been streamed into small groups. The English department is one of the many departments in the academy – geopolitics, operational planning, strategy, and others.

Over several years, the English program's low approval ratings from students suggested that the curriculum and teaching methods were not meeting their expectations. Within this learning environment, the communicative and transactional approaches (Cleret, 2018; Leaver & Cleret, 2018; see also Leaver, this volume) had reached their limits.

7.1 Understanding that Challenges Lie in the Learning Environment

To apprehend the risks, challenges, and caveats, it is important to understand the cultural, professional, and academic context in which a transformative approach is undertaken and how this specific context will shape practice (Taylor, 2009). The key adaptive challenges flowed from all figures in the equation: the learner (our priority); the chain of command and the military faculty; the English teaching team; and the course designer – who is also the head of the English department.

In order to be motivated and active, learners must feel comfortable in their learning environment and, ideally, perceive that their career needs are being met. The course was a one-size-fits-all curriculum designed according to the communicative approach. Instructions were given in the target language. The emphasis was on understanding meaning rather than concentrating on form. The focus was on using "authentic material," that is, news podcasts, talk shows, and other materials prepared by native speakers for native speakers. Teachers provided communicative situations, focusing on pair work, role plays, and so on. Errors were tolerated as a natural development of fluency.

This communicative approach had been chosen because French students unanimously complained that their English courses at school focused too much on linguistic patterns and grammar rather than oral communication. It seemed like the right choice. Nevertheless, this approach was not making the learners feel comfortable at all. They stated in their feedback that they felt they were never given opportunities to express how their needs could be met.

So, why was there such dissatisfaction? In fact, it appears that the question "How can we motivate learners?" was the wrong one because it leads pedagogical staff and teachers to make choices on behalf of learners that often result in artificial and inappropriate answers. The right question is the opposite one: "What makes learners lose their natural motivation?"

All learners should be motivated to master a foreign language and, in reality, it is most likely that everyone is. Few would contest that speaking a foreign language is an advantage. The motivation-killer was not necessarily the approach in itself, but the way it was imposed. This cause of demotivation could be called "anticipated" teaching – all aspects of prepared teaching are predetermined ahead of the act of teaching. This anticipated teaching takes many forms – "manuals," "syllabi," or "curricula" – and they all operate in the same way – a one-size-fits-all approach. Yet, however well designed, a course that is pre-written and then forced on the learner is likely to impair motivation.

The solution seemed to lie in redesigning the syllabus using a transformative approach. The École de Guerre decided to introduce TP into its foreign language programs in May 2016 so that the newly designed programs could be launched in September 2016. The military directing staff were also very reluctant to accept this looming change and demonstrated resistance, if not hostility.

In the preface to *Transformative learning in practice*, Jack Mezirow and Edward W. Taylor (2009, p. xi) write that "transformative learning has become the dominant teaching paradigm discussed within the field of adult education." While this may be true in the USA and other countries, it is not the case in France. US schools enjoy a tradition of learner self-empowerment, hence the great number of student-led clubs in most schools. Teachers are requested to point out achievements instead of inadequacies and will put particular effort into creating a positive learning environment.

In France, the sage on the stage spoon-feeds knowledge. Understanding and acquiring that knowledge is a solitary process for the learner. Culturally, learners do not debate with a teacher (just as, importantly in this context, you do not with a higher-ranking officer). In this vertical structure, students expect teachers to force them to work and to spotlight their failings using tests. Students see progress purely in terms of grades; this means that nearly all the feedback students receive is negative. In the case of foreign-language learning, students are disparaged every time the slightest mistake is made, and the self-confidence needed to speak erodes.

Language is taught via the grammar-translation method. While this approach allows students to acquire knowledge of grammar rules and master long vocabulary lists, it does not offer the opportunity to practice speaking. It does not favor the self-confidence necessary to be effective communicators in L2. Students thus experience the frustrating paradox of sitting in English classes for over seven years and never being able to sustain a conversation.

French learners can be reluctant to learn English for historical, linguistic, and cultural reasons. The most salient point is that the French identify the English language with the English people, who have mostly been their violent enemy. This long-lasting rivalry has infused proverbs, sayings, and idioms. The French language underwent huge phonetic changes between Old French and the modern language: the loss of final consonants and strong stress, the weakened pronunciation of vowels and diphthongs, and so on. Thus, the English language often seems counterintuitive to the French learner. This is one of the reasons that they tend to retain a strong accent.

In the École de Guerre, the cohort seems to form a homogeneous group that perpetuates the long-lasting tradition of who in society would access a commission – male, Caucasian, Catholic, well-read, sharp minds from upper-class or aristocratic families, and usually from military dynasties. Their views are strongly grounded in prescriptive assumptions: tight-knit communities and defenders of national values. Toning down differences is a survival reflex, especially in a group that always needs to show that they can move forward as one. This becomes all the more necessary in the light of recent terrorist attacks in France, which have led the military to close in and protect itself from the press and the body politic. In addition to the learners' national culture and academic background, it is necessary to add military culture into the equation.

For the learning process to be successful, it was important to help students learn through a process that would transform their narrow frames of reference to more inclusive ones that are open to change (Mezirow & Taylor, 2009); the focus also needed to be on challenging the military administrators and teaching team. Getting a green light from the military chain of command is an external challenge to the English program. Although aware of what needed to be changed and why, they had to be convinced to support the chosen strategy and process. Explaining the different stages in a student-led transformative learning process would most likely be useless as it differs significantly from the military drill used to acquire skills such as folding a parachute. The temptation is to apply the drill to other domains. Using examples of potential outcomes such as honing cross-cultural understanding and becoming more effective when working with US or British counterparts proved effective, especially since administrators were aware of the ineffectiveness of the English program in achieving these outcomes. Military culture is very pragmatic: the approval of a course of action is by reference to observable outcomes.

Bringing the teaching team on board was crucial. The English teachers are the cornerstone for implementing student-led TP. Teachers' cultural and academic backgrounds facilitated the task. Being from English-speaking countries, they were trained not to be the sage on the stage, and as civilians, they were used to operating in more horizontal structures and had also experienced tensions in their classroom arising from their instructional methods.

Two stumbling blocks remained. First, with their seemingly incompatible profiles, having teachers and learners work together risked creating sociolinguistic insecurity for both groups. Second, the head of department (and course designer) was placed in a situation where she had to question her own long-held assumptions about foreign language education.

A few years ago, one was taught to plan lessons using three steps that involved only the teacher's view: "What do I want the students to learn?"; "What teaching and learning activities will I use?"; and "How will I assess progress?" All these questions are in the first-person singular, the needs analysis is filtered through only the teacher's framework. The process is not fit for adult learners because it leaves them out of the equation by not valuing their experience, not addressing what they regard as useful, and not discussing a learning contract with them. As a result of this process, the course designer was putting the École de Guerre students into the learning environment that they had loathed, viewing the syllabus and teaching team as threats. In their feedback, they often stated that they felt that they were being told that British or US culture was better than French culture. This had never been the intention; it resulted from a syllabus being forced upon them, creating a barrier between the students and the teachers.

If the curriculum has the virtue of making teachers interchangeable, it also eliminates their role as educators and turns them into mechanical lecturers. The impossibility of assuming one's role as educator to better relay a curriculum is a strong factor in teacher demotivation. The personal and emotional disengagement of the teacher in the learning process is bound to create a contagious demotivation for the learners.

7.2 Transformative Pedagogy to Meet Learners' Needs and Bridge the Faculty–Student Gap

Pedagogy and teaching methods are merely concepts until adapted to a particular learning environment and its goals. Essential first steps include understanding the concepts and studying the specificities of TP: analyzing cases of its successful implementation; maintaining awareness that what works in one context cannot be copied into another; and accepting that open-architecture lesson-planning allows the syllabus to evolve, meaning that some teachers may never find their comfort zone.

The English department was introduced to the concepts of TP, open architecture curricular design, and the counterintuitive nature of teaching and learning for upper proficiency levels by Dr. Betty Lou Leaver, then Provost of the Defense Language Institute Foreign Language Center (DLIFLC). It was striking to realize that the operative word was "counterintuitive." It was necessary to be open to go against what had become an intuitive construct of what teaching should be. The English department was given the opportunity to look at the designs of the DLIFLC's courses for advanced Korean, Arabic, and Spanish, all using Transformative Instructional Approaches (TIAs).

Superimposing a US-born theory onto a rather opposite culture would have jeopardized its chances for success. As such, a paradox arose: TP and open architecture could solve problems but the cultural context itself seemed incompatible with both.

An approach that would mark such a strong break with a top-down classroom environment could not be forced upon the students. They would resist developing a heuristic and metanoic process. Imposing a transformative approach to replace a monolithic system would be fruitless. To refer to the first of the ten phases of learning identified by Mezirow (1978a, 1978b), the teaching team could not brutally confront them with a disorienting dilemma.

The journey had to start on the opposite side of the spectrum, in the vertically structured classroom that students disliked. This would take into account the students' academic culture, allowing the context to shape the practice of transformative learning (Taylor, 2009). In effect, the curriculum itself would become what the philosophy was preaching.

The grounds are laid from day one even though the first classes follow a transmission educational philosophy. The teachers try, step by step, to bring in the seven conditions identified by Mezirow to help students engage freely and fully participate in discourse to achieve transformation.

The first module puts the teacher in a directive role but already preparing for transformative learning by adopting rituals, assigning and rotating roles to create an idioculture because trust within the group – teacher and students – is crucial to fostering transformation, that is, to creating "a willingness to seek understanding, agreement, and a tentative best judgment as a test of validity until new perspectives, evidence, or arguments are encountered and validated through discourse as yielding a better judgment" (Mezirow and Associates, 2000, pp. 13–14). They are gradually given "more accurate and complete information" (Mezirow and Associates, 2000, pp. 13–14) as to how the teacher hands over tasks and decisions to them. Being from a different cultural background, the teacher will always suggest their point of view, explaining how one's cultural bias triggers "openness to alternative points of view and empathy and concern about how others think and feel" (Mezirow and Associates, 2000, pp. 13–14). The content is oral presenting and discussing, which are basic skills for officers.

The second module moves into a transaction mode using a more communicative approach. The use of inductive activities, especially debating, offers opportunities to trigger critical dialogue. This hones "the ability to weigh evidence and assess arguments objectively," as well as the "awareness of the context of ideas" (Mezirow and Associates, 2000, pp. 13–14) and taken-for-granted assumptions. As formatted public-speaking, debate generates "equal opportunity to participate in the various roles of discourse" (Mezirow and Associates, 2000, pp. 13–14) and cultural awareness of ways of reasoning that contrast with a Cartesian construct. More advanced students are often very comfortable with the structure and rules of formal debating.

The third module will turn to a student-led approach. The teacher facilitates a discussion where students suggest what and how they want to learn. They do so by consensus, free "from coercion and distorting self-deception" (Mezirow and Associates, 2000, pp. 13–14). The students and teacher will regularly discuss lesson content. As TP relies on collaborative discussion, teachers become active listeners, gathering information and building their understanding of students' cultural mindsets and career needs.

The gradual process from transmission through transaction to transformation shows that the approaches do not have a paradigmatic relationship as they are not interchangeable. However, in our present case, they definitely have a syntagmatic relationship because it is the transition from one to the other that allows the metanoic process to happen and the transformation to operate: the students realize that it is not about becoming someone different, but about transforming their frame of reference to be able to read another culture – and that is when their motivation to learn L2 soars.

7.3 The Ripple Effect: Adapting TP to Multiple Contexts

Implementing TP must have broad support and bringing it in with a heavy hand could prevent transformation and have toxic consequences. At this stage, it is vital to focus on people rather than concepts.

At the École de Guerre, the chain of command imposes a certain subject matter, while the structure of the course remains structurally vertical and culturally biased. This is a challenge for the English TP program. It was decided that the English program and the overall course would not be mutually exclusive. Students are encouraged to bring into the classroom topics imposed by the chain of command in other domains. The teacher and students then see how they want to tackle the topics, invariably drawing on their operational experience. During the collaborative discussions, the teacher always points out the portability of the skills that they are acquiring within the English program to other areas of their professional environment. The administration is invited to attend activities or events that are the outcome of student-led projects. Remaining open to the rest of the course that originally seemed so opposed to TP proved to have a very positive impact. The military faculty decided to start exchanging best practices with the English department and to implement certain activities within a transformative approach.

Adapting TP to a specific context makes it more effective and creates a ripple effect within the organization, bringing positive change across the curriculum. Fully consistent with TP, student-led activities are no longer extracurricular activities done in the dark and in an attic after duty, but now fully integrated into the curriculum. The department has extended the activities with projects such as debating, academic writing, and networking.

The debate program brings international recognition that the military command cannot ignore. Its success is due to coaching administrators to question their assumptions, whether cultural, academic, or military. The key is to encourage the students – through asking questions rather than giving answers – to turn assertions into analysis and logic into persuasion.

This self-inquiry extends to the teaching team. Even abandoning TP in certain contexts may become an option. Interestingly, the collaborative discussion that it relies on means that it can detect its own limits. Learners can choose to reject it in favor of grammar-translation exercises, for example. However, the difference is that this will be a negotiated choice and not imposed upon the learners.

7.4 Conclusion

This experience has led us to understand that the solutions for implementing TP are found within the process that leads to the meta-concept described earlier. TP mainly comes down to teachers ascertaining student aims (language, skills, subject matter, exams) and students accepting their responsibility in building lessons; teaching then follows a transformative student-led approach, with constant reference to cultural insights. The main constraints on students being open to new learning methods are their level of English and their exam objectives. Weaker students tend to ask for teacher direction and scaffolded activities within traditional pedagogical approaches; straying outside this might be considered "transformative," or simply much-needed fun. Preparation for specific exams – increasingly demanded for career development – leans heavily on grammar translation and drills. In the project-related groups, students lead on tasks discussed with external partners in a mix of autonomous learning, project management, cultural awareness, and communication skills. Where TP flourishes is in the intermediate-level (and above) English groups, where students are not taking exams and just want to enjoy speaking English. As for teachers, they take to it readily and find it liberating. TP is a broad and open field, which is exactly what the École de Guerre needs.

DISCUSSION QUESTIONS

1. If you wish to shift to a transformative approach in your language program, how would you prepare the teaching team for the challenges of this pedagogy? What training, workshops, and activities would you design and carry out?
2. What assessment tools should the course designer and head of department use to check that the collaborative dynamics are in place for the transformative approach to be effective and deliver the right outcomes?
3. What actions should be carried out to get effective feedback on the positive impact of this approach in the long term? What are the necessary means to investigate how effective this approach is in relation to the officers' needs for their careers as military leaders and decision-makers at the strategic level?

PART III

Transformative Language Learning and Teaching Applications in University Programs

8

Authentic Resources and Written Reflection as Contributors to Transformative Learning

Stacey Margarita Johnson

For language teachers who are already convinced about *why* to include transformative learning goals, this chapter will help to clarify what we know about *how* these sometimes-elusive learning goals can be scaffolded within our existing instruction. Language teachers interested in including transformative learning goals in their language classes should know that the transformative process is difficult to predict and to measure. However, instructors can intentionally and even successfully nurture transformation without straying far from widely accepted classroom practices by taking a more critical approach.

The nature of transformative learning makes teaching toward it challenging for several reasons. First, transformation typically takes place over much longer periods of time than instructors have with their students. Many language students may only understand the deep learning that has taken place after time has gone by and the process is complete. Second, because the early stages of transformation are largely internal, the instructor is not always aware that it is happening. In some cases, the instructor may have no idea that their students are experiencing such profound change (Johnson, 2015), while others (Crane et al., 2018) may be aware that something special is happening in addition to the typical language-focused learning objectives. Additionally, transformative learning is an integrative experience that draws on experiences from across a student's life and is not limited just to what happens in the classroom. Every student's experience of transformation will be as different as the knowledge, attitudes, relationships, and assumptions that they bring with them. With this in mind, a growing body of empirical research indicates that language teachers' choices do have a potentially significant impact on their students' experiences of transformation.

Mezirow's (1991) original model of transformative learning includes ten distinct steps. This discussion will begin with a focus on three stages of that model that recur in the empirical literature and in various other models of transformation: *disorienting dilemmas*, *critical reflection*, and *taking action*. These three stages are also integral to a Freirean perspective on transformation, which positions "people as subjects, not objects, who are constantly reflecting and acting on the transformation of their world so it can become a more equitable place for all to live" (Taylor, 2008, p. 8). Whereas Mezirow's conception of transformation is focused on the individual experiencing it over time, likely years of development, Freire and others conceptualize the individual as in an ongoing state of transformation of the self and action upon the environment. In a Freirean conception, transformation becomes social change and not just an ultimate experience of self-actualization. If imagining transformation as a process that is both personal and social in nature, and in which the student-self is both the actor and the acted-upon, what is the role of the teacher in such a deeply personal learning process? Randolph and Johnson (2017) echo Freire (1970) in arguing that while transformation is the domain of the student, critical pedagogy – meaning teaching approaches that center on social justice and highlight power relationships in and through language education – is the vehicle through which teachers can best support student transformation.

In both the personal and the social models of transformation, there is an event or a cluster of events that precipitate transformation, often termed a *disorienting dilemma*, followed by a process of critical reflection and, finally, action. Transformative learning theories can provide teachers with an understanding of the underlying learning processes that bring about transformation. However, teachers seeking concrete steps will benefit from knowing what specific classroom practices are associated with disorienting dilemmas and critical reflection in the research literature, as well as how to take a critical approach to established language teaching practices.

8.1 Promoting Disorienting Dilemmas

Mezirow's (1991) term *disorienting dilemma*, also referred to as a *trigger event* by Brookfield (1987, p. 26), comes into play when a person finds that their existing frame of reference is no longer useful for making sense of their situation. Before one can become open to perspective transformation (Mezirow, 1991), or conscientization (Freire, 1970), one must first be aware that one's own perspective is not sufficient to make sense of one's current reality. As described by Clevinger (1993), a *crisis event* can cause an individual to realize that an existing meaning perspective is not useful for resolving the current problem.

In a world that is full of potentially disorienting experiences, people encounter many opportunities to experience a disorienting dilemma every day. Yet, actual disorienting dilemmas are rare because our brains identify patterns in our experiences and then interpret all subsequent input through our understanding of those patterns and associations (Beitman, 2009; Thomas, 2012). This human ability to make sense of the world by collecting and analyzing data and then extrapolating from patterns is the core of our meaning perspective, or our ability to interpret experience through our own individual lens. The link between our own language and culture and our meaning perspective is very strong. As we grow and are socialized into a community of speakers, we develop a common sense, or a *mental model* (Johnson-Laird, 2010), to interpret our experiences. We absorb the collective wisdom of our language/culture group, and we see our own meaning perspective as the default: "Mental models help people make sense of the world – to interpret their environment and understand themselves. Mental models include categories, concepts, identities, prototypes, stereotypes, causal narratives, and worldviews" (World Bank, 2015, p. 62). Learning a new language and culture presents a remarkable opportunity to make sense of another way of interacting with the world, and to start to see one's perspective as linguistically and culturally embedded. More so than teachers of other subjects, it can be argued that language teachers have the opportunity to help students see how mental models shape experience and reinforce social hierarchies. This, in turn, can help students make sense of disorienting dilemmas that lead to perspective transformation.

Research gives us some clues about how to facilitate disorienting dilemmas. In Johnson's (2015) study of college-level language learners, quite a few initiators of disorientation were uncovered in the language class, including differences in lexico-grammar, differences in pragmatics or social interactions, cultural differences, students confronting their own difficulty in learning a language, and life circumstances. The same study, as well as others, including De Santis and Willis's (2016) study of learners of Russian, reported that contact with L2 community members through authentic resources is a core practice.

8.2 Authentic Resources

Authentic resources, also called authentic texts, are classroom materials, whether written, audio, video, or visual texts, that originate from and are intended for members of the target language group as part of authentic communication. Galloway (1998, p. 133) described them as "written by members of a language and culture group for members of the same language and culture group." These resources might include movies, magazines, social media posts, infographics, advertisements, and many other forms of communication.

While using authentic resources may seem like a common practice in language classrooms, there can also be many reasons as to why teachers do not use them. Many classrooms exclusively use commercial textbooks, which rarely include authentic resources, often for copyright reasons, but also because they are designed to be easily digestible so as not to cause the sort of cognitive dissonance that might serve as a disorienting dilemma. In addition, for the last several decades, teachers who use certain communicative approaches might also have rejected, or at least questioned, the notion of authentic texts in the lower levels of language study, instead focusing on teaching students to personalize their learning and talk about themselves and their own experiences. More recently, teachers who focus on input-oriented, acquisition-focused models of instruction might prefer to use texts specifically written for learners in order to achieve near-100 percent comprehension of every text. While authentic resources are a common practice in some classrooms, in other classrooms in a variety of settings and for a variety of reasons, the usefulness of authentic texts has been criticized.

Despite these objections, authentic texts that highlight the experiences and attitudes of L2 community members serve an important role by decentering the learner's own perspective and centering the perspective of L2 speakers. When students come into contact with people whose mental models interpret reality in unfamiliar ways, the potential for disorienting dilemmas increases. One key practice in critical pedagogy is consciousness-raising, which simply means helping students to become aware of issues that had previously been invisible to them, in other words, helping students to see the hidden realities around them. Presenting the perspectives of L2 community members through fiction, such as literary works or television shows, and/or non-fiction, such as news stories, Instagram posts, or even images, can all be consciousness-raising. From a critical pedagogy perspective, resources should not only serve the linguistic purposes of the course, but also explicitly highlight power relationships, culturally embedded first-person accounts, and L2 community activism (Glynn et al., 2018). Including the words and stories of community activists, perhaps by mining authentic resources from their own writing or social media accounts, is characteristic of transformative teaching (Kumaravadivelu, 2003). A useful authentic resource in the transformation-oriented classroom amplifies the voices of people whose lives and ideas are outside of the realm of experience of students.

The complex, compelling nature of authentic resources is useful for generating the type of cognitive dissonance that can lead to transformation. However, care should be taken to ensure that authentic resources are comprehensible to students rather than overly linguistically challenging. Glisan and Donato (2017) and Conlon Perugini (2017) recommend the following practices to help make authentic resources accessible to even novice students: choose appropriate resources; design feasible tasks; and pair authentic texts and feasible tasks with comprehensible teacher talk or learner-oriented texts.

8.2.1 Choose Appropriate Resources That Are at the Learners' Cognitive *and* Proficiency Level

While a children's book might show an authentic first-person account of life in a country where the target language is widely spoken, a group of college students would not find that resource at their *cognitive* level. Furthermore, while a newspaper might give interesting culturally embedded information about current events that could lead to a disorienting dilemma for some students, novice learners at the early stages of language acquisition will not find a newspaper at their *proficiency* level.

8.2.2 Design Feasible Tasks That Learners Can Do with Their Current Linguistic Resources

A novice learner will not be able to use the target language to explain in detail the cultural differences, for example, in breakfast foods between two countries. However, a novice certainly could look at a picture of a real family eating breakfast in another country and make a list of the foods the family is eating. That list, contrasted with a list of the foods most commonly eaten for breakfast by students in the classroom, might make for a meaningful and potentially disorienting experience without overtaxing the students' linguistic resources. A critical approach to this activity might be to ask students if rich people and poor people generally eat the same breakfast foods, or if all people in the same country always eat the same breakfast foods, and comparing how the target culture may be the same or different from the students' own.

8.2.3 Pair Authentic Texts and Feasible Tasks with Comprehensible Teacher Talk or Learner-Oriented Texts

If you want to use an authentic resource that is not accessible enough to students, consider pairing that text with teacher talk that is completely comprehensible to ensure that students do not feel linguistically overwhelmed and can focus their mental attention on the consciousness-raising activities embedded in the authentic text-based lesson.

8.3 Facilitating Critical Reflection

Critical reflection is a process that is often referred to as an ultimate goal of education (Bailin & Siegel, 2003). Yet, how many educators feel confident that they can effectively engage students in learning that requires or inspires students to carefully and critically think about a text, an experience, or their own reactions? There is much evidence that critical reflection of the type that leads to perspective transformation requires more than just rational exploration from students. Exploring one's own emotional experience is also an essential part of the process (Brooks, 1989; Cochrane, 1981; Coffman, 1989; D'Andrea, 1986; Goulah, 2006; Taylor, 1993), and there is also evidence that relationships contribute to the process and may even be a key element (Cochrane, 1981; D'Andrea, 1986; Harper, 1994; Holt, 1994; Johnson, 2015; Kamisky, 1997; Saavedra, 1995).

A key component of critical reflection is the ability to engage in critical thinking. So, what does critical thinking entail? Brookfield (1987, pp. 7–9) identified several components:

- identifying and challenging assumptions;
- challenging the importance of context;
- imagining and exploring alternatives; and
- arriving at reflective skepticism.

Instructors who understand these components of critical thinking can make space in the curriculum for reflective practices that encourage critical thinking about what students have experienced or are learning. For example, in a language classroom, students who engage with authentic resources might encounter a cultural product or practice that is different from their own. Initially, the student might experience a disorienting dilemma, accompanied by disgust or rejection. Passing through this dualistic phase is a normal part of diversity development (Chávez et al., 2003); yet, through critical reflection, the same students can learn to identify and challenge their own emotional and rational responses. They might begin to imagine what life would be like if they came into contact with or even adopted that cultural product or practice.

Abrami et al.'s (2008) meta-analysis of instructional interventions demonstrated that there is a range of interventions that can and do promote critical thinking skills and dispositions in the classroom. What such successful interventions have in common is that they must include making the expectation of critical thinking explicit in the course goals and implementing structured instruction on how to engage effectively in critical thinking. For teachers, this means building a consistent practice of: (1) reflecting on authentic texts; (2) identifying one's own emotional and rational responses; (3) imagining alternatives; and (4) questioning assumptions.

8.4 Written Reflection

Scheduling opportunities for students to respond to written prompts, in the target language when possible or in their first language throughout the semester, is a key practice. In one interesting study (Kamin et al., 2002), students who participated in an online discussion that took place entirely in writing scored higher in a measure of critical thinking than did those who participated in a face-to-face discussion that was entirely oral. This may indicate that the act of writing out ideas forces students to analyze and articulate them with more care. More recently, researchers have found that reflective writing in the language classroom is a useful tool for transformation (Crane, 2018; De Santis & Willis, 2016; Johnson, 2015; see also Crane & Sosulski, this volume). In Crane's research, students were encouraged to think deeply about their learning experiences through guided writing assignments in English rather than the target language. Among the findings in that study, Crane (2018, p. 68) reported that students became more aware of their own experiences with and assumptions of German language and culture, they became more aware of how German is used in the world outside of the classroom, and they experienced "a deepening understanding of the self in relationship to the course content." Johnson found that the reflective activity that beginning Spanish students completed in their first language on a weekly basis – an activity that was originally intended as a data-collection method for the study and not necessarily as a learning tool – was frequently cited by students as an essential part of their transformative learning. Asking questions like, "What did you learn this week?," "How did you learn it?," and "Were you shocked or surprised by anything you learned?" helped students think through their own learning in important ways. At higher levels of proficiency, this sort of reflection could be done in the target language to bring transformative and linguistic goals together. However, for students in the aforementioned studies, short, periodic first language reflection promoted the kind of critical reflection that leads to transformation.

8.5 Next Steps

After students have examined an authentic resource, processed the resource linguistically, and had the opportunity to critically reflect on the resource, both individually and in small, collaborative groups, what comes next? One action step that could be feasible at a range of proficiency levels is to ask students what their next step would be if they could take any action. Imagining hypothetical next steps may be just the push that students need to move into the later, more action-oriented, phases of transformation on their own.

In my own first semester Spanish classroom, I took advantage of the food unit to ask my students the essential question (McTighe & Wiggins, 2013): "What responsibility do we as consumers have in ensuring ethical food production?" After examining simple, easy-to-understand authentic resources in class, such as infographics, video with limited narration, and images that explored the traditional and modern methods of producing chocolate, students reflected on the resources in both the target and first language. Their consciousness had been raised on the issues of unethical labor practices, including slavery, in modern chocolate production. While students cannot reasonably take action to end slavery directly, they were asked as a presentational writing task to explain what small step they could take that same day to combat the unethical labor practices in the production of the food that they would eat that day. The responses were in simple language, things like write a letter, send an email, post on social media, or read the label before buying. Several students in that class went on to take those steps in their own time after class. One student even asked the manager of the campus snack bar to stop selling chocolate from manufacturers who did not commit to transparent and ethical labor practices. Hypothetical questions can lead to real action for students who are ready to engage.

8.6 Conclusion

While transformative learning is far too complex to be micromanaged and neatly divided into lesson plans, it can be promoted by teachers through the thoughtful integration of key practices. Many common L2 classroom practices either already do or, with some modifications, can encourage students to embrace difference, question assumptions, and integrate new perspectives into their own meaning perspective. In particular, authentic resources and written reflection are two widely used practices that can help students maximize the potential for transformation in the language classroom. Choosing accessible authentic texts that center L2 community members' voices can be useful not only for language development, but also for helping students to explore cognitive dissonance. Additionally, reflecting on learning experiences through written reflection can provide students with essential opportunities to critically evaluate their own assumptions and explore alternative ideas. Once students have thoroughly explored authentic resources and reflected on their learning, teachers may consider giving students one more push toward transformation by asking learners to imagine next steps. Using language appropriate to the students' proficiency level, how will they change their routines or interact with the world differently knowing what they know now? This final element of helping students to imagine future actions may be the push that some students need to put their integrated perspective to work in the world. After all, students interacting with the world in new ways is the ultimate goal of transformative language education.

DISCUSSION QUESTIONS

1. How are you currently using authentic resources in your teaching? If you are not using them transformatively, what adaptations in approach or activities could you make to encourage a process of transformation?

2. How do your resources highlight L2 community perspectives? Are there ways in which you could further center L2 perspectives through authentic resources?
3. Think of a specific lesson or unit from your course where it might make sense to ask students what their hypothetical "action step" would be. How might you include this practice?

9

The Community as Transformative Classroom

*Nelleke Van Deusen-Scholl and Stéphane Charitos**

Social pedagogies, which seek to establish a connection between individual learning and the sociocultural context in which that learning takes place, are increasingly prevalent within postsecondary education, including foreign language classes (Bass & Elmendorf, 2010, 2012). These approaches, which include both project-based and service learning, provide students with meaningful opportunities to interact with the broader communities outside the classroom. For many students today, this means connecting with an increasingly urban, multicultural, and multilingual environment, where various groups, communities, and individuals negotiate and embed their identities.

In this chapter, we draw on examples from language programs at two institutions to illustrate how students can explore the world beyond their classrooms and discuss how social pedagogies, in particular, place- and community-based approaches, can connect learners more meaningfully with the languages spoken and lived there. Engagement with the communities that shape and are shaped by the geographic and historical spaces that they inhabit can be transformative for both the learners and the community, and can contribute to a critical social awareness (Charitos & Van Deusen-Scholl, 2017). However, this does require designing and implementing rich pedagogical practices that extend the formal classroom and provide opportunities for learners to engage in authentic interactions in their local communities.

9.1 The Role of Place and Space in Language Education

Recent decades have witnessed several major "turns" in applied linguistics, including the social turn (Block, 2003; Ortega, 2010), the multilingual turn, and the spatial turn, which have had a profound impact on language pedagogy (Charitos & Van Deusen-Scholl, 2017). Starting in the mid-1990s, researchers

* We would like to thank Sybil Alexandrov and Angela Lee-Smith from Yale University for generously allowing us to use their materials and to showcase their innovative and exciting projects. Stéphane Charitos would also like to acknowledge Lee Abraham, with whom he co-taught the course "Mapping Astoria," and whose passion for the life of languages in the city has been an inspiration.

challenged the narrowly focused cognitive and psycholinguistic perspectives in second language acquisition (SLA) and called for a greater emphasis on the sociocultural context (Firth & Wagner, 1997; Ortega, 2011). This led to a broader understanding of second language (L2) development which recognized "that human cognition (and thus human mind/brain) is *formed and transformed* as the individual is interdependently embedded in a world that is necessarily interactive, social, cultural, and historical" (Ohta, 2017, p. 65, emphasis in original). Subsequently, the multilingual turn sought to address the prevailing monolingual bias in SLA research (Ortega, 2010) and situated "multilingualism, rather than monolingualism, as the new norm of applied linguistic and sociolinguistic analysis" (May, 2014, p. 1).

Finally, the spatial turn brought forth new perspectives on the role of place and space. The term was first introduced in the mid-1990s by Soja (e.g., 2003), who drew upon the path-breaking work of Henri Lefebvre (1991). Their perspectives on spatiality influenced a range of disciplines, including sociolinguistics and applied linguistics. Johnstone (2012, p. 210), for example, notes how current sociolinguistic research has begun to examine: "how physical spaces shape social spaces, and vice versa; how place and 'place identity' are created and reflected in discourse; and how people's experience of place may shape their linguistic behavior and ideology." Furthermore, within the broad context of globalization, a new "sociolinguistics of mobility" (Blommaert, 2010, 2013; Blommaert & Rampton, 2011b; Creese & Blackledge, 2010) has emerged, which is concerned with the mobility both of people and "of linguistic and sociolinguistic resources," resulting in a combination of "territorialized" and "translocal" or "deterritorialized" patterns of language use (Blommaert, 2010, pp. 4–5).

These shifts have had profound implications for language education (Firth & Wagner, 2007; Kramsch, 2014), as both the context and the goals of language education have changed dramatically in recent years. As Kramsch (2014, p. 296) notes: "globalization has changed the conditions under which foreign languages are taught, learned and used ... destabilized the codes, norms, and conventions that foreign language (FL) educators relied upon to help learners be successful users of the language once they had left their classrooms." Current post-communicative approaches must therefore acknowledge the complex multilingual and multicultural context in which languages are learned and engage students in a critical awareness of the social and historical spaces in which languages are used.

In a Teagle Foundation White Paper, Bass and Elmendorf (2012) laid out a framework for social pedagogies that connect students with authentic learning opportunities inside and outside the classroom. Their model offers an iterative cycle of student engagement, with an exploration of disciplinary concepts that allows them to discover how "acts of communication and representation connect authentic tasks to learning processes, learning process to adaptive practices, practices to learning environments and intellectual communities and how the constellation of these elements help [them] integrate their learning by connecting to larger contexts for knowledge and action" (Bass & Elmendorf, 2011). Focusing on the social dimensions of learning and authentic learning contexts, social pedagogies have gained increasing interest within language education.

The 2017 American Association of University Supervisors, Coordinators, and Directors of Language Programs (AAUSC) Volume *Engaging the world: Social pedagogies and language learning*, edited by Sébastien Dubreil and Steve Thorne, seeks to address the question: "How can we more dynamically integrate the vibrancy of linguistically mediated social engagement outside of classroom settings with the pedagogical efficacy of instructional activity in the classroom?" (Dubreil and Thorne, 2017, p. 2). The contributions in this volume discuss a broad spectrum of pedagogical initiatives that exemplify the potential of community-engaged learning. The editors point out that "[t]he boundaries of L2 use have shifted, and it is incumbent upon L2 educators to make a case for the relevance of emerging communicative contexts in a world increasingly marked by the neoliberal ideology of productivity and consumerism at the expense of fostering empathy and building sustainable relationships in multicultural, multilingual societies" (Dubreil & Thorne, 2017, p. 9). This perspective aligns well with the main tenets of transformative language learning and teaching (TLLT) to challenge "sets of fixed assumptions and expectations (habits of mind, meaning, perspectives, mindsets) – to make them more inclusive, discriminating, open, reflective, and emotionally able to change" (Mezirow, 2003a, p. 58). Mezirow's framework identifies four types of learning: elaborating existing frames of reference; learning new frames of reference; transforming habits of mind; and transforming points of view (Kitchenham, 2008, p. 120). TLLT involves a range of skills, such as "interdisciplinary thinking, problem solving, team working, and holistic thinking" (Thomas, 2009, p. 245), and requires approaches that promote critical thinking skills through problem- or project-based learning (PBL) (see Leaver, this volume). For language pedagogy, place- and community-based approaches offer opportunities to forge a critical connection with social issues in the community (Sobel, 2004). These approaches can create learning experiences for students that are intellectually challenging and enriching, while promoting active involvement with their local communities. McInerney, Smyth and Down (2011, p. 3) argue that place-based education must be informed by a more critical perspective that challenges prevailing assumptions about place, identity, and community, noting that:

> [i]t may seem something of a paradox that in a globalized age where notions of interdependence, interconnectedness and common destinies abound, the "local", with its diversity of cultures, languages, histories and geographies, continues to exercise a powerful grip on the human imagination. The ties that bind us have global connections but are anchored in a strong sense of locality.

If designed appropriately, these approaches can contribute to greater intellectual, social, and cultural engagement in the learning process, and may foster values (including empathy) that are largely absent from a more traditional pedagogy (McInerney et al., 2011).

Dubreil and Thorne (2017, p. 1) suggest that "instructed language education would benefit from greater integration with a variety of lifeworld contexts and communities," and Byrnes (2011, p. 291) similarly notes that "[l]anguage learning is no longer to be primarily of and in the classroom alone but of, with, and for the 'community.'" However, this requires rethinking the balance between formal and more naturalistic learning. Language learning beyond the classroom (Benson & Reinders, 2011; Richards, 2015) may encompass, as Benson (2011, pp. 13, 14) characterizes it, a range of *settings* – an "arrangement for learning, involving one or more learners in a particular place, who are situated in particular kinds of physical, social, or pedagogical relationships with other people (teachers, learners, others) and materials or virtual resources" – and *modes of practice* – a "set of routine pedagogical processes that deploy features of a particular setting and may be characteristic of it." Richards (2015) points to some limitations of classroom-based learning, including the lack of opportunities for authentic communication and a focus on narrowly defined curricular outcomes. Furthermore, he notes that out-of-class learning may promote greater learner autonomy and offer learners additional benefits (see Little, this volume), such as managing their own learning, enhancing their experience, and reflecting their needs and interests (Richards, 2015, p. 20).

Naturalistic or non-instructed learning contexts can refer to a range of environments, including study abroad programs, community schools, service learning (Lee et al., 2018; Leeman et al., 2011), technology-enhanced learning, or telecollaborative arrangements. In recent years, mobile learning and online gaming in particular have also been increasingly inspired by place-based language learning (Holden & Sykes, 2011; Kukulska-Hulme, 2012; Thorne et al., 2009).

In this chapter, we focus primarily on approaches that connect classroom-based or instructed language learning with the physical and social spaces in the surrounding community through collaborative or project-based activities (Bruzos, 2017; Pellettieri, 2011). While PBL has been around for a long time, it has recently gained renewed momentum among language educators (Tavares & Potter, 2018). The National Foreign Language Resource Center (NFLRC) at Hawaii-Manoa, for example, is offering many professional development activities on project-based language learning, including online modules and summer institutes.[1]

Tavares and Potter (2018, p. 7) note that "it is important to understand that, when using PBL, the ultimate goal is to have students design and present a product, or a solution that can make a difference, be it by educating others, by raising awareness to important issues, by informing and proposing solutions to real-life problems, and, most importantly, by inspiring others to do the same." They identify five key elements: real learning with a focus on meaningful content; challenging questions that involve students in design, problem-solving, and decision-making; a focus on process rather than product; collaboration; and assessment, including peer and self-assessment. These approaches align with TLLT in their emphasis on learning "how to think" (Thomas, 2009, p. 245), critical reflection (Kitchenham, 2008; Mezirow, 2003a), collaboration, and problem-solving.

9.2 Place-and Community-Based Language Learning at Columbia and Yale

Recognizing the importance of its location in one of the world's major cities, Columbia University seeks to connect its research and teaching to the resources afforded by this city. This means devising courses and curricula that ensure that the Columbia experience is more than just formal classroom instruction.

"Mapping Astoria" is a course that helps students think about language practices in spatial terms and reflect critically upon the linkages between language, space, and identity in an urban context. While it is not a language course, it provides an opportunity for students to enrich and extend their language study by taking their experiences "out of the classroom."

Focusing on the history and present state of language communities in the New York landscape, the course explores urban multilingualism through a variety of critical, theoretical, and cultural lenses that focus on the relationship between the spatial organization of a city and its linguistic profile. Balancing readings, in-class discussions, and presentations from guest speakers with off-campus field trips, the course challenges students to develop the competences needed to engage with multilingualism and creates practical opportunities

---

[1] Further information can be found at: http://nflrc.hawaii.edu/projects/view/2014D/.

for them to explore Astoria, one of New York City's most ethnically and linguistically diverse neighborhoods.

The goals of the course are threefold: to help students understand the limits of analyzing urban linguistic communities based on simplified or static geographic views of language; to experience how a network of dynamic language practices shape and mold complex, urban environments; and to collaboratively construct a platform that visualizes how linguistically diverse communities lay claim to space and negotiate a sense of place within the hyper-diverse environment that characterizes global cities such as New York.

This platform draws upon methodologies of "thick mapping" to create a composite of geo-located layers populated with census and other archival data, as well as images, videos, and recordings that highlight alternative, spatially informed linguistic repertoires. Taken together, these layers present a rich, intertextual digital narrative that documents the nexus of situated language practices structuring the language spaces of Astoria.[2]

The course yielded interesting outcomes in terms of transformative learning. It has been noted that the drive and dedication that compel Columbia's students to pursue excellence in their academic careers also inhibit them from exploring their broader surroundings. Many of them have limited interaction with the city outside the boundaries of the university and confine themselves to a four-block radius around the Morningside Heights campus. Additionally, students are intensely consumed with grades and tend to compete with each other rather than work collaboratively. "Mapping Astoria" provided them with an opportunity to more fully immerse themselves in the city and break out of their individualized learning shells.

By asking students to investigate how languages exist(ed) in the city as embodied, situated practices, the course required them to identify, catalog, and curate the routine symbols and habits of language that characterize a linguistic community. Thus, students fused theory and practice by expanding what they had learned in the classroom through tangible experiences and by collaboratively creating a map of Astoria. Compiling a precise linguistic profile of a city and the "linguistic repertoires" of the people who live in it, as well as describing, analyzing, and visualizing how linguistic diversity is organized in urban settings, required students to interact with each other to invent new ways of visually exploring the individual trajectories that make up today's multiethnic, multilingual urban environments.

Finally, the course encouraged students to reflect critically on the traditional ideologies that expressly link a geographical place to an imagined community (e.g., a nation) and to a specific language. This helped them invent different

[2] A visual representation of this narrative can be found at the Cambridge University Press website.

ways of visualizing the multilingual and hyper-diverse reality that characterizes modern urban centers in ways that challenge the traditional tenets of a national ideology (i.e., one language, one people, one nation).

9.3 Project Modules for Language and Culture Learning (ProM) (Yale)

In a second example of programs that focus on place and space, several language programs at Yale University began to rethink their curricular goals and objectives for language and culture learning by incorporating more project-based activities centered around the notions of place and community. This was accomplished through a series of collaborative professional development activities over several years, including intensive workshops (on the topics of community-based language education and teaching culture), a symposium,[3] and faculty fellowships.

At the start of this process, nine language faculties participated, representing seven different languages. Their projects focused on engaging heritage learners with community members and/or community resources (Chinese, Spanish, and Vietnamese), exploring socially engaged practices (e.g., social businesses in Israel [Hebrew] and sustainability in Germany [German]), and working with young learners in the community (teaching Arabic and German). In 2018, 16 instructors participated in a total of 13 projects in nine languages, including collaborations across languages. The projects explored a range of topics that engaged learners in project-based, place-based, and community-based language learning activities.

In fall 2018, two faculty members (Spanish and Korean) obtained a Yale University Center for Language Study (CLS) fellowship that provided them with course-release time to collaborate on the development of a repository of pedagogical modules for language and culture learning intended to become an open educational resource (OER). The modules will be made available on an open online platform designed to share existing work and to invite future contributions from language instructors at Yale and other institutions.[4] The modules are based on the *World-readiness standards for learning languages* (The National Standards Collaborative Board, 2019) and on the multiliteracies framework (Paesani et al., 2016), and are categorized thematically into art, community, heritage learners, multiliteracies, and place. They follow a consistent set of design principles that provide the broad pedagogical

---

[3] The program can be found at: https://campuspress.yale.edu/consortiumforltl2017/program/.

[4] See: https://campuspress.yale.edu/projectmodules/.

parameters, such as approach (e.g., genre-, literacy-, place-, or community-based approaches), project goals, duration, and outcomes, as well as specific criteria, such as language, proficiency range, and instructional setting. The modules are intended to be replicable and adaptable across languages.[5]

The major goals are to encourage students to apply what they learn in the classroom through tangible experiences and to engage more thoroughly with the material through exploration and immersion in the local environment. Students are expected to not only be consumers of resources, but also provide concrete evidence of transformed perspectives and practices. For example, the students in Angela Lee-Smith's Korean course created a campus tour of Yale in Korean and translated the campus brochure into Korean. The students then conducted the tour with Korean visitors. The learners in Sybil Alexandrov's Spanish for heritage speakers class engage in a variety of reflective activities that connect them closer to the local community through the module "My [New] Haven," in which they explore different parts of the town through the lens of their heritage identity and connect their personal experiences more tightly with the surrounding community. These are not simple, stand-alone projects, but intended to forge more extended and deeper engagements with the world beyond the classroom, elicit critical reflection, and promote collaboration both among the students and with the community.

9.4 Implications

At Columbia and Yale, both private institutions, students have traditionally been relatively isolated from the communities surrounding them. Place-based approaches have the potential to help them build meaningful connections to these communities, promote critical social awareness, and have a transformative impact.

As we have tried to demonstrate in this chapter, place- and community-based approaches and social pedagogies have become increasingly relevant in language education. These approaches can help move students out of their academic bubble and deepen their engagement with the broader urban, multicultural, and multilingual communities surrounding them. Not only do they provide opportunities for authentic interactions with real audiences outside the classroom, but, more significantly, they also foster a greater awareness of the languages and histories embedded within the local communities.

---

[5] A listing of these modules can be found at the Cambridge University Press website.

DISCUSSION QUESTIONS

1. Read two or three current articles on SLA theory (e.g., by Ortega or Ohta) and reflect on how perspectives in SLA connect with TLLT. What specific aspects of the transformative learning model are particularly useful for thinking about second language teaching and learning?
2. Provide three examples of language learning activities beyond the classroom. In what way(s) can they contribute to raising students' critical awareness and transforming their perspectives?
3. What are some possible ways in which instructors could engage K-12 learners to connect more meaningfully with the multilingual and multicultural environments in which they live?

10

Cultural Transformation

Virtual Communities, Autonomous Contact, and Intercultural Competence

Thomas Jesús Garza

In his foundational work *Pedagogy of the oppressed*, Freire's (1998c, p. 162) commentary on the interaction between worldviews that is required to move from "cultural invasion" to "cultural synthesis" is at the heart of critical pedagogy in general, and of intercultural competence (IC) in particular. For the world language (WL) learner, the movement from mimicking prescribed content to interacting with the products, practices, and perspectives within the environment of native speakers lies at the core of developing linguistic and cultural competence. Freire's approach to pedagogy also emphasizes the role of the learner as "active," and not simply as a repository for information provided by authority models – a proposition also held in proficiency-based models of WL instruction. Implicit is equal access to information, instruction, and resources for learners to be empowered participants in the educational process. All of these tenets come into play in the transformative experience of WL learners as they undergo the cultural synthesis that emerges from negotiating meaning autonomously, self-directing their study in authentic linguistic and cultural contexts.

The ACTFL's (1986) *Proficiency guidelines* provided the language teaching profession with a "common yardstick" by which functional competence in WLs could be measured. However, before the publication of these proficiency-based descriptors, Rivers (1973, p. 26) described "autonomous production," when learners interact spontaneously and critically with native speakers of the language and culture in an authentic context, challenging their existing notions of meaning and "norms" to arrive at a negotiated cultural synthesis. Rivers's dialogic notions of "autonomous contact" and "spontaneous interaction" preserve face validity in digital-age communication, though now with a crucial update of the media and materials available to learners. With easy access to virtual realities and global communities, autonomous contact with the language remains at the core of new iterations of WL acquisition in and out of the classroom. Such learner interactions with the authentic linguo-cultural content of the web-based virtual communities of WL native speakers can yield transformative learning experiences, in addition to supporting overall proficiency gains and the development of IC.

This chapter discusses the personal and cognitive transformation that WL learners may undergo when exposed to environments for autonomous contact with native speakers, situations, and contexts. As learners progress from transactional toward transformative learning, these environments – both domestic and abroad – provide the contexts and content necessary for learners to proceed to advanced and even superior levels of proficiency. The chapter proposes alternatives to study abroad for developing autonomous interaction and facilitating spontaneous contact with the language and culture: courses within domestic WL programs that utilize available interactive technology and related media to increase access to opportunities for IC proficiency gains.

10.1 The Study Abroad Experience as Transformative

Few question the educational and personally transformative value of the well-designed study abroad experience for university students in general, and for WL learners in particular. Angulo (2010), for example, examined 200 undergraduate students from the University of Texas at Austin (UT) who were engaged in semester-long study abroad programs, focusing on the transformative changes in the participants' personal identities and ways of thinking about the world. Using various theories of identity and metacognition, the study concluded that students abroad "changed more than a matched-control group spending the semester at UT," and described study abroad as a "unique and transformative experience" (Angulo, 2010, pp. ix, 85). Pellegrino-Aveni (2005) and Benson, Barkhuizen and Bodycott (2012) describe a similar, though often complicated, transformation of identity and self-presentation, especially through metacognitive learning in the study abroad context.

The transformative experience for learners of WLs and cultures abroad has been most acutely demonstrated in the Language Flagship Program (LFP). The recent experience (2002–present) of the LFP through the National Security Education Program empirically supports the unprecedented proficiency gains attained by the majority of participants who complete the program, which includes a capstone program abroad (Murphy & Evans-Romaine, 2017). During this year-long period of intensive in-country study, participants submit language utilization reports (LURs), which document language use and weekly learner reflections on cultural challenges that happen in both academic settings and free time. Davidson and Lekic (2010) describe the interactive settings (time spent with friends, homestay-related activities, reading for pleasure, and so on) that provide the "acquisition-rich environment" (Davidson & Frank, 2012; see also Davidson et al., this volume) for autonomous contact and interaction with the language and culture and lead to the most significant proficiency gains.

The linguistic, extralinguistic, and cultural benefits of academic experiences abroad are incontrovertible; however, access to these opportunities is too often restricted by interrelated variables, including socioeconomic background, ethnicity, and race. As 2016/2017 data from the Association of International Educators (NAFSA) indicate, the number of US students studying abroad – including those in WL programs – increased by 2.3 percent over the preceding year; however, the overall number studying abroad (at 332,727) still represents only 1.6 percent of all students enrolled at institutions of higher education in the USA (Institute of International Education, 2018). Furthermore, in their report of the Open Doors data, NAFSA (2018, p. 1) remarks that "Although the diversity of study abroad participation has increased in recent years, minority students are still greatly underrepresented in study abroad." Abraham (2018) echoes this position, citing cost as the primary reason for the lack of participation and diversity in study abroad.

However, the disparity in access to study abroad programs does not mean that students who cannot afford or accommodate study abroad as part of their education cannot reap the benefits of authentic contact with the language and culture and, thus, experience the spontaneous interaction that culminates in a transformative learning experience (Frye & Garza, 1992). Judicious, thoughtful utilization of media-based technology during WL instruction can provide many more learners with the materials and contexts for cultural synthesis as they progress to full learner autonomy.

10.2 Virtual Realities: An American in Moscow

The issue of equal access for WL learners to the opportunities to experience the benefits of autonomous contact with the source culture in context has been significantly ameliorated with the development of advanced technologies in communication and information. The growing availability of data equipment and Internet access to learners nationally and globally[1] provides virtual alternatives to study abroad and an affordable and efficacious means to benefit from autonomous contact with native speakers of WLs in authentic environments.

One of the most salient forms of information transmittal in the digital age is video media as visuals are particularly well-suited for conveying multilayered meaning in communication. Osborn (2006, pp. 91–94) brings together visual,

---

[1] As of June 2018, 55.1 percent of the world's population has Internet access. In the USA, 76.2 percent of the population reported having access to the Internet in 2018 (see: www.internetworldstats.com/stats.htm).

semiotic, and social considerations in making the case for incorporating visual media in WL education in ways that require the learner to examine critically, challenge, and respond to the language, images, and content of authentic media. Kern and Develotte (2018, p. 2) see the use of visual media as essential to "distinguish between cultural learning, which implies acquiring knowledge about another culture, and intercultural learning, which involves reflection on one's personal engagement with multiple cultures and developing an awareness of one's own cultural assumptions and interpretative logic in relation to those of others." It is precisely this intercultural perspective that is the desired result and that visual media can facilitate. As Liddicott and Scarino (2013, p. 29) contend, an intercultural perspective implies the transformative engagement of the learner in the act of learning, moving learners away from their established conceptions and assumptions and toward a new intercultural identity: "The borders between self and other are explored, problematized, and redrawn." Ehrman (1996) applied work in the field of psychology on ego boundaries (Hartmann, 1991) to WL learners as well.

Interactive media allow us to design and create access to virtual environments, materials, and interlocutors that were once only available through study abroad. One can imagine learners of Russian, for example, accustomed to accessing authentic online materials early in their study of the language, engaging with Russian peers in Moscow via FaceTime to prepare a self-designed final project on youth and political activism, and conducting interviews and discussing their assumptions using a social media platform. The "American in Moscow" is no longer required to be physically abroad to benefit from a virtual in-country experience.

10.3 Creating Virtual Communities

Students need no introduction to the utility and breadth of Web 2.0 capacities; however, the switch to using WL sources, search engines, and websites – in the WL – requires some instruction. Nemtchinova (2014) and Garza (2017) present two exemplars of training models that use created programs, such as Café Russia, and existing web-based interfaces, such as the inquiry-oriented lesson format WebQuest, to build on Russian learners' existing Internet abilities and incorporate meaningful authentic content. Such programs build computer literacy skills in the WL and accustom learners to perform routine online tasks and use social media in non-English platforms. Once learners are comfortable working in the WL web-based milieu, they can begin to use these skills both to perform structured assignments and tasks, and to explore the web in learner-centered and learner-directed activities and projects – the spontaneous interaction necessary for developing proficiency and IC.

By working collaboratively with instructors to first learn how to identify, access, and interact with these online sources, learners can then proceed to achieve and maintain autonomous contact and interaction with the WL and culture. The creation of WL virtual communities is necessary to simulate the in-country experience afforded by study abroad but in a much more accessible medium and environment. The "traditional" WL classroom is now reimagined as a hybrid, blended model that shifts seamlessly between live communication in class to virtual interactions that utilize authentic websites, blogs, and chat rooms. In a similar vein, homework and independent inquiry takes the learner into virtual environments of autonomous contact with native speakers and cultural artifacts: texts, speech, images, ephemera, and so on.

Autonomous contact with the language and culture in virtual communities aligns well with the Vygotskian notion of self-transformation via mediating artifacts – tangible or psychological – that are in the appropriate (i.e., authentic) social and cultural context (Vygotsky, 1978/2013). For Vygotsky (1978/2013, p. 55), these "internally oriented" signs are "a means of internal activity aimed at mastering oneself." While in-country experiences inherently provide learners with immersion in the language and culture, authentic materials available online on WL websites can furnish the learner with comparable virtual benefits. The stimuli contained within authentic online sources become the impetus both for self-transformation and for linguo-cultural development.

10.4 Autonomous Contact and Cultural Transformation

The process of moving toward learner autonomy in WL courses has informed several iterations of IC, beginning with Byram's (1997) multidimensional model. This exemplar is useful in emphasizing the need for WL instructors to act as a "go-between" in designing and constructing new kinds of classes and content. Byram and Wagner (2018) suggest that instructors of WLs should use both face-to-face interactions and self-directed work to guide learners to make new discoveries – both linguistic and cultural – about the "other" (the native speaker) and, equally important, about themselves. In particular, they point specifically to how learners' identities are changed by this kind of interaction (Byram & Wagner, 2018, p. 144). Another influential model of IC that describes the aim to transform learners and learning is Deardorff's (2011) process model of intercultural competence, which focuses on the continual development of learner attitudes and knowledge, while targeting and assessing internal and external outcomes. Finally, Moeller and Nugent (2014, p. 14) present IC as an integral part of the WL learning process in which "learners experience how to appropriately use language to build relationships and understandings with members of other cultures." This "transformative" model places the learner on an extended journey, where "the learner continues to learn, change, evolve, and become transformed with time" (Moeller & Nugent, 2014, p. 6).

Such models of IC and their place in WL curricula and course design have informed and contributed to the creation of innovative courses that integrate the goals of cultural competence and language proficiency. Against the grain of conventional wisdom, these courses introduce authentic texts, audio, and video materials from the first days of instruction in order to accustom learners to authentic linguistic and cultural content from the very beginning.

10.4.1 From Novice to Intermediate: Breaking Barriers

Learners can be exposed to – and become accustomed to – engaging with authentic materials in original contexts that are available to them "live" online. At the ACTFL novice and intermediate levels of proficiency, online virtual communities can be employed to simulate face-to-face interactions and move learners toward autonomous interaction, requiring them to assess, question, and reevaluate preconceived notions of linguistic and cultural singularity. Johnson (2010), for example, uses authentic materials and a computer-based interactive video interface to train military personnel linguistically and culturally prior to deployment. For learners in this context, intercultural skills training "requires knowing about culture that is operationally focused as well as *operator-focused*, i.e., focused on what an individual military operator (service member in the field) needs to know and be able to do to be effective in the intercultural situations they are likely to encounter" (Johnson, 2010, p. 189).

In several WL classes at UT, learners are required to prepare cultural portfolios or, more specifically, e-portfolios (Lee, 1997; Shrum & Glisan, 2015; Zapata, 2018), demonstrating their contact and interaction with online sources based on their own interests and reasons for studying the language. A learner taking intensive first-year Russian, for example, might be a petroleum engineering student. Her e-portfolio might contain, among other things: digital online maps of oil-producing areas of Russia, annotated with geographic information provided by the student; self-recordings of pronunciation practice with a new content-specific lexicon; a video file of a simple autobiographical interview with a Russian student at Gubkin Russian State University of Oil and Gas; and a collection of images collected from various sites of various types of rigs and drills, described comparatively with simple annotations. Such products of learner-directed interaction with authentic online sources can then be evaluated as part of a larger profile of progress in the course. Much like the LURs used in the LFP overseas programs, portfolios offer a learner-centered, self-directed, and introspective venue for both instructor and learner, and, as such, contribute to the transformative experience.

10.4.2 From Intermediate to Advanced: Building Bridges

Bringing learners to higher levels of proficiency requires the engagement, interaction, and cultural synthesis that can be created domestically using interactive media to place the learner into domains of direct contact with native speakers in country. In this context, domestic classes must go outside the frame of traditional "language courses" and broaden their reach to embrace interdisciplinary topics and material within content-based and "language across the curriculum" courses. They must challenge learners critically to stimulate their transformation to autonomous participants. In this connection, Glanville (2017, p. 71) identifies the "independent learner," which he defines as the "precursor to full learner autonomy" and actively participatory as a partner in the process of learning. He goes on to acknowledge that the development of independent learners in WL classes can facilitate transition to higher-level content courses taught entirely in the language (Glanville, 2017, p. 86). These are the courses that are designed to develop learner autonomy and IC.

For example, a course might use debate as the thematic and structural frame for an advanced WL course. Brown, Balykhina, Talalakina, Bown and Kurilenko (2014) describe a methodology and curriculum for an interdisciplinary course that incorporates the higher-order thinking skills (analysis, assessment, production) required for executing parliamentary-style debate with the linguo-cultural content necessary for conducting research, creating relevant briefs, and executing persuasive argumentation. Topics for global debate in the WL classroom provide contexts that require examination and discussion through a variety of critical lenses and perspectives. Learners are not therefore restricted to a single perspective, but rather asked to engage with the material in a way that is much more individuated for all learners and identities (Garza, 2018). The debates themselves are transacted first using internet resources to research the topics and then using Skype to facilitate the actual debates between learners in the USA and their in-country Russian counterparts.

Instant messaging technology is also proving fruitful in developing proficiency in writing and IC. Bain and Spring (2017) describe using BRIX, an open-source courseware system developed by the National Foreign Language Resource Center and the federally funded Language Resource Centers, to create online "cafés" for Russian and Chinese LFP students at the advanced level. Based on the "Cultura" project (Furstenberg et al., 2001), participants in the LFP cafés interacted with student peers at in-country universities over six- to eight-week periods using a text-based messaging interface. Based on participant responses, the interactions were found to be "a rich resource for promoting intercultural awareness and competence" (Bain & Spring, 2017, p. 131). Crucially, as Kramsch and Thorne (2002) reminded us in the early

2000s, success in online interactions for language learning relies on informed instructor mediation of the virtual discourse, as well as on critical reflection on the part of the learner following each interaction.

Instructor-mediated content courses conducted in the WL offer opportunities to bring interdisciplinarity and critical breadth to the curriculum. As Reagan and Osborn (2012, p. 80) argue: "Although collaborations with other disciplinary specialists within the academic setting may seem restricted because the fluency required to discuss complex topics in the second language often eludes students, in reality the newest standards and mandates provide multiple opportunities for connections and comparisons in the second language classroom." Publications such as the *World-readiness standards for learning languages* (The National Standards Collaborative Board, 2019) and the application of the "Five Cs" to curricula and courses can provide necessary scaffolding to create effective environments for WL learning. For example, an advanced Russian content course at UT considers the lyric, musical, stage, and filmic works of the bard Vladimir Vysotsky during Brezhnev's reign. With direction and guidance from the instructor, learners in this course are required to conduct limited research online into topics related to the works and period, though in their own areas of interest, and to conduct live interviews with their Russian peers at the Moscow International University. After instructor review and commentary, the final projects are then presented to the entire class, showcasing the information gleaned from the web-based resources.

Each of these approaches attempts, in Freire's terms, to resolve the contradiction between disparate worldviews in the attainment of cultural synthesis. As learners become accustomed to making autonomous contact with authentic materials that challenge their domestic identities and understandings, they become more and more comfortable with and adept at negotiating the meaning that arises from recognizing and appreciating the similarities and differences between disparate languages and cultures. Learner reflection protocols, such as LURs, can assist instructors in assessing when cultural synthesis is operative: when learners acknowledge cultural difference not in opposition, but rather in synthesis one with the other. Such are the results usually associated with successful study abroad but attainable domestically through carefully designed web-based hybrid courses that exploit the benefits of well-incorporated online authentic materials.

10.5 Conclusion: If We Build It, They Will Come

One solution to the issue of access to the benefits of study abroad is to create new or redesign existing programs that are more affordable and inclusive. Federally funded programs such as the National Security Education Program and the

Critical Languages Scholarship Program for university-level students have been effective in creating access to study abroad for students at Tribal, Historically Black Colleges and Universities, Hispanic-Serving Institutions, and Two-Year Colleges, and other learner populations that have been historically underrepresented in study abroad. A collaborative effort between the Center for International Programs and the Educational Opportunity Program at the State University of New York at New Paltz has embedded study abroad in the support work provided to disadvantaged students, reinforced by peers and supported through scholarships (Lane, 2015, p. 1). New programs such as these provide access to more students but such opportunities are few in the USA; also, as mentioned earlier, cost still remains the primary reason given against studying abroad.

Given the demonstrable results in proficiency and IC attainable in study abroad programs, and given the statistically small number of students, including WL learners, who actually participate in study abroad, creating domestic alternatives that promote autonomous contact and interaction would address issues of access and equity in WL education. Designing courses that employ online multimodal authentic materials from the beginning of instruction can provide students with the contextualized input necessary to begin the transformative journey toward proficiency and IC. Through structured, mediated, and autonomous contact and spontaneous interaction with authentic linguistic and cultural difference, learners can confront, reflect on, and expand their capacities for cultural synthesis and successful language learning.

DISCUSSION QUESTIONS

1. Examine any textbooks and materials used in your language program and consider how the subject of "culture" is treated. Assess to what extent these materials facilitate increased proficiency in intercultural communication. Do they encourage, in Freire's terms, "cultural synthesis," requiring learners to interact with the products, practices, and perspectives of the culture within an authentic environment? What might be done within the parameters of your program to increase authentic contact with the new culture?
2. Consider ways to facilitate and mediate learners' use of already-familiar social media platforms (Facebook, Snapchat, Instagram, Twitter, etc.) in the WL being learned. What kinds of tasks, projects, or activities might best serve the development of linguistic and cultural proficiency in the WL?
3. What might be the components of an interdisciplinary, instructor-mediated hybrid WL content course? Consider how technology can facilitate and enhance autonomous contact with the WL and when face-to-face interaction is most necessary for language and cultural proficiency gains.

11

Designing Learning Environments to Facilitate Transformative Language and Culture Learning in a US Language Flagship Program

Karen Evans-Romaine and Dianna Murphy

A transformative approach to language education calls for an expanded understanding of curriculum and program design that leverages potential learning environments both inside and outside the classroom – in academic, residential, and social settings – to support language and culture learning. This chapter provides an overview of the curricular and co-curricular learning environments designed by the University of Wisconsin–Madison Russian Flagship (UWRF) that offer affordances for transformative language and culture learning for its students. Elements of the program's design that facilitate transformative learning include: (1) positioning students as independent language learners striving to meet programmatic and personal goals; (2) providing a continuum of opportunities for language and culture learning in formal instructional environments, individual and small-group tutorials, and residential and social contexts in which students engage in meaningful interactions in Russian with various interlocutors, reflecting the concept of open architecture curricular design (OACD) for learning (see Leaver, this volume; Campbell, this volume); and (3) offering spaces for reflection in supportive, low-stakes environments, potentially leading to transformative change (see Leaver, this volume).

The UWRF is one of 31 undergraduate language programs, including eight Russian Flagships, currently funded by the Language Flagship (see: www.thelanguageflagship.org), a program of the National Security Education Program (NSEP) in the US Department of Defense, with the goal to "change the way that Americans learn languages" (Nugent & Slater, 2017, p. 11). Through federal funding that supports curricular innovation, student scholarships, and new partnerships between US and overseas universities, the Language Flagship aims to "create a pool of educated university graduates with demonstrated professional-level language proficiency" (Nugent & Slater, 2017, p. 10) in languages identified as being of critical national need. Professional-level proficiency in the Language Flagship is defined as ACTFL Superior (ILR 3: General Professional Proficiency).

11.1 The UWRF Program

To enable students to reach learning goals, all Language Flagship programs share characteristics in their design, summarized by Murphy, Evans-Romaine, Anishchenkova, and Jing-Schmidt (2017, pp. 34–35) as follows:[1]

1. A persistent focus on language development and proficiency-based assessments throughout the student's course of study;
2. Options for intensive and accelerated programs of study, as well as advanced coursework on the student's home campus that prepares them for advanced overseas study;
3. Opportunities for disciplinary learning in the L2, connecting the students' L2 development with learning in other subject areas;
4. Focused attention and support for individual learners, including individual or small-group tutoring in the L2;
5. Extensive co- and extra-curricular programming that provides opportunities for language use outside of traditional classroom environments;
6. Articulated domestic and overseas programs of study, with direct enrollment and professional internships during advanced overseas study on a capstone program that targets ILR 3 proficiency in the L2.

The UWRF follows this model. The domestic portion of the program prepares students to reach ACTFL Advanced (ILR 2); students then apply to participate in a nine-month, capstone Russian Overseas Flagship (ROF) program (Davidson & Lekic, 2010; Davidson & Shaw, 2019; see also Davidson et al., this volume) at Al-Farabi Kazakh National University (KazNU), located in the "super-diverse" (Blommaert & Rampton, 2011a) multilingual, multiethnic, and multicultural city of Almaty, Kazakhstan (see also Smagulova, 2017, p. 744; Smailova, 2011, p. 20).

The ROF, which is administered by American Councils for International Education, consists of at least 20 hours per week of formal coursework in Russian on various aspects of Russian language and culture, four hours a week of one-on-one tutoring with KazNU faculty plus two hours a week with peer tutors, introductory coursework in the Kazakh language, a fall-semester "direct-enroll" course in each student's major academic area from the regular curriculum offered to KazNU students, a spring-semester professional internship, a co-curricular program of activities such as excursions in Almaty and elsewhere in Kazakhstan, and a homestay with a Russian-speaking family.

The UWRF domestic component is designed to prepare students for study at KazNU, for the professional internship, and for daily life in Almaty, as well

[1] See also Spring (2015).

as for possible future study or work in the Russian-speaking world. Taking an expansive approach to curriculum and program design, reflecting aspects of OACD key to transformative learning and teaching (TLLT) (see Campbell, this volume; Leaver, this volume), the UWRF offers students a range of curricular and co-curricular experiences in academic, residential, and social learning environments, in both face-to-face and virtual contexts. Formal courses include: 1st- through 4th-year Russian (or the equivalent, completed during the academic year and summer, at UW-Madison and overseas); a two-semester sequence on the history of Russian culture; a preparatory course for advanced students ("Intercultural Introduction to Kazakhstan"); and one other advanced course (a senior capstone course on Russian literature and culture, focused on reading, or an advanced Russian media course, focused on listening). Co-curricular learning environments include: individual and small-group tutoring; individualized "Russian across the curriculum" (RAC) tutorials; an online intercultural exchange using the bilingual *Cultura* approach (Furstenberg & Levet, 2014); online modules based on cultural scenarios; co-curricular programming in various settings; and a residential Russian-language floor within the university's International Learning Community (ILC). The remainder of this chapter focuses on those aspects of the program that provide opportunities for transformative learning outside of the traditional four-year language and advanced course sequence.

11.2 Tutoring

One of the key components of Language Flagship programs is non-credit tutoring, which UWRF students regularly cite in program evaluations as one of the most, or even *the* most, effective aspect of the program (Murphy et al., 2012). Tutoring takes place in weekly individual sessions for students in 3rd-year Russian and above, and in weekly small-group sessions for all students. Tutoring is designed to be transformative, positioning tutors as counselors and students as clients (see Leaver, this volume), who develop as independent learners monitoring their own learning. Bown (2006, p. 647) suggests that learners with an internal locus of learning (i.e., attributed to learners themselves) "believe that learning is a process that occurs within the individual learner, that the individual constructs knowledge on his or her own, perhaps with the facilitation of an instructor." Glanville (2017, pp. 71–72) defines an independent learner as "an active partner in the learning process, rather than as a passive consumer": an independent learner "monitors and evaluates personal language use," "sets goals for improvement and evaluates progress in achieving these goals." The UWRF tutoring guidelines prompt students to be "responsible for coming prepared to tutoring sessions with ideas for topics to discuss or aspects of

Russian language to practice." They advise students that "tutoring sessions should be primarily driven by you." Both students and tutors report that this can be a challenge; preparation for tutoring sessions requires that students develop the ability to self-monitor and assume personal responsibility for their learning. This transformation from what Glanville calls a "passive consumer" to a conscientious agent in one's own learning – akin to Mahatmya et al.'s (2014, pp. 32–33) concept of students as clients, active in shaping their own learning trajectories – is essential for the achievement of professional-level proficiency and for transformative learning.

11.3 Russian across the Curriculum Tutorial

In addition to weekly non-credit tutoring, advanced UWRF students enroll in a one-credit RAC tutorial, which reflects the goal of OACD to promote "selecting curricular materials in accordance with individual learner interest and need" (see Campbell, this volume; Leaver, this volume) and enables transformation by challenging students to cross several types of borders: disciplinary, linguistic, and cultural. The RAC tutorial (Freels et al., 2017, p. 63; Murphy et al., 2017, p. 43; see also Spring, 2012) requires that students work one-on-one with a tutor, a disciplinary specialist, on a semester-long research project and write a five-page paper in Russian. (The tutorial is either an "add-on" to a concurrent or previously taken course, or an independent research project in the student's academic area.) Project topics reflect the breadth of disciplines studied by UWRF students in the humanities, social sciences, and scientific and technical fields. Students are required to cite scholarly literature or other relevant resources in Russian, consulting with RAC tutors on their research and discussing readings during tutorials.

The most successful RAC tutorial papers demonstrate deep thinking not only about the topic, but also about its treatment in Russian-language sources, from media discussions, to official policy statements, to scholarly literature. Analysis of these sources requires an openness to new perspectives, an exploration of the historical and cultural context of policy decisions, and an examination of the register and of the structure of arguments in scholarly and other articles. Research projects reflect transformative learning when they do not merely translate arguments from English to Russian, but demonstrate both deepened scholarly knowledge and expanded cultural awareness, that is, reflection on both the home culture(s) and on the culture(s) under study. In the short term, RAC tutorials are intended to prepare students for the "direct-enroll" course and professional internship in Kazakhstan. In the long term, they are intended to prepare students to analyze information and ideas from a bilingual and bicultural, even multicultural, perspective. In one successful example, a UWRF history major who completed an RAC tutorial paper on Soviet- and post-Soviet-era Russian history textbooks then applied this knowledge in the ROF internship, teaching history in a Russian-language high school in Almaty. The combination of research on Russian and Kazakhstani history textbooks and teaching Kazakhstani high school students provided enlightening new perspectives for this student on formative events in US and Soviet history. Such transformative experiences cannot be replicated in a home country setting.

11.4 Intercultural Introduction to Kazakhstan

The most direct preparation for study in Kazakhstan is provided to students through a one-credit "Intercultural Introduction to Kazakhstan" course,[2] which has been piloted in three formats: as a non-credit group tutorial conducted in Russian; as a one-credit course taught in English to all interested students in the ILC; and as a one-credit course taught in Russian to students preparing to participate in the ROF in Almaty the following academic year. This course was developed in response to annual student evaluations of the Russian Flagship program, in which students requested deeper preparation in Kazakh culture in order to prepare them for study and homestay experiences in Kazakhstan. Authentic Russian-language course materials consist of online resources, including articles, official government statements, news reports, and informational videos. Course learning objectives express some of the goals of transformative pedagogy: to reflect on the cultural assumptions and beliefs that may underlie observed behaviors; to consider the possible consequences of different responses; and to interpret homestay and academic expectations in a Kazakhstani context. The course includes affordances that enable students not only to learn about the history, geography, and culture of Kazakhstan, but also to interact with Kazakhstani students via an online intercultural exchange, and to consider potentially challenging situations through online cultural scenarios.

11.5 Virtual Intercultural Exchange

The virtual intercultural exchange, created as part of the Flagship Culture Initiative (FCI),[3] pairs cohorts of advanced UWRF students with students at

---

[2] The first version of the course was developed by Ainur Ainabekova, Dianna Murphy, and Uli Schamiloglu. The course has been taught by Jambul Akkaziev (in 2017), Assel Almuratova (in 2018 and 2020), and Gulnara Glowacki (in 2019).

[3] The FCI is an interinstitutional curriculum development project administered through the University of Maryland (Valerie Anishchenkova, PI) and focused on intercultural learning before and during study abroad.

Nazarbayev University (NU), an English-medium university in the Kazakhstani capital of Nur-Sultan, to participate in a series of activities designed to raise the students' critical cultural awareness and to provide a forum for cultural exploration.[4] Modeled on the *Cultura* project (Furstenberg & Levet, 2014), the four-week exchange includes units on national symbols and national identity, media, International Women's Day, and student and family life. Specific activities in the platform used for the exchange, Class2Class,[5] include word associations, sentence completions, scenarios, and discussion in Russian (NU) and English (UWRF). These activities provide students with opportunities to problematize national symbols, celebrations, cultural stereotypes, and issues that have associations with national culture and also cross national borders (such as views on marriage). Since all activities include options (e.g., to respond to four out of eight prompts), students select prompts of greatest interest to them; thus, they may also avoid topics that they consider too sensitive. The choices themselves offer opportunities for discussion under the guidance of faculty moderators. In addition, students participate in faculty-moderated, synchronous discussions on subjects related to the units. The exchange provides opportunities for students to express their views on topics that may be challenging to discuss, and to reflect both about their own culture(s) and about the ways in which others may view their culture(s). In feedback on the exchange, students expressed the desire for more synchronous discussions – a sign of eagerness on both the US and Kazakhstani sides to learn more about each other's cultures.

11.6 Scenarios for Intercultural Exploration

In transformative education, students are challenged to face and reflect on "disorienting dilemmas" (Mezirow, 1991). As part of the FCI, the UWRF is piloting a series of scenario-based, online learning modules[6] that present students with such dilemmas and provide framing and reflection questions

---

[4] The exchange was conducted in 2018 by Evans-Romaine and Victoria Thorstensson (NU), in 2019 by Thorstensson and Gulnara Glowacki (UW-Madison), and in 2020 by Evans-Romaine and Thorstensson.

[5] The authors thank the creators of Class2Class (see: immerseu.class2class.com) and the Flagship Technology Center at the University of Hawaii at Manoa for providing access to this platform.

[6] Russian-language scenario authors and consultants are Evans-Romaine, S.A. Karpukhin, Gulnara Glowacki, William J. Comer, Dianna Murphy, Moldir Oskenbay, and Anna Tumarkin. The FCI scenario platform is designed by Julio Rodriguez and Stephen Tschudi, Flagship Technology Center, University of Hawaii at Manoa, with assistance from Ruslan Suvorov and Dmitrii Egorov.

to stimulate role play and discussion. The Russian-language scenarios – developed following an anonymous online survey and focus group discussions on perceptions of the cultural preparation needs of students on Language Flagship Capstone overseas programs (Davidson & Garas, 2018) – present students with potentially challenging dilemmas for which a range of outcomes is possible. The scenarios, which take place in classroom, homestay, internship, and public settings, describe interactions that illustrate possible challenges, for example: in greeting and leave-taking; classroom and professional hierarchies; sharing food; concepts of personal space; giving and taking advice; and social expectations at home and in academic, professional, and other formal settings. Each scenario is presented with three possible actions that learners might take. Students make acceptability judgments about these actions, and then compare their ratings with acceptability ratings from those knowledgeable about the region. Feedback presents possible consequences and implications for each course of action. Reflection questions ask students to compare scenarios with similar situations that they have encountered at home in order to reflect on what they might do in a similar situation abroad, and what they might expect of others in both cases. The intent of the modules is neither to present learners with a set of "do's and don'ts," nor to present all possible outcomes of each course of action, but to encourage reflection on the values and beliefs that underlie and inform the actions or behaviors that they might observe, and more broadly on their own culture(s) and their positioning relative to their own and other culture(s). The ideal setting for exploring these scenarios is small-group discussion, where participants can compare their reflections under the guidance of a culturally informed moderator.[7]

11.7 Opportunities for Social Interaction

In addition to the more formal academic environments for transformative learning described earlier, the UWRF has designed learning environments to promote language and culture learning in informal settings, through co-curricular programming involving diverse speakers of Russian. Programming includes "tea and conversation," game or film nights, holiday celebrations open to the local Russian-speaking community, mini-lectures and discussions in Russian with visiting scholars, and summer conversation partnerships with visiting

---

[7] While overseas, ROF students participate in roundtable discussions, moderated by the resident director, also based on scenarios and role plays, designed by academic director Maria Lekic, in which students discuss, in English, the possible meanings associated with the actions taken by characters in the scenarios (see Davidson et al., this volume).

students from NU. Students are challenged through these events linguistically and culturally, and can select the kinds of interaction that best suit their academic and personal goals, while deepening their knowledge of Russian-speaking cultures.

11.8 Residential Language and Culture Learning: Russian House

UW-Madison's ILC offers a partial immersion environment in its Russian-language floor (*Russkii dom*). Russian House residents participate in Russian-language social events organized by a resident graduate student and take a class taught in Russian in the dormitory. This class, graded on a lower-stakes credit/no-credit scale, brings together students at all levels, positioning peers as mentors and enabling less advanced learners to participate in a minimally stressful environment (Evans-Romaine et al., 2020). In addition, ILC events bring together all residents studying various languages, including international students studying English. This multilevel, multilingual, and multicultural residential setting provides opportunities for cultural encounters and potential transformations as students take on new roles using language.

11.9 Conclusion: Transformative Practices and Learner Agency

By taking an expanded approach to curriculum and program design, the UWRF strives to offer students wraparound language learning environments that can foster transformative learning. Key to the affordances in these environments are student engagement and student agency: students must be willing and able to take responsibility for their learning. Although courses and program components such as tutoring are required, student engagement is necessary for them to succeed. RAC tutorials can be challenging, even transformative when students choose to dive deeply into Russian-language research and discussion, and to apply their research abroad. Co-curricular offerings involve choices at every turn: formal or informal interactions; small-group discussions or large gatherings; and lecture hall or residential settings. Students can remain within comfort zones in any of these parameters or step out of them. As educators, we strive to create learning experiences that encourage students to step out. How far they go is up to them. That agency is key to transformative pedagogy.

DISCUSSION QUESTIONS

1. The affordances discussed in this chapter involve choices for learners. How might educators encourage learners to leave their comfort zones in order to promote deeper and more meaningful transformative learning?
2. Review Leaver's chapter in this volume. In what ways do the affordances discussed in this chapter reflect the characteristics of transformative pedagogy outlined by Leaver?
3. Review the five identifiable stages of transformative learning presented by Davidson et al. (this volume). What would need to take place during and after the affordances presented in this chapter to allow for the learner to experience the five identifiable stages of transformative learning identified in that chapter? Which of these stages of transformative learning can feasibly take place during study on a home campus, and which are more likely to take place in a study abroad immersion setting?

PART IV

Transformative Language Learning and Teaching Applications in Immersion Programs

12

Transformative Language Learning in the Overseas Immersion Environment

Exploring Affordances of Intercultural Development

Dan E. Davidson, Nadra Garas, and Maria D. Lekic

Overseas language immersion programs have the potential to make both formal and informal learning of the target language and culture sufficiently personal, nuanced, and memorable to enable dramatic gains for the learner, both in second language (L2) proficiency and in critical thinking skills. These abilities are essential if learners are to recognize and respond appropriately to the culturally bound behaviors of representatives of the host country while maintaining awareness of their own personal and home cultural contexts.

Within the popular literature, study abroad experiences were often called "transformative" well before theories of transformative education occupied the prominent position that they do today in educational research precisely because of the close connections that such programs can provide for learners between their academic study and the day-to-day, real-life experience of the target culture. With respect to foreign language learning at advanced levels, a growing body of empirical evidence supports the claim that well-designed overseas immersion programming, such as the Language Flagship Capstone[1] year, can produce high-functioning bilinguals, that is, individuals capable of communicating meaning with high levels of precision, building and maintaining professional relationships with locals, and mediating differences in culturally appropriate ways.[2] The Capstone programs have been shown to be effective in preparing traditional and heritage students with the linguistic, cultural, and cross-cultural skill sets, as well as with attitudes and knowledge base, essential for global professionals in diverse fields.

This study will examine some of the existing empirical evidence for these claims through the lens of transformative theory. Current research and practice based on transformative theory within foreign language education build on established principles of communicative and competency-based teaching

---

[1] The Language Flagship is an initiative of the National Security Education Program (see: www.thelanguageflagship.org; see also Evans-Romaine and Murphy, this volume).

[2] Compare also the use of the term "contextual intelligence" in the field of international management, as well as the term "cultural intelligence," defined as the "ability to shift perspective from one's own to other personal, cultural, and organizational contexts" (Khanna, 2014).

methods, as well as on concepts and practices from the fields of psychology and human development (Crane, 2018; Dirkx, 2008b; Johnson, 2015; Jung, 1921; Mezirow, 1991; Rogers, 1969/1986; Vygotsky, 1978/2013; see also Leaver, this volume). Foreign language teaching is transformative when it brings learners into direct and meaningful contact with cultural difference, which is an experience that can be unsettling or disorienting for learners, requiring reflection, analysis, and, ultimately, a new or broadened understanding of another culture, as well as the underlying value systems, traditions, and belief structures that inform it.

Vygotsky's concepts of the zone of proximal development (ZPD), learner-centered instruction, and self-management principles are central to transformative learning more generally. ZPD presupposes the existence of a set of affordances that permit learners to safely and successfully navigate the challenges that learners at this level of preparation encounter, in this case, as students, interns, and residents in a cultural setting that is notably different from their own, while relating these challenges to a larger process of their own intellectual, cultural, and linguistic growth. A number of the affordances developed for the Capstone program will be noted in the following.

Within the context of advanced language study in the overseas immersion context, transformative learning has been observed to encompass five identifiable stages:

- A *disorienting dilemma* shakes students' culturally conditioned expectations, pre-existing judgments, or current attitudes regarding a cultural matter, causing them to reflect about it.[3]
- *Premise reflection* (see Crane & Sosulski, this volume; see also Dirkx, 1997, 2012; Kember et al., 1999, p. 23; Mezirow, 1991), in which learners reflect on the causes of their own reactions to the particular behavior in question on both the cognitive-analytic and emotional-integrative levels.[4]
- *Critical reflection* on the cognitive dissonance and emotional disequilibrium experienced by learners as a result of the dilemma leads to a re-examination of their assumptions about the inherent meaning of a particular word or utterance, behaviors, or social practices observed within the target culture.
- *Reframing* is a cognitive tool for processing the data revealed by the disorienting dilemma and for re-establishing a degree of cognitive continuity by learners on a different (higher) level.

---

[3] Mezirow (2000, p. 22) identified ten potential stages in the process.

[4] Lawrence and Cranton (2009, p. 316) note that "transformative learning can be both cognitive and imaginative; it can be collaborative and individually based; it can include depth psychology alongside a more practical reflective approach." Dirkx (2008a) and Oxford (this volume) address overt interactions of cognition and emotion in the context of transformative learning.

- *Revised strategy (action plan)* for integrating the new or revised perspective into their communication and interactional strategies in the target culture on the basis of conditions dictated by their new perspective.

Within the overseas Russian Capstone program, transformative learning is ongoing, nonlinear, and cumulative in nature, resembling what Mezirow (1994, pp. 229–230) characterized as "a set of progressive transformations in related meaning schemes," alternating with occasional setbacks. Through increasing numbers of personal and social interactions, as well as the more nuanced and extended exchanges of views and ideas that are made possible by the learner's growing linguistic and cultural proficiency, participants sharpen their ability to recognize and anticipate cultural, cognitive, or attitudinal differences across cultures, and develop their capacity for reflection on those differences, as well as on their own personal or culturally bound reactions to difference. The transformative foreign language learning experience is successful when the students have reached a stage of intercultural development that permits them to shift from the home-culture perspective to that of the target culture in order to communicate effectively and appropriately across cultures, just as the accomplished speaker learns to shift smoothly between the mother tongue and target language as necessary.

As a multi-institutional US national program informed by the principles of transformative learning, the Flagship Capstone program administered by the American Councils for International Education at Al-Farabi Kazakh National University incorporates affordances for participants (US undergraduate students of Russian at the advanced to professional levels CEFR B2 to C1/C2; ILR 2–3) within a relatively "open architecture," which includes intensive language study, individual tutorials, self-selected courses in their fields of specialization, professional internships, a year-long residence with local families, integrated cultural programming, and 24/7 immersion in the language(s) and culture(s) of the host country.[5]

While study abroad alumni often do refer to their immersion year as "transformative," most alumni also readily concede that their language and cultural growth included periods of cognitive overload and emotional unrest, when their sense of status, personal identity, or how things work fell into doubt (Pellegrino-Aveni, 2005). For most immersion learners, at this level at least, transformative learning *without* disorienting dilemmas is relatively rare. For that reason, a well-scaffolded transformative language program should provide the affordances that enable learners to recognize, negotiate, and eventually anticipate disorienting dilemmas. For example, in 2016/2017, the Russian

---

[5] Language utilization reports document 57–85 hours per week of L2 utilization of Flagship students at Levels 2+ to 3 (Davidson & Lekic, 2012).

Capstone program introduced moderated bimonthly roundtable discussions, supported by the Flagship Culture Initiative (FCI), using case studies and role plays based on actual (anonymized) cultural dilemmas previously reported by Flagship students in their online journals. The topics reflect behaviors and practices encountered within the host culture related to health, hospitality and reciprocity, gender, family life, workplace and classroom etiquette, the role of social status, attitudes toward time and rules, and understanding of what are appropriate subjects for conversation.

12.1 Online Learner Journals: Affordance of Structured Reflection

Given the central importance of premise reflection, critical reflection, goal setting, and strategy selection for virtually all aspects of language learning at the professional level, the role of the online journal is a central affordance for structured reflection within the Flagship Capstone program. Each week over the course of the two-semester program, Flagship students are required to submit written reflections in English on their linguistic and cultural interactions and personal growth over the past seven-day reporting period, while setting (or re-setting) learning goals for themselves for the coming weeks. In addition to completing time/place maps for the past week, the online journals prompt participants to document, in their own words, culturally distinctive experiences (words, conversations, behaviors, practices) that they have encountered, the strategies that they employed in response, and any lessons learned for the future. In the process, students develop skills for observation, self-reflection, critical reflection, and perspective taking, based on their own day-to-day experiences with peers and other representatives of the target culture.[6]

Sample reflections by individual students regarding issues ("dilemmas") that they encountered over the course of a week provide a glimpse into the process of the transformative learning that students undergo in dealing (cognitively and emotionally) with cross-cultural differences. The successive stages through which student reflections progress are tagged for reference.

Sample #1: "Nationality"

Dilemma: This week a lot of people have been asking me about my nationality. I say that I am American, and nobody takes that as an answer. I have to explain why my mom speaks Spanish, I have to explain my last name, and I have to explain which side of the family gave me certain traits.

---

[6] In Crane's research, students were encouraged to think deeply about their learning experiences through guided writing assignments in English rather than the language of instruction.

Premise reflection: This can get a little offensive to someone who grew up in America.

Critical reflection: I realized that it is just something that happens here. People are just curious. They aren't using the information to make judgments about me.

Action plan: I answer the questions and then usually switch the conversation to something else. I think that is a more or less positive outcome. I learned that people have good intentions behind their questions, and I can use that to avoid getting prematurely offended in the future.

Graceful avoidance of uncomfortable topics is often the best choice among available cross-cultural strategies, especially with respect to persistent local interest in an issue like nationality, which is an understandable by-product of living in a multi-ethnic republic and a social culture where ethnicity is still an official part of everyone's passport and family identity.

Sample #2: "Marriage"

Dilemma: In Kazakhstan, a lot of people have asked me if I am getting married soon. Upon hearing that I have been dating someone for a few years, they always tell me that I should get married after this year.

Premise reflection: In the US, there is not the same pressure to get married. In fact, I would say that in my community in the US, getting married in your early 20s is usually considered jumping the gun.

Critical reflection: I learned that it isn't meant to be rude. People here just consider starting a family life a big blessing, and they want me to have that kind of success.

Action plan: I think the situation was resolved well. I just smile and say that I am not in a hurry.

The foregoing reflections (and others like them) by immersion students on their own language and cultural learning provide insight for teachers and specialists into the cultural contexts and speech situations in which young adult learners develop their linguistic and intercultural skills, and negotiate their status within their professional and personal networks.

12.2 Language Proficiency and Intercultural Growth

The primary focus of the Capstone program is the development of professional language and cultural proficiency. As students' speaking, listening, reading, and writing proficiencies develop over the course of the year-long program, so too does their ability to notice, interpret, and negotiate cultural differences and the disorienting dilemmas that often accompany them. With appropriate affordances (such as structured reflection, weekly journals, and individual mentoring) in place, students can learn to navigate beyond their present levels of understanding into their next growth trajectory, engaging higher-level cultural issues that had not previously been accessible to them. Throughout this process, target language proficiency appears to be a critical rung on the ladder of transformative learning and intercultural development.

In order to explore the relationship between L2 proficiency and intercultural growth, a longitudinal study was begun in 2014 by the American Councils Research Center to assess the overall levels of intercultural development of consecutive groups of advanced US students of Arabic, Chinese, and Russian participating in Capstone programs at higher education institutions in Beijing, Meknes, St. Petersburg, and Almaty.

The subjects of the present study are the Russian Flagship program participants ($N = 61$), advanced-level US university students, 56 percent of whom identified as female and 44 percent as male. Participants ranged in age from 21 to 32 years and all had completed at least three years of university-level language study, including a minimum of eight weeks of immersion study in a Russian-speaking country prior to the Capstone program. Virtually all the Russian language students achieved Level 3 by the end of their Flagship program, as shown in the pre-/post-program comparisons in Figure 12.1.

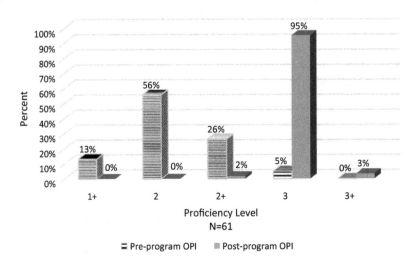

Figure 12.1 Overseas Flagship programs' pre- and post-program Oral Proficiency Interview (OPI) levels. This figure illustrates improvements in tested performance as a result of overseas study.

The instrument selected to assess evidence of their transformative learning was the widely used Intercultural Development Inventory® (IDI), which defines high-level intercultural competence as the "capability to shift cultural perspective and appropriately adapt behavior to cultural differences and commonalities." This online standardized test was administered to participants prior to the start of their year abroad and once again at the end. The IDI generates data on intercultural *developmental orientation* (DO), a measurement of the subject's orientation toward cultural difference and commonalities, one's *perceived orientation* (PO), and the *orientation gap* (OG) between PO and DO. At its core, the test collects and assesses evidence of capacity for cognitive frame-shifting, behavior code-shifting, and other relevant cross-cultural behaviors. Based on the work of Bennett (1993, 2004), Bennett and Bennett (2004), and Hammer (1998, 2009, 2012), the current version of the 50-item IDI generates scores that locate participant orientations along a broad continuum ranging from monocultural mindsets of denial (not engaging with cultural differences) and polarization ("us" vs. "them"), to a transitional orientation of minimization of cultural difference, and, ultimately, to a well-developed intercultural mindset of acceptance and adaptation (i.e., the ability to shift perspectives and change behavior to act in a culturally appropriate manner).[7]

Table 12.1 presents the results of the IDI data collected before and after the overseas immersion year, listing the mean scores of the PO and DO of participants in the Russian Flagship Capstone program, including those subscales for which statistically significant findings were noted.

A paired sample *t*-test was used to compare the pre- and post-program scores of the participants on the IDI scales. The results of this study show that participants experienced a statistically significant positive shift in their DO scores, moving from 95.83 to 99.36, a gain of 3.53 points ($p \leq 0.001$). The results also point to a positive change in the year-long study at the level of *acceptance orientation*. Critically, these results also indicate a statistically significant change in the direction of growth on the IDI subscale for acceptance and adaptation within the clusters of *cognitive frame-shifting*. Mean scores for acceptance orientation changed from a pre-test score of 3.94 to a post-test score of 4.11 ($p \leq .001$), demonstrating participants' enhanced ability to recognize and appreciate differences and similarities both between and within cultures. The upper-level language learners also show noticeable positive change in the adaptation subscale for cognitive frame-shifting, where the mean student profile score increased to 3.76 from 3.64 ($p \leq .0001$). This reflects participants' growing ability to understand and perceive issues from multiple cultural perspectives.

---

[7] Compare also William Perry's (1981) epistemic approach to critical thinking.

Table 12.1 Paired sample *t*-tests for Russian Overseas Flagship program (*N* = 61)

	Pre-program mean (sd)	Post-program mean (sd)	Mean difference	*t* (df = 60)	*p*
Perceived orientation	123.23 (5.656)	124.72 (5.423)	1.49	4.384	.000
Developmental orientation	95.83 (14.926)	99.36 (14.266)	3.53	4.101	.000
Orientation gap	27.40 (9.604)	25.36 (9.173)	−2.04	−3.724	.000
Acceptance	3.94 (0.649)	4.11 (0.656)	0.18	3.618	.000
Cognitive frame-shifting	3.64 (0.666)	3.76 (0.622)	0.12	2.413	.017

While it is salient for the present study to demonstrate measurable positive change in the overall intercultural development and cognitive frame-shifting abilities of consecutive groups of Flagship Capstone participants, the question remains as to whether this development is connected with the students' speaking, reading, or listening levels during this period. Hence, a further round of analyses was performed comparing student speaking, listening, and reading proficiency scores pre- and post-program with the pre- and post-IDI data reported earlier. These results demonstrate a close relationship between end-of-program ratings for speaking and DO scores. Post-program OPI proficiency levels (presented numerically with a maximum of 10, which corresponds to ILR 3/3+) on the horizontal axis of the trellis plot show the steep incline or growth in post-program DO at the highest proficiency levels. In short, the higher the post-program speaking proficiency, the higher the intercultural DO is likely to be. This positive relationship (3.23 points gained on the IDI scale for each proficiency sub-level beyond ILR 2 achieved by the student) is presented in Figure 12.2.

Higher post-program speaking proficiency is also correlated with positive overall growth in DO, regardless of the student's initial DO score. For this analysis an IDI-DO "change" variable was created to help in further examining the relationship between language proficiency levels and intercultural development (see Figure 12.3).

Given the strong correlation between the students' speaking attainment and their post-intercultural development scores, tests were also performed to determine whether there was a relationship between the *pre-program* speaking, reading, or listening levels and final DO scores. Regressions revealed that both pre-program reading and pre-program listening are correlated with higher post-program DO scores (see Figure 12.4).

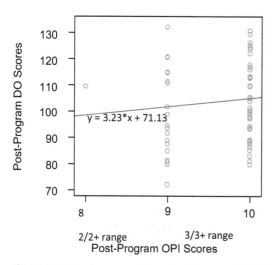

Figure 12.2 Post-program OPI and post-program DO. This figure illustrates post-program OPI scores and post-program developmental orientation scores.

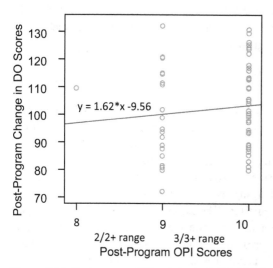

Figure 12.3 Post-program OPI and change in DO. This figure illustrates post-program OPI scores and change in post-program developmental orientation scores.

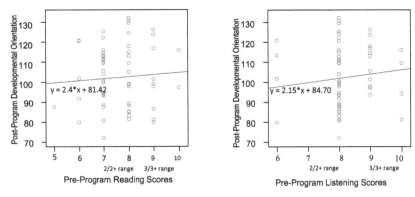

Figure 12.4 Post-program Reading and Listening Post-program DO. This figure illustrates pre-program reading and listening scores and post-program Developmental Orientation scores.

For each sub-level difference achieved by the entering student on the pre-program Flagship reading test, that student's predicted end-of-program DO can be expected to increase by 2.4 points. The pre-program listening proficiency is also a predictor of DO gain, with a 2.15-point gain.[8] From the data reported here, it follows that good baseline L2 reading and listening skills bode well for students participating in programs grounded in transformative theories with a strong focus on intercultural growth.[9]

12.3 Conclusions

The present study has examined strategies employed by the Russian Overseas Flagship program to foster student reflection on their own linguistic and cultural learning from the point of view of transformative learning. With its relatively open architecture, the Capstone program seeks to meet the needs of ILR 2, 2+, and 3 learners by providing a scaffolded learning environment, designed to foster incremental transformative learning and intercultural growth for all students over the course of two academic semesters. The current study has presented examples of transformative learning as it unfolds within the overseas immersion context, as captured in student reflections in online journals. The second portion of this study sought to provide group-level quantitative data collected over a three-year period documenting the *measurable outcomes* of the Flagship program in the area of

<hr>

[8] Note that the positive cross-skill predictive power of pre-reading proficiency was noted in Davidson and Shaw (2019).

[9] Regarding the role of listening proficiency as a predictor of advanced-level language gain in the study abroad environment, see Davidson (2010).

intercultural growth, defined here as movement of one's cultural orientation away from a monocultural mindset and toward greater awareness of the mindsets of others, as well as of the specifics of one's own particular cultural lens.

The results of the mixed-method exploratory analyses regarding the application of transformative principles within the context of the Russian Overseas Flagship are positive and encouraging of further study in this area.

The current analysis also points to a relationship between language proficiency and the learner's intercultural development. The most accomplished speakers in the cohort also tended to score highest on the IDI and/or register the greatest gains in IDI over the course of the year. Moreover, and of no less significance, among entering students in the Capstone program, those who had achieved higher levels of proficiency in reading and listening in the pre-program tests were also most likely to be among the high-scoring IDI performers at the end of the program. Furthermore, students, especially those with strong reading and listening skills, appear to mobilize their interpretive and linguistic skills upon arrival in the country to strengthen their ability to notice, reflect on, and interpret the meanings behind the linguistic and cultural input that they hear, read, and observe. Target language proficiency also appears to function as a primary affordance of intercultural growth for participants in the Russian Capstone Program.

The present study has provided evidence that by the end of their course of study, Capstone students are able to sufficiently engage in cognitive frame-shifting and cultural adaptation to take into account the effects of local cultural differences, manage their own intellectual and emotional reactions to those differences, and generally understand the intentions and worldviews of their hosts. As a result of these transformations, they are better positioned to respond and behave effectively and appropriately as global professionals.

DISCUSSION QUESTIONS

1. Based on your reading of the chapter, what would you identify as the key interventions for ensuring that overseas immersion programs succeed in advancing the language and intercultural learning of their participants?
2. The present volume provides several approaches to the possible assessment of transformative language learning. To what extent do the measured differences in ILR and IDI test scores, as well as the sample learner diaries, provide evidence in support of the claim of transformative learning in this case? What other forms of evidence of student learning might one elicit?
3. The focus of this chapter is on the advanced to professional levels of language training and the study abroad context. How might the design of the program be changed to accommodate the needs of learners at other levels, such as beginning-level or lower-proficiency learners?

13

Transformative Dimensions of Community Engagement and Service Learning during In-Country Immersion

Amer Farraj

In 2007, faculty and administrators began to inject transformative language learning and teaching (TLLT) practices into programs within the Arabic Department in the Directorate of Continuing Education (CE) at the Defense Language Institute Foreign Language Center (DLIFLC).[1] The Arabic Department taught intermediate and advanced (I/A) courses to military cohorts, with the target goals of achieving interagency language roundtable (ILR) Level 2+ and Level 3, respectively, in listening and reading comprehension.[2] The TLLT approaches used in the I/A Arabic classrooms were exemplified in two specialized programs: short-term in-country immersions in Jordan, Egypt, and Morocco; and distance-learning courses. These programs included the expected components of TLLT: open architecture curricular design (see Campbell, this volume; see also Leaver and Campbell, 2020); full authenticity with grammar "taught in the wild," that is, within the context of the authentic materials themselves but delving more deeply into grammatical usage than in a focus-on-form approach (Doughty & Williams, 1998); learner empowerment/ development of learner autonomy (see Little, this volume); real-life cross-cultural scenarios that create disorienting dilemmas and segue to the remaining nine phases of transformative learning; the role of teacher as advisor, mentor, and coach (Leaver, 2018; Rogers, 1978); formative assessments, including diagnostic assessment (DA) (Cohen, 2014; Sternberg & Grigorenko, 2002)[3]

---

[1] TLLT in the Arabic program was based loosely on practices associated with Mezirow (1991), the most pertinent phases being disorienting dilemmas, reflection with affective responses, and change.

[2] The ILR (2012) Language Skill Level Descriptions, which delineate levels of proficiency using a scale from 0 through 5, informed the development of the ACTFL proficiency guidelines scale from novice/low through distinguished. For more information, see: www.govtilr.org and www.actfl.org/publications/guidelines-and-manuals/actfl.

[3] Cohen (2014) describes DA as used at the DLIFLC to assess in a formative manner (feedback and planning) the gaps in learners' proficiency at the next higher level of proficiency, that is, what will it take in terms of linguistic and cultural knowledge and behavior to reach that level? Sternberg and Grigorenko (2002) describe dynamic testing as a targeted aspect of diagnostic assessment that identifies language specifics that learners are most ready to learn; the DLIFLC incorporates dynamic testing as a component of diagnostic assessment.

with continual feedback, and occasional summative assessments (projects, presentations, contracted assignments, and portfolios) that integrate outcome and process, rather than separate them; and attention to learner differences and individual needs (Ehrman et al., 2003).

13.1 The CE Arabic Department Immersion Programs: History and Salient Features

The first iterations of the community engagement and service-learning components took place in the CE Arabic Department overseas immersion programs. Later, a similar overseas immersion program was also organized in the context of a language for specific purposes (LSP) course at a separate government installation. The successes of the former were a key source of information for the design and execution of the latter program.

Prior to the adoption of TLLT practices in CE in 2007, success in immersion programs had been difficult to achieve. In fact, in 2006, the pre- and post-immersion score comparisons of learners participating in an immersion program at a private language school in Egypt showed a loss in proficiency in all learners by an average of half a proficiency level, from 2+/2+/2 (2+ in listening comprehension/2+ in reading comprehension/2 in speaking) to 2/2/1+ (and in one case, 0+). For a number of learners, fluency had increased but accuracy levels were inadequate for the requirements of upper-level proficiency. An analysis of the immersion program showed that the instructional emphasis on typical communicative activities such as simple role plays (without formative evaluative feedback) and excursion programs was more touristic than educational in nature.

A robust plan to increase proficiency was imperative given learners had only six weeks to attain the 3/3/2+ graduation goal but were now a full proficiency point away. Together with the teacher, the learners developed a plan to review the content domains taught in the course. Instruction included one-on-one mentoring over Skype evenings and weekends. The DA results showed that most of the learners were visual learners, so materials were first presented in written form, with an assignment of 10–20 pages of authentic materials nightly. The results? On the Defense Language Proficiency Test in reading and listening comprehension, 100 percent of the learners achieved 3/3 (3 in listening comprehension and reading comprehension); on the Oral Proficiency Interview (OPI), which measures speaking, 90 percent of the learners achieved 2+. One learner "failed," with a 3/3/1+ (3 in listening comprehension, 3 in reading comprehension, and 1+ in speaking); however, that learner had been waived into the class at 1/1/0, when the prerequisite for the course was 2/2/1+. (The faculty considered her 3/3/1+ to reflect remarkable progress, nonetheless.)

Thus were planted the first seeds of TLLT in the I/A course but, first, the administration put the immersion program on hold, being determined to discover the reasons for the loss of proficiency while in-country for learners in six of seven groups. At a DLIFLC-CE summit, external experts were presented with the collected data. The experts considered the length of the immersion (four weeks) too short for advanced learners; their recommendation was either to lengthen the immersion to a full semester (a non-starter due to the costs involved) or shorten the immersion to two weeks and change the goal to cultural exposure.

The administration and faculty decided to shorten the course to two weeks but, in that time frame, to experiment with a full TLLT program. When the first two-week TLLT course at the University of Jordan found learners improving on average by half a point in listening comprehension, reading comprehension, and speaking, the course was increased to three weeks, and then to four weeks. In one remarkable example, a very weak learner, tested by the DLIFLC Testing Division at 2/2/1 before the four-week Jordan immersion, returned at 3/3/2+ (and was retested by tester trainers, who confirmed this exceptional progress). Other learners made less remarkable progress but all recorded measurable increases in proficiency in an unusually short amount of time.

So, what had changed? The classroom teachers were the same; the cohorts of learners were similar; and the availability of Arabic-language resources remained constant. However, one factor was new: the revamped programs had adopted TLLT principles. In every group:

- empowered learners articulated specific, unique goals;
- teachers coached learners in drafting a map of the course (immersion) content; and
- teachers provided tools to learners that scaffolded their language and culture skills, building the abilities needed for participation in native-learner content classes taught by professors in a variety of disciplines. Equally important, learners developed the cross-cultural skills needed to cope successfully with on-site disorienting dilemmas. The skills included:
  - conveying and understanding spoken opinions;
  - reading copious amounts of authentic materials rapidly; and, ultimately,
  - interacting appropriately in-country with native Arabs.

13.1.1 Before the Immersion

Before starting their immersion, learners identified their immersion goals. Then, coached by their teacher, they mapped out their program, which included the kinds of materials and topics to be studied, not unlike the advanced "50/50" course taught by Shekhtman at the Foreign Service Institute (see Campbell, this volume). Learners searched for the appropriate materials, and teachers guided them in how to tell which materials they were most ready to learn, following the concept of the zone of proximal development (Vygotsky, 1997). At this point, teachers guided learners in the use of each of Shekhtman's (2003) communicative tools by:

- ensuring the accuracy of learner monologues ("islands"), rehearsed with learners;
- coaching learners in rehearsing ways to adjust for where they may be caught off guard while mingling with native Arabic speakers in the host country ("shifting gears");
- guiding learners in giving extended responses;
- providing learners with opportunities to practice simplifying;
- putting learners in situations where they could become comfortable with breaking away, that is, letting go of translation;
- teaching learners how to embellish; and
- prompting learners to "show your stuff" (using everything that has been learned or is known).

These tools build linguistic flexibility to support the emotional resiliency needed for challenging in-country experiences.

In the pre-immersion phase, learners and teacher planned the curriculum to be studied in-country and readied themselves for it. After studying the authentic material identified in their course maps, learners conducted research in Arabic about the topics of interest. Then, the teacher planned a meeting with a specialist in the content area to visit class and discuss/debate in Arabic the learners' findings and conclusions. The hope was that this initial discussion with an Arab content specialist would ameliorate in advance some of the cognitive dilemmas that learners might encounter in their in-country content classes: the way in which the classes are conducted; the expectations of the other learners; and the mindset of the typical Arab in the country of immersion.

Also, teachers conducted DAs in the pre-immersion phase to compare with the post-immersion results. The DAs had multiple purposes. Pre- and post-assessments indicated linguistic progress while abroad. More than proficiency gain, the results showed specific areas of strength and weakness within a proficiency level, and the dynamic testing component of the DA allowed assessors to determine which components of the next/higher proficiency levels learners were most ready to acquire. The results, where it mattered, also pointed to activities, lessons, and so on that went wrong in the immersion for the purpose of informing the training of the next cohort. The DA instrument in use at the DLIFLC also included demographic information and the E&L Cognitive Styles

Construct tool (Corin & Leaver, 2019; Ehrman & Leaver, 2002) for determining participant's learning styles. When combined with linguistic information, this additional information helped teachers better understand and advise students in their learning.

13.1.2 During the Immersion

The resident I/A courses last 47 weeks, of which four weeks are spent in an Arabic-speaking country. From 2007 to 2011, when the author was associated with the I/A Arabic in-country immersion, DLIFLC-CE enrolled learners at local universities, where they studied the same materials as their Arab counterparts, though not together with them.

In the morning, learners attended a language class on the local dialect (Jordanian, Egyptian, or Moroccan), followed by a lecture in the local, traditional instructional approach, conducted by a university content professor, using the same notes and instructional techniques as for their local learners (often, a two-hour lecture, though in such cases, the professor was asked to leave time at the end for discussion given that it is not customary to do so). Popular topics included comparative law, political science, sociology, and history. In the afternoon, learners participated in excursions related to the morning's lecture. For example, if learners studied law, they would hear three days of morning lectures and in the afternoons would: (1) visit a tribal sharia expert; (2) meet with a civil lawyer; and (3) discuss honor killings with a journalist crusading against them. A one-hour post-excursion meeting with the accompanying teacher-mentor[4] consisted of discussing authentic readings (provided by the university professor) for the next day's lecture in order to acquire the vocabulary and grammar that they would need, preparing questions (local professors were not generally used to working with non-native speakers, so questions needed to be posed with precision by the students), and discussing the cultural phenomena that had been encountered.

Separately, as homework, learners wrote one-page analyses of each day's experiences, which were corrected by the teacher-mentor, revised, and sent to the primary instructor back at DLIFLC. These became the basis for presentations in Arabic that learners gave to other learners, faculty, and visitors upon their return to their regular programs. In their presentations, individual learners reflected on their experiences and the ways that these experiences transformed their understanding of the culture of and interactions with Arabs.

---

[4] Abarbanel (2019) advises study abroad professionals to talk to learners about in-country emotional challenges and ways to increase their resiliency.

13.2 LSP Immersions

The government LSP immersion programs from 2008 to 2012 followed the format of scenario-based instruction (for a discussion of scenario-based instruction at DLIFLC, see Corin, this volume), roundtable discussions, and volunteer activities found in the I/A immersion programs (Corin, 1997; see also Corin, this volume). Preparatory work during the pre-immersion phase paralleled the CE I/A courses. However, the activities during LSP immersion took a different shape, that is, an immersion model based on a heuristic, roundtable discussion, and volunteer activities.

13.2.1 Use of a Heuristic

In-country, learners in the LSP immersion program applied their knowledge and skills to authentic scenarios, mingling with Arabs and using Arabic only. In this phase, learners used the communicative tools that they had learned. Learners gained local friends who could help them navigate the disorienting dilemmas that they encountered, develop deeper cultural awareness, and take a big step toward biculturalism.[5]

By way of example, in 2011, the author accompanied a group of learners to an Arab-speaking country. They had a clear goal: accurately emulate cultural behavior so as to be readily accepted by their counterparts. Learners had prepared for this trip by repeating real-life scenarios to the point that the range of probable communications came as easily to them as repeating their own names – the automatic–correct language that one expects from Level 4 performers (Shekhtman & Leaver, 2002). At the end of each day, the learners and the author gathered to interpret the in-context feedback that they had received (or gaffes that they had noticed) in order to give them feedback on how to improve their language use and to rehearse scenarios associated with their individualized real-life goals for the next day.

These goals varied. In one case, a history buff, working on culturally appropriate persuasive skills, was tasked with talking the guard at a historical site into granting him gratis entry. The learner went to the historical site, held the rehearsed conversation with the guard, and gained entry without paying any entrance fees; not only that, the guard gave him his personal phone number, offering to help him whenever he wanted to access historical sites. How did

---

[5] Shekhtman and Leaver (2002) posit that learners go through four phases of language control as they approach near-native proficiency: (1) not automatic–not correct (new learners, native language influence); (2) not automatic–correct (memorized rules); (3) automatic–not correct (fossilization); and (4) automatic–correct (the goal).

this happen? The following heuristic, implemented by empowered, autonomous learners who were coached by a teacher-mentor, was used in the preparation and conduct of real-life tasks:

- Establish a real-life goal.
- Build and practice a culturally appropriate scenario (multiple times, with pertinent variations).
- Try out the scenario with the host family.
- Accomplish the task.
- Report on the experience.
- Receive cultural and linguistic feedback.
- Establish a new or follow-on real-life goal.

The controlled rehearsals gave the learners the confidence to approach uncontrolled real-life situations, using acquired language and tools. The pragmatic result was an accomplished task important to real-life job requirements. The affective result was a change in how learners viewed and approached language learning and in how they viewed and approached native speakers.

13.2.2 Use of Roundtable Discussions

For each topic in the program, learners conducted research in Arabic, presented information that each had learned to the teacher-mentor, fellow cohort members, host families, and others, and received language and culture feedback from the teacher-mentor. Learners followed up by conducting more focused research, presenting new or supplemental information, and receiving additional feedback. Once in-country, learners reviewed the authentic material on the relevant topic the night before a meeting with a specialist on the topic, practiced discussing the topic with their host families, and rehearsed questions and talking points for the meeting with the cohort.

13.2.3 Use of Volunteer Work/Service Learning

Barbara Jacoby (1996) describes service learning as a form of hands-on education in which learners take part in activities targeted toward human and community needs followed by opportunities for reflection upon the experience of those activities. Such service-learning concepts undergird the volunteer portion of the in-country immersion experience, which provides learners with activities connected with community engagement while putting them in the position of developing their cultural awareness by helping others. Service learning differs from in-country internships in that: (1) they are intended to provide unpaid community service; and (2) they involve the conscious achievement of learning goals (as opposed to the less-focused learning that is typical in many internship or work environments, where the development of language skills and cultural awareness is incidental to the job itself). In service learning, learning goals are expressed initially, analyzed in process, and reflected upon in retrospect, with the assistance of the teacher-mentor.

The volunteering component of the LSP immersion program sought to balance service goals, that is, providing benefit to a group within the community or to the community as a whole, and learning goals, namely, proficiency enhancement (Furco, 1996; Sigmon, 1979, 1994). The results from volunteer work showed that learners at ILR Level 2 gained the most in proficiency from participating, considerably more than learners at lower levels. However, all learners improved their language skills, and learners at higher levels volunteered for work that demanded more sophisticated language skills, for example, at a customer service shop that required dealing with customers from a range of socioeconomic and educational backgrounds.

13.3 After the Immersion

After returning from both the I/A and LSP immersions, learners discussed their experiences with their teachers, reviewing the original course mapping, comparing the scenarios that they had rehearsed with the scenarios that they had encountered, and more. They reflected upon the cultural awareness that they had developed and the discomfort that they had felt linguistically and emotionally in particular situations. Finally, they assessed the ways in which the experience had changed them.

Additionally, learners took a DA to determine proficiency gain and, to the extent that the proficiency scale can make such judgments, the maturation of cultural understanding. This information helped learners to plan their future study. Likewise, teachers used this information to assess the efficacy of the immersion program and take appropriate actions for future program modification.

13.4 Conclusion

Mingling in-country with native Arabs, engaging with them in rehearsed conversations and unrehearsed offshoots, and joining with them through volunteer activities can create many levels of transformation if learners remain open-minded about the local culture – not always easy with a military cohort whose real-life jobs are not always limited to peacekeeping or humanitarian relief. The immersions described in this chapter did indeed bring about change in the learners: knowledge of cultural norms (e.g., eating food in authentic ways – in Arab countries, often with the hands rather than with utensils), proficiency gain, and a step toward biculturalism from understanding the culture, becoming comfortable within it, and absorbing a part of it into their own personality, in great part due to living with host families and volunteering at workplaces.

The success of the immersions described in this chapter emanated from a goal-oriented organization, course mapping undertaken by learners and teachers, rehearsing anticipated in-country experiences in advance, having a teacher-mentor on-site to help interpret experiences and provide timely corrections and training, and the post-immersion collaborative analysis by teachers and learners in which internal changes experienced by the learners could be processed in the safety of their classrooms. A typical transformation that took place was the conversion from uneasiness with a culture often considered "enemy" to these military students to genuine friendship and a desire to build bridges and use the language for collaboration.

DISCUSSION QUESTIONS

1. Read Boris Shekhtman's (2013) book *How to improve your foreign language immediately.* Discuss the importance of building "islands" and point out ways to have students stay in control of the conversation while mingling with native speakers.
2. Interview two to three teachers with lengthy study abroad experience about the importance of immersion and what challenges they face during the stages of planning and implementation and placing students with host families.
3. Discuss with language teachers how they can balance fluency and accuracy during in-country immersion, and list ways and methods to sustain accuracy while in the country.

14

Immersion and Transformative Pedagogy in the French Language Department of the French War College

Jérôme Collin

Located in the facilities of the Military School, in the very heart of Paris, right in front of the Eiffel Tower, the War College's French Language Department offers an immersive language learning environment, both from a linguistic and a professional perspective. The officers are plunged into the linguistic capital of the francophone world,[1] within their professional space.[2] In theory, this immersive situation enhances active, participative, and transformative pedagogies. However, it can conceal obstacles that might slow down, if not prevent, language learning and the learners willfully and responsibly taking charge of their learning. The objective of this chapter is both to delineate obstacles to the application of transformative pedagogy in the immersive situation and to suggest several remedies.

14.1 Obstacles to the Application of Transformative Pedagogy

This section will describe two obstacles to the application of transformative pedagogy: pedagogical disengagement and sociolinguistic insecurity.

14.1.1 Pedagogical Disengagement

In the world of professionals sent as learners to the War College's French Department, the professionals' profile is all-important. The learners are not linguistic students; they are senior military officers, selected by their military leadership, who come to France from various French-speaking countries to undertake professional training, some for the very first time.[3] The language is

---

[1] The headquarters of the International Francophonie Organization is in Paris on Avenue Bosquet, 650 meters from the War School; that of the Alliance Française on Boulevard Raspail is less than half an hour away on foot.

[2] The French Language Department classrooms are in the same building as the War College classrooms.

[3] Their educational backgrounds are highly varied, depending upon their culture of origin. Some have an education background that can differ radically from the products of the educational system in France, including individualized instruction by preceptorship or, at the opposite extreme, in rigidly teacher-centered classrooms. Additionally, some are committed to ultimate military service from very young ages.

not the objective; rather, it is the means to reach the objective. Consequently, the learners typically have little curiosity or interest in the language. They do not wish to become French specialists. In some cases, they may even be forced to learn French against their wishes. Therefore, they tend to rely on the teacher to take full charge of their training, for example, determining the appropriate learning strategies. Not wishing to get involved in the didactic problems that may be beyond their grasp and faced with a native speaker who has all the sociolinguistic keys of the target language, the learners find themselves in a situation of *pedagogical disengagement*.

This disengagement manifests itself in a variety of ways. First, it is a shift from confidence in oneself to full confidence in the teacher. The result is a blocking of any internal transformative process. In the case of pronunciation and intonation, for example, learner disengagement greatly diminishes chances of progress because good diction cannot be acquired without a strong personal investment and confidence. The same can be said for the mastery of idiomatic expressions.

Second, disengagement occurs when learners sacrifice their personal learning needs related to their mother tongue in order to accommodate the learning needs of the group. The result is a further withdrawal from the learning process because they do not want to be a blocking factor in the group – one that distorts the pedagogy for one's own needs to the detriment of others' needs. Instead, they delegate their pedagogical strategizing to the teacher, who (alone) will know how to build an adapted pedagogical process of benefit to all.

Third, in the specific case of the French language, the feeling of pedagogical disengagement also comes from the relative absence of any margin of creativity for the learner. Either the form is given by usage and is accepted, or usage never integrated the form or abandoned it, and so it will be considered incorrect.[4] This absence of creativity in French can also be seen in the lexicon (difficulty in creating compound words and neologisms) and in syntax (word order rigidity). Any deviation from usage will be considered a mistake with respect to grammar or other norms of contemporary usage.

The immersive context and the presence of native teachers living in the country of the target language make the learner much more sensitive to the notion of norms. The teachers know what the French "that is spoken" or "that is written" is. Whatever the pedagogical options, the teachers will be seen as guardians of both prescriptive and descriptive norms.[5] As soon as the use of

---

[4] One of the reference books for knowledge of the French language is called *Le bon usage*, by Maurice Grévisse (1936), first published by Boeck/Duculot in 1936.

[5] The speech of teachers who come from countries where French is not the *lingua franca* can stray from both classically correct French grammar and accepted norms of the colloquial language, that is, it can be either linguistically wrong or not in accordance with cultural usage.

the language is sanctioned by a norm – this goes for French as well as for any other language – it strongly impairs the autonomous training of learners, who convince themselves that without in-depth knowledge of the norm (which is the domain of the native teacher), they do not have the legitimacy to commit themselves fully to active and practical learning.

14.1.2 Sociolinguistic Insecurity

Transformative pedagogical methods do not just concern memory and the ability to repeat lessons learned by heart. Quite the contrary, they require a reappropriation of the deep and personal teaching process that must reach the learner at the core of their motivation, that is, of their intellectual – and even spiritual – investment in training. This deep investment requires favorable dispositions towards the learning process to give way in the learner to the energy of emotion and action.

In an immersive situation, the tough reality of daily life overseas can broadly block this investment in the learner by creating a feeling of *sociolinguistic insecurity*. The sociolinguistic insecurity, for example, can express itself in financial difficulties that make the learner lose their autonomy and decision-making capability and increase their loss of responsibility. This situation can bring them to put themselves entirely in the hands of their sole comprehensive and understandable contact in the protected space of the classroom – the teacher – and to trigger a demotivation process that the latter will be hard-pressed to reverse.

Immersion can also create in the learner an overload effect regarding the culture of the host country. In the case of France, the officer comes to a country that is very proud of its culture. In the classroom, through the use of authentic materials, the learner is further exposed to French culture. Even if France is open to international news and to other cultures of the world, it grants a major interest to its own history, its own news, its own culture, and its own language. With the language class as an entrée to the culture of the target language, learners engage in a process of cultural impregnation. When the impregnation is limited to the space of the classroom, it can spur curiosity or interest. However, in an immersive situation, the target language culture goes beyond the classroom, invading the entire living space of the learner.

The impregnation continues while learners are discovering the culture. However, transforming oneself to take charge of one's own language learning is more than discovering a culture; it is opening oneself to a linguistic universe in order to reconfigure one's own cultural profile so that the language might speak from within. Motivation does not come from without, but from within. The transformation must not be the consequence of the learning, but its cause.

In the case of immersion in a culture that permeates learners brutally, and without concern, they can feel like they are in a forced *pact* with this other culture. To speak the language is to transact with the culture that uses it and that created it. The feeling of cultural overload can bring on a feeling of disgust and of rejection, and totally paralyze linguistic learning. The transformative pedagogy will then be entirely counterproductive: learners will only tolerate the learning as far as is strictly necessary and their sentiment will translate into total passiveness and a voluntary limitation of investment.

However, even if the learning is in a comfortable social situation and easily adheres to the target language culture, the feeling of sociolinguistic insecurity can come from another factor: the discrepancy between the classroom space and the outside world. In a structured situation, one basically teaches a "written" language – a scholastic, clear, regular language adapted to linguistic discovery and learning. However, as soon as learners leave the structured space of the classroom and hear the "real" speakers speak the "real" language, they risk losing faith in the pedagogy because of major difficulties in understanding. Each constituent element of the language – the pronunciation, the lexicon, and the syntax – seems different to them.[6]

There are three reasons why the language of spoken interactions in French is almost never taught. First, teaching often focuses on the scholastic written languages, codified in great part during the educational campaigns of the massive schooling of children at the end of the nineteenth century and the beginning of the twentieth century.[7] Second, language teachers often speak "teacher talk": they have studied linguistics, literature, and language science; they have in-depth knowledge of the language, of its structure, and of how it works; they belong to a cultivated and educated socio-professional group; they are metalinguistically attentive to their written and spoken expression; in the classroom space, they tend to practice and to teach a highly didactic language; and they typically even dislike teaching and practicing the degraded forms of spoken interaction, considering them unworthy to teach.

Third, there are few grammars or dictionaries that refer to the rules of syntax, pronunciation, and lexicon specific to the spoken language. The main origin of this difficulty lies in the absence of a body of study. Even the study of audiovisual documents in the classroom is most often limited to exercises of oral comprehension, then of restitution in scholastic French, and not an analysis of French as it is spoken by real speakers in the real world.

---

[6] The language of spoken interactions is not only spoken on the street and in the metro; it is spoken in the professional world, in hallways, at the coffee machine, and in-between conferences by cultivated and educated persons.

[7] In France, it corresponds to the French in the scholastic grammars of the Third Republic.

Why insist so much on this point? Transformative pedagogies are anchored in life experience, felt within the language and its learning by the learners. In the situation of learning a second language in a non-francophone country, one can become impassioned to learn "scholastic" French and muster all one's resources to take charge of the pedagogical process. However, in an immersive situation, even with the best of transformative pedagogies, if the learners discover upon leaving the classroom that the learning does not allow them to understand what speakers say to each other in society, or to be understood when speaking to others outside of the classroom, the major investment will seem a total loss. The result is that learners find themselves in a situation of major sociolinguistic insecurity, where they lose both faith in the pedagogy and the energy to become further involved in the learning process.

14.2 Pedagogical Engineering: A Response to the Obstacles

This section will describe two responses to obstacles to the application of transformative pedagogy: pedagogical engagement and sociolinguistic security.

14.2.1 Pedagogical Engagement

For learners to feel fully engaged in the learning of a language, it is necessary for their *scholastic and linguistic profile* to shape the pedagogical strategies. Small groups both allow the teacher to get to know each learner and enhance interactions among the learners, thus avoiding a centralized class oriented toward the teacher. Experience shows that a format of six to eight learners seems to be the optimal format to constitute a group.

The scholastic profile corresponds to the learning habits that the officer has acquired throughout life. The diversity of learner backgrounds in an immersive situation often makes these profiles quite varied. Some learners may have had little schooling. Others will have experienced extremely constraining and coercive teaching methods. Still others will be accustomed to more interactive and transformative methods. Imposing active learning methods too quickly can totally disorient certain officers.

One pedagogical option for the immersive situation is open architecture curriculum design, which consists in using a curricular framework with a thematic syllabus that will allow teachers and learners maximum flexibility to adapt by adding, deleting, and switching activities. The teacher must systematically adapt their teaching to the level and learning pace of the learners in their group. Each evaluation helps identify the needs and characteristics of the speed and quality of each learner's learning. It is the learner who sets the pace and who "pushes" the teacher, not the teacher who anticipates their sequence and "pulls" the learner.

To succeed in building a satisfactory pedagogical progression with open architecture curriculum design, it is necessary to recruit teachers who are autonomous and motivated in order to avoid the implementation of counterproductive routines. Routine quickly settles in inside a durable team. Recruitment using regularly renewable contracts[8] makes each session, each group, and each learner a new challenge that teachers must position at the heart of their teaching.

With no static curriculum, teachers work exclusively on authentic materials, focusing on the professional themes of interest to the learners. The materials must come from the most recent news and professional documents. Regarding subject matter expertise, teachers do not need to be specialists in the field; rather, the learners become the specialists, collaborating with teachers both to judge the quality of the themes and materials, and to select linguistic tools for speaking, discussing, and expressing opinions.

All these measures aim to put learners at the heart of teaching, their scholastic profiles, and their needs and professional competencies. The native speaker in the target language country acts as a learning reference. It is the learning pace of the learners and the expression of their professional needs that quantitatively and qualitatively determine the nature of each activity suggested by the teacher and/or learners, and negotiated by the group. Immersion is therefore seen as an accommodation to a professional setting rather than to a linguistic one. Learners are thus fully engaged, exercising their legitimacy in the language learning process.

14.2.2 Sociolinguistic Security

The feeling of sociolinguistic insecurity is strongly tied to the socio-professional situation of the learner. Reducing the feeling of sociolinguistic insecurity in the high-ranking officers of the intensive French language training program at the War College starts with a solid introduction to French institutions. The introduction is adapted to their socio-professional profile, that is, the officers' particular work duties and responsibilities in their countries. Knowledge of institutions always allows for a better understanding of the general spirit of a country. The visits to the institutions allow learners to become more familiar with the processes within the heart

---

[8] At the War College, recruitment of the pedagogical team is conducted every year. The retention rate is approximately 85 percent.

of these institutions, where French heritage and power preside. The result is a feeling of greater connection to the host culture.

Teachers conduct sociocultural training in the course, continually asking learners for suggestions about activities, topics, and more. For example, in the context of "news topics," each learner chooses a topic corresponding to a contemporary event that they wish to discuss in the classroom space. This practice provides an opportunity to elucidate in groups the implicit culture or social practices, and for each learner to detect sources of misunderstanding or insecurity. Through the reading of billboard ads, storefronts, and leaflets distributed in the street, learners witness all sorts of social and cultural events that are brought back into the classroom space.

The complexity of the language of spoken interactions makes it imperative that teachers, sensitive to the learners' feelings of sociolinguistic insecurity described earlier, address not only academic language, but also commonplace language, even in its most degraded forms. For example, officers participate in field trips where they interact with the local populations that typically speak a language replete with colloquialisms and regionalisms. These trips highlight one of the main advantages of an immersive class: the ability to extend the learning space outside of the classroom.

Finally, the risk of cultural overload must be taken quite seriously. The pedagogical engineering of an immersive class must try to multiply the opportunities for learners to validate their own cultural references and their own national pride. Activities such as formal presentations in an amphitheater about each learner's country and tastings of the culinary specialties of the country are important events. This cultural showcasing by learners creates a multicultural linguistic learning climate that is favorable to everyone's greater fulfillment despite "homesickness." Events such as these relieve the learners of the cultural overload that is part of the immersive situation and help them find within the necessary energy to continue learning. These concrete solutions to obstacles to the application of transformative pedagogy, identified through pedagogical engineering by the management of the intensive French language program of the War College, allow officers to take full advantage of their training in Paris, gradually becoming autonomous learners engaged in and enjoying speaking French.

DISCUSSION QUESTIONS

1. Develop a questionnaire to profile incoming students' academic and cultural characteristics that will help you anticipate the difficulties that the students might encounter during an immersion, including what might hinder the success of an immersion utilizing transformative education.

2. Audiovisual materials can be rich for developing spoken language yet are commonly exclusively used for listening comprehension. Using sample audiovisual materials, design activities that will allow students to discover – and apply – the characteristics of the spoken language.
3. What kind of extramural activities will put the learner in direct contact with the local population, improve their language interaction skills, and reduce their sociolinguistic insecurity? Make a thorough lesson plan to accommodate these kinds of activities, including development, pedagogical supervision, and evaluation.

15

California's K-12 Dual Language Programs

Transforming Teachers and Learners, Improving Educational Outcomes

Mary Ann Lyman-Hager, Sally Rice Fox, and Farid Saydee

California[1] is one of the most diverse states in the USA in terms of ethnicities, languages, cultures, and political and economic agendas. Consensus about statewide priorities can therefore be difficult to achieve. Nevertheless, at a California-wide Language Roadmap Forum held in June 2010, attendees had the opportunity to meet with teachers in related disciplines, with the goal of finding common ground in building dual language programs, which differ significantly from the bilingual programs that dominated California classrooms for decades. Unlike the programs that preceded them,[2] "rather than approaching bilingualism from a deficit model, dual language programs aim to build on the native language of students while a new language is introduced and eventually used equally in instruction" (Hunt, 2009, p. 1). For both language majority and minority learners, dual language programs encourage full bilingualism, biliteracy, and multicultural understanding (Freeman et al., 2018; Pérez, 2017; Torres-Guzman, 2002). The connections established at the Forum – for example, those among colleagues at San Diego State University's (SDSU's) College of Education's Dual Language and English Learner Education (DLE) Department (see: https://education.sdsu.edu/departments/dle), the SDSU Language Acquisition Resource Center (SDSU-LARC), and the San Diego County Office of Education – have yielded a number of grassroots efforts throughout the state to support early language education, the expansion of

---

[1] While this article focuses on the programs known personally to the authors, K-12 dual language programs that use principles of transformative language learning and teaching (TLLT) have exploded in popularity in the past decade and can now be found across the USA and worldwide, for example, an Albanian/Macedonian program in Macedonia (Tankersley, 2001) and French–English programs in Canada (Cummins, 2019), among others.

[2] Programs labeled "dual language" did not appear without precedent. As early as the 1980s, a few "bilingual" programs, often referred to as "two-way partial immersion programs," reflected the characteristics of today's dual language programs. For example, the K-6 language immersion program at Key School in Arlington, Virginia, established in 1987, taught mornings in English, using US-produced textbooks, and afternoons in Spanish, using textbooks from Mexico (Von Vacano et al., 1992).

dual language programs, the creation of the Seal of Biliteracy,[3] and, in the area of teacher education, the exploration and implementation of cross-disciplinary approaches to dual language teacher education based on the principles of transformative language learning and teaching (TLLT), whose primary goals include: (1) personal transformation that results in both bilingual/bicultural competence; and (2) learner autonomy.

The transformation in question, which is rooted in significant cognitive and/or emotional change, requires the development of increased learner self-awareness and autonomy in the learning process (see Little, this volume), the successful resolution of what Mezirow (2003b) termed "disorienting dilemmas,"[4] the identification of cognitive distortions[5] and affective dissonance[6] (see Salyer and Leaver, this volume), and individuation (Dirkx, 2012).[7] These concepts differ from currently widespread language teaching practices, just as the premise of dual language programs is distinct from traditional bilingual language programs.

In many cases, perhaps even most cases, for teachers to create the conditions needed for learner transformation, they themselves will have experienced the heuristics of linguistic, and especially cultural, transformation. They will have developed the personal strategies to recognize and resolve the disorienting

---

[3] California was the first of 32 states to offer a State Seal of Biliteracy (SSB) to formally acknowledge high school students' attainment of high levels of proficiency in one or more languages in addition to English, focusing on speaking, writing, and reading. The SSB primarily uses available instruments of assessment, including the California Assessment of Student Performance and Progress for English Language Arts, World Language Advanced Placement (AP) Tests, and International Baccalaureate (IB) language tests. Students must maintain grade point averages (GPAs) and pass the Scholastic Achievement Test (SAT) world language exam, as well as complete four years of language study with an overall minimum GPA of 3.0 in the language. For more information, see: https://sealofbiliteracy.org/steps/3-define-criteria-granting-awards/high-school-state-seal-biliteracy/.

[4] For a detailed delineation of Mezirow's ten principles, of which the resolution of a disorienting dilemma is one, see Crane and Sosulski (this volume), Johnson (this volume), Kearney (this volume), Kramlich (this volume), and Oxford (this volume), among others.

[5] An example of cognitive distortions is binary thinking, in which the learner believes everything is black or white, that is, either one thing or its opposite, overlooking gray areas that tend to dominate in cross-cultural and linguistic environments. Learners with distorted cognition struggle with grammar, where they expect all language use to follow "the rules" without deviation and are floored by exceptions.

[6] An example of affective dissonance is negative self-talk, in which a student tells themselves frequently enough that they cannot learn the language and that, originally inaccurate, self-talk turns into reality.

[7] Individuation refers to transformations underlying the development of a unique and integrated self, which are necessary, in the opinion and experiences of the authors, to becoming a bilingual/bicultural person successfully.

dilemmas faced in encounters with another language and culture. The authors personally witnessed examples of personal transformation experienced by language teachers in the two teacher education programs informed by the principles of TLLT described in this chapter, as well as their effects at the home schools of these enlightened teachers and administrators.

15.1 Transforming Language Teachers

At the time of the California Language Roadmap Forum, California had been facing the additional challenge of the decade-long legacy of Proposition 227 (Sifuentes, 2008).[8] This initiative had been placed on the ballot in 1998 to eliminate transitional language programs in languages other than English and to institute "English only" in public schools. The challenges of educating an ever-growing population of school-aged children whose primary language was not English led to innovation and transformational policies in certain California schools where the tenets of Proposition 227 had produced unsatisfactory results. The disconnect between "English only" policies and the realities experienced by teachers and their students in the classrooms of these schools led to parental involvement in demanding dual language education opportunities for their children.

Among programs responding to these demands for changes is STARTALK.[9] STARTALK is a US government initiative aimed at both drawing more learners into languages of concern for national defense, diplomacy, and international economic competition (often in under-enrolled, less commonly taught languages) and developing high-quality instruction and highly knowledgeable teachers for them (Ingold & Hart, 2010). The SDSU-LARC Teacher and Student Summer Workshops provided opportunities for recruiting and training both teachers and learners in critical languages. Application of TLLT principles, presented in these workshops, frequently resulted in observable changes in attitudes and mindsets among the teacher and learner participants, which contributed to significantly improved proficiency and/or performance results for learners.

The STARTALK teacher training program at SDSU-LARC focused on transformative learning theory. After completing the workshop, the teachers, through critical reflection,[10] were able to demonstrate, through application in

---

[8] Proposition 227 was repealed by Proposition 58 in November 2016 by 73 percent of Californians voting in that election. Proposition 58 gives schools more latitude in assisting limited English proficient students, permitting instruction through bilingual environments or in English-only classrooms.

[9] The name of the program is "STARTalking," generally abbreviated to "STARTALK."

[10] Critical reflection is one of the ten phrases of transformative education suggested by Mezirow (1990a). For a detailed example of critical reflection tasks, with rubrics, see Crane and Sosulski (this volume).

the classroom, their understanding of practical and experiential instructional approaches. The curriculum included units about:

- discourse strategies to help learners think critically (Mezirow, 2003a);
- techniques for creating disorienting dilemmas, applying reflective analyses and using reframing activities;[11]
- *World-readiness standards for learning languages* (The National Standards Collaborative Board, 2019);[12]
- teacher-centered versus learner-centered instruction;
- resource-sharing with and among learners, including learner-developed resources; and
- long-term collaboration on projects.

Encouraged by the transformation observed among teachers during the STARTALK workshops, the SDSU Language Training Center (LTC), where military personnel attend intensive short-term language courses, adopted a similar curriculum.

Historically, the LTC programs have hired native speakers as teachers. Having been educated in their native country, where traditional instructional approaches characteristic of the transmission educational philosophy (see Leaver, this volume) dominate, they expect learners to be passive. This expectation follows them into their US classrooms, influencing and guiding their in-class practices (Borg, 2003; Freeman, 1989; Saydee, 2016). Given that the majority of American learners have experienced instructional approaches based on either transactional or transformative educational philosophies (for definitions, see Leaver, this volume), the LTC teachers faced a conflict between the learners' instructional expectations and their own (Cazzell et al., 2014). The conflict constituted a "disorienting dilemma" for them.

Aside from analysis of such dilemmas, using critical reflection techniques, teacher participants in the workshop discussed how to lead learners to critically evaluate their assumptions about the target language community. Questions such as the following encourage learner reflection about their assumptions:

- Why do you think that way? (What motivates your thinking: personal experience motives, belief system motives, habituated motives, etc.?)
- What do you value and why?
- Why are those values important to you? Are they important in general and, if so, why? Are they important to representatives of the target culture and, if so, why?
- What other perspective might be taken on these issues?

---

[11] Detailed examples of reframing can be found in Salyer and Leaver (this volume).
[12] *World-readiness standards for learning languages* is the product of The National Standards Collaborative Board (2019), a group of 14 national associations responsible for each language-specific standard, one of which (the publisher of this book) is ACTFL.

Once learners are able to transcend their prevailing beliefs, they better understand the life conditions of the target language people (Imel, 1998). For example, non-Muslim learners of Arabic who originally felt uncomfortable going to a local mosque to observe Friday prayer and interacting with the Imam (who leads the prayer) later indicated that once they felt more knowledgeable about Muslims and their ways of life, the uneasiness and even fear that they had prior to the trip abated. Post-assessment student surveys and end-of-course reflections indicated that language learners believed that TLLT practices such as the questioning of assumptions about the target language community had enhanced their critical thinking and boosted their self-confidence.

Teacher participants in the workshop came to understand how learning can become learner-directed, autonomous, and self-managed (Candy, 1991). Workshop instructors observed the ways in which teacher participants "transformed" over the course of the training – because the context made them change in order to achieve equilibrium – just as they could expect their language learners to change when presented with analogous disorienting dilemmas.

15.2 Exploring TLLT-Based Dual Language Programs at Nestor, Chula Vista, and Sherman Heights Schools

The following are three examples of ways in which TLLT has been introduced via dual language programs in the San Diego area.

15.2.1 Nestor School

While Proposition 227 discouraged Californian schools from offering transitional bilingual language programs, Nestor School in South San Diego was a notable exception. Nestor had introduced a dual language track just before the passage of Proposition 227, a year-round, two-way, Spanish–English 90–10 (90 percent of instruction in Spanish and 10 percent instruction in English) in kindergarten, which gradually changed to 50–50 by the upper grades. This new program type was offered, in addition to a mature transitional bilingual education track and two English-only tracks. The new dual language program included an approach to instruction that incorporated the major elements of TLLT.

Shortly after the passage of Proposition 227, Lynda Malek, Nestor's principal, spoke at a district board meeting about the school's impressive academic achievement scores. She relayed to one of the authors that she had been asked by a board member: "Why aren't we offering dual immersion at all our schools?"

It was a good question, asked some 20 years ahead of its time amid the powerful "English only" movement of 1998. Some 20 years later, Nestor's two-way dual language immersion program is so successful that it fills the entire school and has prompted the creation of a charter school in order to provide a middle school program within the K-6 district.

15.2.2 Chula Vista

As Nestor was starting its two-way 90–10 program, parents and community leaders in the neighboring city of Chula Vista were also advocating for a TLLT-focused, dual language immersion program in their district. Under the visionary leadership of Dr. Jorge Ramírez, the group created a highly successful charter school – the Chula Vista Learning Community Charter School (CVLCC) – implementing a Spanish–English two-way 50–50 model (50 percent of instruction in each language). Key to the school's success has been a long-term relationship with SDSU's College of Education, especially the department that prepares Spanish bilingual teachers and awards certificates and master's degrees in dual language education. Over time, CVLCC has been academically successful and has expanded into K-12 to meet the demand for dual language development through high school. Today, the entire Chula Vista public elementary school district has begun including dual language strands in its non-charter schools and is known for high levels of achievement. Taketa (2018) cites impressive results: 64 percent of the district's learners met or exceeded state standards in English language arts, and 52 percent did so in math, surpassing county and state averages in both subjects for elementary school grades. Chula Vista Elementary School District (CVESD) was cited as the only school district in San Diego County and one of only 23 statewide to be named as an "exemplary district" in 2018 by the California Department of Education. District programs have attracted the attention of state and national education think tanks and research foundations, such as the national Learning Policy Institute (LPI).[13]

15.2.3 Sherman Elementary School

The successes of Nestor and CVLCC, both located in what is known as the South Bay Area, informed the program at Sherman Elementary School in

---

[13] The LPI, located in Palo Alto, California, "conducts and communicates independent, high-quality research to improve education policy and practice. Working with policymakers, researchers, educators, community groups, and others, the Institute seeks to advance evidence-based policies that support empowering and equitable learning for each and every child" (see: https://learningpolicyinstitute.org/about). For related research and information, see also the Dual Language Immersion Research Alliance at: www.americancouncils.org/research-assessment/dli-research-alliance.

Central San Diego. Eddie Caballero was one of the educators in the early days of CVLCC's innovative bilingual program. In 2005, Caballero was hired as a vice principal at San Diego Unified School District (SDUSD). He later became a community spokesperson for the district, where he used his Spanish language skills to speak with members of the Spanish language media and to support community and family engagement. In December 2007, he was hired by the Board of Education to reopen Sherman Elementary, which had been the lowest-performing school in the district and had been closed for two years for remodeling.

In January 2008, Eddie started holding monthly parent meetings, where he outlined his experience at CVLCC but indicated that the reopened school did not require a dual language immersion program, especially since many parents were wary of bilingual education programs. Subsequently, an expert from the SDUSD Education Center's Office of Language Acquisition provided background information and a review of research. Months later, a turning point occurred when parents learned that Caballero planned to enroll his own daughter in the school. Parents' interest in a 50–50 dual language model steadily grew, and the Sherman Academy began its 50–50 Spanish immersion program in 2008. Like the other two programs, the Sherman Academy emphasized TLLT principles in its classrooms, where learners probed the realities of another culture, questioning (as they are capable of doing even at a young age) their assumptions about it as they engaged in critical reflection.

By 2012, Sherman was demonstrating significant success: a 139-point rise in student performance points on the California Academic Performance Index (API), as highlighted in "Promising practices in education" (The National Clearinghouse for English Language Acquisition 2012, p. 2). Several years later, the Academy was recognized by the California Department of Education as a Gold Ribbon School. The school has raised achievement levels for Latino students by 189 API points, socioeconomically disadvantaged students by 188 API points, and English learners by 195 API points, results that surpass overall district-wide and statewide averages.

15.3 Improving Learning Outcomes through More Effective Language Education in California

While the "English only" Proposition 227 officially discouraged bilingual programs, San Diego County's Office of Education (SDCOE) continued to meet the needs of developing bilingual/bicultural language users, offering a Dual Language Institute in 2001 that has inspired hundreds of K-12 teachers each year since that time. From the 1990s through the present, the SDCOE has provided training for teachers earning the English learner authorization

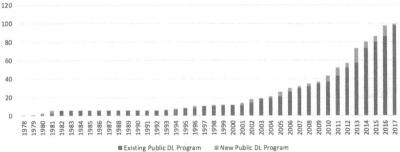

Figure 15.1 Dual language programs in San Diego County. This figure illustrates the growth in the number of programs from 1978 to 2017.

on their credentials through the State's Bilingual Teacher Training Program. (Fox worked with the SDCOE on this initiative from 2006 to 2019.) In 2008, the county superintendent (a former bilingual teacher himself) launched a strategic planning process, including community outreach and research. In 2009/2010, specific transformative approaches were articulated for San Diego public schools that included both English learners and native English speakers learning another world language. Excerpts from the 2009/2010 *SDCOE board goals and strategic plan* are listed as follows:

> Strategy IV: Board Goal 4: We will develop and implement means to ensure global workplace readiness for all students.
> Specific Result 4.3: In partnership with one or more districts, initiate global language study opportunities for early grade students.

A determined, systematic effort by the SDCOE, SDSU, and forward-thinking teachers has resulted in unprecedented growth in dual language programs in the county, as reflected in Figure 15.1.

15.4 Conclusion

This chapter has described the personal transformation experienced by teachers in teacher education programs where principles of TLLT underlie the curriculum. It has also reviewed curricular and policy changes brought about by enlightened teachers, administrators, and parents. In the former case, degree programs like the SDSU DLE and events like the Dual Language Institute sponsored by the SDCOE since 2001 graduate professionals who have been transformed to guide learners towards becoming bilingually/biculturally competent language users empowered to take ownership of their language and cultural learning.

Institutional changes like those described in the San Diego County area schools have occurred when transformed teachers and administrators have worked, both individually and in groups, using both overt and subtle means, to bring about those curricular improvements and innovations. The program examples cited, where principles of TLLT were an influence, call to mind the statement by Margaret Mead (2008) about the power of a small, dedicated group to bring about change: "Never doubt that a small group of thoughtful, committed citizens can change the world; indeed, it's the only thing that ever has."

Transformed teachers are committed to their learners' cognitive development, attainment of high levels of academic achievement and language proficiency, enjoyment of authentic cultural products from around the world, development of metacognitive and metalinguistic skills, increased communication with more people in English and other languages, and cultural understanding, where bias and prejudice have no place. They can and do influence the institutions in which they work in significant ways.

DISCUSSION QUESTIONS

1. How might a hiring committee gauge an applicant teacher's level of commitment to implementing TLLT in the language curriculum? Discuss your approach to this situation in a context where an applicant may be a native speaker of the language that he or she teaches and may be more familiar with traditional approaches.

2. Based on transformative learning approaches introduced by Jack Mezirow and elaborated upon in this volume, discuss at least two assessment strategies to measure the effects of implementing TLLT approaches on student learning and outcomes.

3. In this chapter, we have highlighted the accomplishments of pioneering schools in California (whose learner outcomes have surpassed expectations), stressing their having led the way for others. In your opinion, are there more effective ways to bring about desired curricular reform, particularly adapted to your local context?

PART V

The Learner

16

The Language Classroom as Transformative Response to the Unique Needs of Migrants and Refugees

Deborah J. Kramlich

In 2017, the number of international migrants reached 258 million, including 25.4 million refugees (Vidal & Tjaden, 2018). Moving to, living in, and working in a different country is a transformative act, reflecting both positive and negative aspects of the cross-cultural experience. All immigrants learning the local language face unique challenges in the world languages classroom setting. Teachers and their instructional styles can confirm the immigrant's sense of stigma and insecurities, or they can positively support this adjustment phase. Transformative learning theory assists those seeking to make meaning of their new lives as they cross cultures (Taylor, 2008). The underlying reason for moving influences the challenges of entering a new culture. Intercultural adjustment is affected by identity, acculturation orientation, and more. Formal or informal requirements by the receiving culture can be difficult to determine – some "rules" are learned as a part of growing up in the culture, and such knowledge is later assumed and often not readily available to the immigrant. Loss or change in status can negatively affect self-esteem and, along with other affective experiences, create mental health challenges (Bhugra & Becker, 2005). The list goes on.

An example is Bina,[1] who came to Sweden from Congo as an asylum seeker and spent six months waiting for a residence permit. She came alone, not knowing the status of her family. Had she not been granted permission to attend "Swedish for immigrants" classes (Henry et al., 2015), she would have had to navigate the rules and expectations associated with successful acculturation without assistance. Needless to say, she was overjoyed by the opportunity. The language classroom would give her a supportive environment to address the unique societal, cultural, and psychological challenges that she faced. The support afforded to Bina and others like her is amplified by teachers who use a transformative language learning and teaching (TLLT) framework in their classrooms.

---

[1] Unless a citation is provided, all names have been changed to protect the privacy of individuals.

16.1 Definitions

Definitions of immigrants and refugees are often politically driven (McBrien, 2005). For this chapter, the term "immigrant" will be used for all peoples crossing cultures. The term "migrant" is used generically to describe people who choose (voluntarily) to cross borders semi-permanently or permanently, while a "refugee" is "someone who has been forced to flee his or her country because of persecution, war, or violence" (United Nations High Commission on Refugees, 2018). Migration is challenging for both groups but refugees can be especially vulnerable, so it is critical to support them in their acculturation. Migrants who leave voluntarily will experience the loss of cultural norms and values, their support system, and identity; nevertheless, they often have greater optimism and opportunity in their host culture (Conchas, 2001). On the other hand, refugees have high uncertainty regarding their future, including status, employment, length of stay in the host country, and options for residency or citizenship.

16.2 Language Learning, the Sources and Influence of Stressors, and the Success of Acculturation

Many immigrants will pursue some level of language study dependent on employment demands, intended length of stay, or interest level. In some countries, refugees are required to study language as a prerequisite for government assistance. Some researchers have posited that the world languages classroom can address many of the immigrant's unique needs by building resilience, providing community, giving opportunities for employment, and building a social network (Capstick & Delaney, 2016). Language teachers can play a significant role in the immigrant's adjustment and language development but often lack the training to see, or address, the outside challenges of the immigrant population (Hilburn, 2014).

Stressors in the receiving culture influence the acculturative process as all immigrants, both migrants and refugees, attempt to attain a satisfactory adaptation to their new context (Taloyan et al., 2011; Ward, 2008). This stress of acculturation puts the immigrant at higher risk of psychological challenges (Hwang & Ting, 2008). Many (especially refugees) additionally face mental health crises due to the nature of their departure and the devastating loss of home, family, and status. A number of factors influence the overall positive or negative acculturative experience of the migrant (Achiume, 2013; Bhugra & Becker, 2005):

- (un)known duration of stay;
- language study;
- cultural distance;

- employment;
- housing; and/or
- social attitudes.

Some migrants plan to remain for a specified time. Others, typically refugees, are unaware how long they will stay. Especially for the latter group, language instruction, such as the free year of language study offered to all migrants in Sweden, plays a key role in acculturation.

A small cultural distance often results in less acculturative stress, while a significant cultural distance compounds acculturative stress. Thus, a Latin migrant will have less difficulty moving among culturally close Latin cultures than migrating to a culturally distant Asian country.

The lack of opportunity for appropriate employment can be either a hindrance or a motivator for language learning and acculturation. Until recently, in Thailand, architecture and civil engineering were protected professions reserved only for the Thais and could not be filled by a migrant, though the migrant might have excellent engineering training and skills. In this situation, the migrant can then feel frustrated and even depressed when required to accept lesser-skilled (and lower-paying) work. Similarly, migrant doctors and lawyers have difficulty meeting state requirements and passing bar exams in the USA. In the case of other occupations, where native-like language skills are needed, motivation for language instruction generally soars.

Finding adequate and affordable housing can be another barrier to acculturation, making it difficult to concentrate on studies or even to rest easy. Some are even lodged in tents or temporary camps, making day-to-day living challenging.

Finally, the attitude of the new country and its policies and procedures toward the home country of the migrant can make acculturation easier (e.g., Germans moving into a historically German émigré community in Minnesota) or more difficult (e.g., Arab migrants moving into Israel). Where migrants are welcomed, stress decreases; where they are looked upon with suspicion, unease increases.

16.3 Transformative Learning Theory in a World Languages Classroom

TLLT prompts learners to release fixed mindsets and presuppositions, while embracing change through developing new thoughts and ideas. These are reflected in the resolution of the disorienting dilemma coming from the clash of two cultures within one individual. This process is "threatening, emotionally charged, and extremely difficult" (Mezirow, 1995, p. 48), requiring a safe and accepting context. All immigrants undergo perspective transformation to some degree as they seek to make meaning within the new culture (Taylor, 2008). The support of a perspicacious teacher, assisting the immigrant to scale emotional-psychological and societal-cultural barriers, can help make this transformative process a positive one (Dekutoski, 2011).[2] This is critical because negative transformations can have devastating long-term effects as well.

As a unique resource for addressing the salient challenges of migrants and refugees, the foreign language teacher can create an emotionally safe environment. Recent research (Capstick & Delaney, 2016) further suggests that the language classroom can provide the needed resources to build resilience, thereby helping to reframe the immigrant's current situation with positive elements.

Unfortunately, many foreign language teachers are not trained in the specific needs of the immigrant. Thus, the language classroom often does not achieve its full potential (Capstick & Delaney, 2016; Hilburn, 2014). Understanding and implementing key principles from transformative learning can provide a framework for the language teacher to address some of the key societal, cultural, and psychological needs of immigrants.

16.3.1 Addressing Societal Barriers

TLLT provides a process for learners to make sense of their new situation by providing (or affording) the possibility of stepping outside of their previous frames of reference. As immigrants are already in disequilibrium, the TLLT teacher understands the importance of creating an environment where learners can process their challenges in the community, both in the ethnic community and in the new community of their language classroom (Capstick & Delaney, 2016). Transformative learning theory encourages teachers to develop a deep authentic relationship with their learners – supportive, nurturing, and genuine – which contributes to the development of community in the classroom (Cranton, 2001).

Since the language classroom connects the host and immigrant communities, it can be a pivotal setting for interaction between these two cultures (Capstick & Delaney, 2016). Host culture attitudes play a key role in accepting and welcoming immigrants (Tadayon & Khodi, 2016). Informing the host culture about the benefits of refugees or countering their incorrect beliefs has not

---

[2] Fleming (2019, p. 39) contends that transformation requires the ability to perceive the world as personal, political, and social, and to make connections between one's own problems and the social problems of the surrounding community, that is, "one does not understand the world correctly or in a transformative way without personal and social insights."

proven to be effective in reducing discrimination (Dempster & Hargrave, 2017). Rather, a better way is for both cultures to get to know each other and interact together on a personal level (Pettigrew & Tropp, 2008). Learning to share and tell one's story is another practice of transformative learning that can assist in processing trauma (Catalana & Hamann, 2016). Meeting with members of the host culture provides the immigrant with the opportunity to relate their experiences and to help themselves process these events. The emancipatory nature of transformative learning is rooted in Freire's (1970) philosophy and pedagogy of liberating the oppressed. It is particularly appropriate for the immigrant as it supports the shift from learners as passive objects accepting the world as it is, to subjects actively engaged in changing both themselves and existing social structures (Taylor, 1998). As this acculturating personal paradigm shift happens, immigrants can begin to assume authority over their lives and become more proactive, autonomous thinkers (Mezirow, 1997).

16.3.2 Addressing Cultural Barriers

Many immigrants experience a sense of bereavement and confusion related to their cultural identity (Eisenbruch, 1991). Transformative learning theory encourages teachers to find out about their learners' backgrounds and stories, affirming and welcoming their experience in the classroom (Brookfield, 1990). This includes supporting learners' heritage language and culture, and attributing them with value and worth. One practice gaining support is translanguaging (García & Wei, 2014), where learners are allowed to use all of their known vocabulary, regardless of language, to assist in making meaning. Language learners are encouraged to verbalize their experiences in their mother tongue, as well as to use literature in their heritage language, using either the new language or the mother tongue. Teachers are urged to refer to their learners as emergent bilinguals (Catalano & Hamann, 2016; Martínez, 2017), positively framing their multilingual abilities rather than limiting their identity as single language learners.

In a time of cultural stress, it is important that the teacher gives value to the heritage language and culture of the learners. The common practice of asking learners to leave their heritage culture and language at home has proved detrimental to learners' linguistic development and cultural identity (Catalano & Hamann, 2016; Seals, 2018). For example, Jim – a graduate of such programs and now a college graduate from a selective school – cannot communicate with his Korean grandparents (Polinsky & Kagan, 2007). Learners fare better when they maintain a relationship to and pride in their heritage culture and languages, with language teachers supporting the heritage languages in the classroom. Schools in Sweden, for example, recognize the value of this and offer free *hemspråksundervisning* or heritage language instruction in school.

TLLT teachers with intercultural experience and previous language learning experience tend to be more self-aware (having gone through their own transformation) and empathize better with their learners (Brookfield, 1995; Catalano & Hamann, 2016). Equally important, a teacher's personal attitude toward immigrants and their heritage languages invariably has an impact on both the learners' motivation and their cultural identity (Dekutoski, 2011; Walker et al., 2004). In transformative learning, "cross-cultural relationships are encouraged ... the teacher's role is that of a collaborator with a relational emphasis on group inquiry and narrative reasoning that assist the learners in sharing stories of experience and revising stories in the process" (Taylor, 2008, p. 9). Value is placed on a diverse, inclusive, and global community in transformative learning.

16.3.3 Addressing Psychological Barriers

The language classroom can serve as a therapeutic place, helping the immigrant develop resilience. The Regional Refugee and Resilience Plan (3RP) defines resilience as "the ability of individuals, households, communities, and institutions to anticipate, withstand, recover and transform from shocks and crises" (3RP, 2015, p. 17). Developing resilience through language study can be beneficial for processing past trauma, as well as managing future challenging circumstances. Migrants and refugees can experience empowerment and greater independence through improved language ability, increasing the possibility of positive intercultural adaptation.

Examples of the language classroom as a therapeutic place abound. One instance occurred in a language class in Sweden, where a group of Balkan women ignored the teacher, quietly chatting on their phones and with each other. The teacher and class grew frustrated as this group did not complete assignments or participate in class. Sympathies rose when the teacher and learners realized that the women were illiterate and separated from their children, some of whom were not safe. Every day, the women regularly checked their phones, hoping to hear information about family members. Learning this, the teacher was able to make adjustments to the class to work on literacy skills and allow times for phone calls.

Many refugees need mental health support not provided by their host country. The language classroom emotionally supports learners by providing structure, a network of friends, and necessary language skills for future employment (Capstick & Delaney, 2016). Being alone in a foreign country without meaningful work can be harmful to those already struggling with mental health issues. The neurobiological theory of transformative learning addresses mental health concerns. Medical imaging of patients who had been previously traumatized demonstrated that the brain changed as the patients were learning new things. Janik (2005) postulated a distinct connection between transformative learning and trauma, where the learner was able to transform a traumatic situation into a nontraumatic one. This transformation occurred through a process of discovery under the supervision of a mentor. Such mentoring could be meaningful for the refugee to redefine and process traumatic experiences.

Transformative learning encourages holistic teaching and values the affective and intuitive side of the learner, making space for the learner's emotions and feelings in the classroom (Dirkx, 2006; Taylor, 2008). Yorks and Kasl (2006, p. 46) encourage welcoming "'the whole person' into the classroom environment, the person in fullness of being: as an affective, intuitive, thinking, physical, spiritual self." Boyd and Myers (1988, p. 280) recognize the value of "grieving as a critical condition for the possibility of personal transformation." By teachers supporting affect in the classroom, immigrants have the opportunity to share their feelings and struggles – the initial steps of emotional transformation. The cultural constructs of a bereaved person (such as a refugee) need to be known and considered in order to assist the immigrant to begin the process of healing.

16.4 Implications for Teachers, Schools, and Host Countries

Given the nature of transformative learning as learner-directed, the TLLT classroom accommodates as many of the learners' needs and interests as possible (Brookfield, 1990; Cranton, 2001), fulfilling necessary purposes in the immigrants' lives and building resilience as learners gain tools they need to successfully work and thrive in the new culture (Capstick & Delaney, 2016). Learners' success and motivation increase as language learning, life, and work connect. Henry et al. (2015) propose that learners' motivation will rise as it is linked to their goals and visions of their future selves.

The teacher can shift power to the immigrant student by highlighting their prior education and culture in specific topics (Freire, 1970; Weimer, 2002). This could include an Iranian doctor commenting on health topics or a Thai student explaining Buddhism in a German classroom. Such recognition and value increase their self-worth and social standing in the classroom.

Likewise, school administrators aware of the particular needs and challenges of the immigrant population can ensure that teachers receive appropriate training in keeping with the findings of the British Council report on language for resilience for refugee populations:

- Every language used by refugees helps them to build resilience at the individual, family, and community levels. Both home and their additional languages matter.

- Proficiency in additional languages provides new opportunities for education and employment.
- Proficiency in key languages gives people a voice to tell their story in various contexts.
- Language-learning can bolster social cohesion and intercultural understanding.
- Language-learning activities can be supportive interventions to address the effects of loss, displacement and trauma.
- Building the capacity of language learners can strengthen the resilience of the formal and the non-formal education systems in host countries. (Capstick & Delaney, 2016, p. 5)

The immigrant population is increasing and creating a growing impact on public attitudes toward refugees and migrants (Dempster & Hargrave, 2017). If immigrants do not integrate well into a society, resultant problems may remain unresolved for generations. The United Nations Development Program (Capstick & Delaney, 2016) states that "the core of resilience-based development response is supporting national systems in the context of language … this means identifying the needs of institutional providers of language and education programs and supporting them with resources that could help to build their capacity to support learners to learn in multicultural environments," thus providing more protection for the vulnerable refugee and migrant population. If countries welcoming migrants recognize the importance of the language classroom, the result could be revolutionary for both the host country and the immigrant.

16.5 Conclusion

Moving across cultures is a big undertaking. Immigrants often bring hidden needs into the language classroom that their teachers, due to a lack of awareness or training, do not always see. Nevertheless, the potential of a language class as a place of transformation for the immigrant is pivotal. For Bina, the move to Sweden and opportunity to learn Swedish gave her a framework and focus for her adjustment and acculturation. She said, "80% of the time, I wanted to be busy with the language" (Henry et al., 2015, p. 20). Her progress was rapid and after a year of Swedish, she was able to successfully enroll in a Swedish university.

Teachers who create community and respect the heritage languages and cultures of their learners can help mitigate psychological stressors and support the development of resilience. Both immigrants and teachers would benefit by implementing practices of transformative learning in the language classroom.

The TLLT teacher is equipped in being attentive to these unseen needs and can create a safe, nurturing atmosphere honoring the cultural values and heritage languages that an immigrant brings to the classroom. Through this nurturing community, as well as linguistic instruction, the immigrant has a greater possibility for a positive transformation that will ease and support the stages of acculturation in the new culture.

DISCUSSION QUESTIONS

1. How can refugees learn to share their migration stories both to process grief and to create empathy and understanding from the wider culture in which they are living?
2. If contact theory is the key to mitigating hostile attitudes toward migrants and refugees, how can language instruction play a role in bringing both cultures together?
3. How can an immigrant's culture, experience, education, or religion be given place and space in the language classroom?

17

Technology and Transformative Language Learning and Teaching

Donald C. Fischer, Jr.

How are learners persuaded that a language opens the door to a culture and developing professional and personal relationships within that culture? How can language educators convey that the learning process, from its inception through fluency and even expertise, can transform individuals, leading to the betterment of them, of those around them, and of their culture?

17.1 Human Seeking and Consuming and Its Relation to Learning

The learning process is much the same as the courting/mating process and the process of seeking food. An external object stimulates an observer, in this case, another person who looks welcoming. The observer acts to get to know the person. The person signals acceptance, even liking and love, which motivates the observer to continue the process. Dopamine motivates seeking; opioids signal success. Interestingly, these neurochemicals stem from testosterone and estrogen, which are elements of vasopressin and oxytocin, the basic chemicals for the formation of dopamine and opioids.

Can language educators make language learning as basic a need as procreation and food? Probably not, but it is possible to come close. Teachers help learners to see new things, be attracted to them, encounter and work with them, and be motivated to continue to pursue knowledge of the learning object. Learning something new and liking it mirrors the processes connected with what a newborn must do to get the food, care, love, and shelter necessary for survival, as discussed by Lee, Mikesell, Joaquin, Mates, and Schumann (2009) in their book *The interactional instinct*. Need is necessary for motivation and for learning. The teaching task, then, is to present material in a way that creates that need to learn, in this case, a new language and culture, and through that process, transform the learner.

In a neurochemical sense, teaching is presenting learners with objects of desire that motivate them to seek knowledge. Teaching and tutorials should stimulate dopamine production. Each individual has preferences that develop from homeostats that keep the individual in balance, sociostats that regulate social interaction, and automatic and conscious reactions to life experiences (somatics) (Schumann, 1997). Every action, mostly unconsciously, is appraised in light of these preferences. Thus, affect, caused by and based on these preferences, is operative in learning and thereby critical to transformation.

The John Schumann/K.R. Scherer motivation model (Scherer, 1999; Schumann, 1997) articulates five "planes of stimulus-appraisal" that lead to dopamine production, motivation, and a higher probability that learning (synapse strengthening) will occur. These five planes are:

- relevance to individual needs and goals;
- novelty;
- intrinsic pleasantness;
- compatibility with and promoting a positive self- and social image; and
- coping potential (the learner can do the task).

- A transformative approach incorporates individual and communal activities that support the "planes of stimulus appraisal" and increase the probability that learning, and transformation, takes place.

Technology can provide infrastructure and scaffolding to support transformation in learning and teaching. People can live lives without experiencing a different culture. Until the Internet and computing devices, people had to travel to see other nations and peoples.

Today, tools such as Google Maps and Streetview, and conference systems such as Zoom, Google Connect, and Skype, allow people to see the world and talk to others in it. Learning management systems such as Moodle, Canvas, and Sakai, and affordable transportable hardware such as GoPros, smartphones, tablets, and laptops, serve to put citizens of the world in a position to learn about and from each other.

These technologies provide space where people can participate in wider society and offer means to overcome differences in readiness to learn. Learners see virtually and find what they want to experience directly. These tools prepare learners for the "different" and can encourage them to want to experience "the other," permitting extrication from the limitations of their culture and environment to observe, critically analyze, and apply what works for others in their own lives.

Ultimately, these technologies promote transformative experiences that alter worldviews as users/learners reassess their values. In the language learning context, these technologies can lead to personal transformation that results in bicultural and bilingual competence through growth in learner autonomy (see Garza, this volume; Little, this volume).

17.2 Technology Tools that Can Motivate and Transform Learners

The capacity of technological tools to support learning is growing at exponential rates. Millennials expect to use such tools. Adapting these tools to individualized language learning can lead learners to acquire new skills – seemingly effortlessly. On top of developing coping skills during presentation, practice, and production, the tools support integrating learners' individual skills socially through collaborative activities.

17.2.1 Learning Management Systems

Learning management systems allow the arrangement of materials using visual, audio, and text to present lessons. They provide for announcements, linking to resources, and support for video and audio recordings. They permit collaboration through forums and journals. They support assessment and record assignment submissions, and grades to be received for work performed. Learning management systems include Moodle, iLearn, Sakai, Blackboard, and Canvas.

Instructional designers and teachers can use these systems to develop single lessons, content-rich experiences, and entire courses. In a recent attempt to develop tolerance and understanding of a culture, a Pashtun teacher (Muhammed, 2018) developed a Moodle site about Pashtunwali, the customary support and protection shown to visitors and strangers in Pashtun tribal areas in Afghanistan and Pakistan. The site provided cultural and economic information on Afghanistan to prepare military members from a low-context culture such as the USA (Hall, 1976) for engaging with a high-context culture that values oral tradition and nonverbal communication developed through a long history.

The site included readings and introductory language experiences using the Defense Language Institute Foreign Language Center's (DLIFLC's) *Cultural Orientation Series* and the basic tutorial *Rapport*. Each information session was followed by a forum listing issues for further study. Information was presented visually and through voice narrative using the tutorial system Adobe Captivate, context-based visuals, computer-generated voice narration, closed captions, and videos.

Pretest and posttest results showed a doubling of mean scores. The teacher posited the rise in scores to be due to the learning activities. Other data collected during the course, through learner surveys and learner input in class, suggest that prejudices and stereotypes changed in a positive way through the site. Some research has shown that such morals and values education can prompt prejudice reduction (Paluck & Green, 2008).

17.2.2 Recording and Posting of Language Production

Repeated recording of language production supports all of the planes of appraisal. Learners can regularly record themselves speaking. By listening to the series of recordings, the teacher can determine, and the learner can detect, progress. The two can meet one-on-one for tutoring and suggestions. Using a learning management system, recordings can be posted for classmate viewing and listening, and forums can be provided to comment on each other's production, and to see, collectively, common strengths and weaknesses.

Additionally, regular postings provide a "soft" form of accountability that can serve to motivate each learner to contribute to and continue learning, whether individually or in a group. The process, combined with the learner's motivation to learn, can result in higher linguistic and cultural proficiency. This type of work can reflect elements of TLLT. The activity positions the learner at center stage and can be adjusted through tutoring to meet learner needs and interests, which is a core feature of TLLT, especially as it relates to the concept of the zone of proximal development (Vygotsky, 1930/1997).

Teachers may also adjust the online interactions to parallel classroom interactions or a study abroad encounter by representing the target culture. To the extent that the teacher is able to move beyond simple error correction for pronunciation to activities that focus on meaningful tasks, these authentic online interactions can move a learner toward a greater understanding and embracing of other viewpoints.

17.2.3 Cultural Studies through Films/Videos

During a visit to the DLIFLC by 22 Chinese People's Liberation Army officers, the interpreter – a young Chinese female officer – spoke English without an accent, handling all the transactions with cultural appropriateness. Questioned as to whether she had been in the USA as an exchange student or had a similar experience, she answered that it was her first visit and that the bulk of her learning had taken place through movies. While one could be skeptical about the answer, the idea of learning through movies, especially nonverbal and cultural aspects of a society, has merit.

With the encounter as an impetus, a teacher of Persian Farsi (Monazamfar, 2017) embedded an Iranian movie into a tutorial using Adobe Captivate and provided her students with a template to critique the film. Learners saw Iranians dressed in Western clothing, outfitting their apartments with video, audio, recording, and computing equipment, and attending discos (with the strict separation of male and female dancers, and the behavior police in close watch), as well as watching women learn to drive.

With certain exceptions, the use of the target language is a tenet of modern language instruction. However, there are situations where the learner's native language can be judiciously integrated to enhance learning. In this case, material was delivered using the Sakai learning management system and included forums for commentary in English, structured according to Elizabeth Bernhardt's (1983) immediate recall protocol, where students commented on what they were seeing and hearing in Persian Farsi and what they were learning. In addition to the language and culture experience, they used a rubric to critically analyze a film – a useful skill beyond this training.

Participant response showed a change from a hostile, negative view of Iran and its people to a more objective, empathetic view, and a willingness to accept Iranians as a people much like themselves. Reactions were "I enjoyed the learning process," "the movie was interesting and provides good cultural points that help one understand and retain aspects of the culture," and "[I found intriguing] seeing how law enforcement interacts with people." The film provided context for viewing the culture in a different light to which learners found that they could relate, changing their perception of the "foreignness" of Iran. The film criticism template provided structure for parsing the episodes, understanding the culture that drove the behaviors, and identifying similarities and differences in value systems between the USA and Iran. Learners modified their stereotypes of Iranians that had been built by US media and political leaders because of guided, interactive involvement in a culture that they could not, at least presently, experience first-hand.

17.2.4 Apps that Work to Provide Opportunities for Speaking and Collaboration

Apps can help world language learners negotiate meaning with native speakers. Apps can also help learners achieve higher levels of proficiency in their own language and perform higher-level cognitive tasks.

Among the simplest apps to use are conferencing systems such as Skype, Adobe Connect, and Zoom. Zoom Lite offers free 40-minute sessions to anywhere in the world. The business version offers unlimited time, as well as breakout rooms and cloud features. There are no time delays or artifacts, and communication flows nearly as smoothly as being in the same room. Participants discuss directly, share desktops, and collaborate on Google Docs, Dropbox, iCloud, and other cloud-based systems. The author has even performed chamber music with other musicians across thousands of miles on Zoom, with no problems related to tempo, intonation, or "hitting the beat" together.

Along with such conferencing apps, programs are available that allow a learner to slow the tempo of a spoken text without changing pitch to permit pronunciation and comprehension practice. There is also a speed-adjusting capability on YouTube available to anyone. While the YouTube tool makes somewhat drastic speed changes, the Amazing Slowdowner app is more flexible in both speed and pitch. While the software is intended for music, the applicability to listening and speaking practice in the target language is immediately evident.

Apps permitting direct conversation with native speakers include Teletandem, TalkAbroad, Diversity, WeSpeak, Panda Tree, and italki (sic). The application TalkAbroad involves face-to-face encounters with native speakers trained to conduct conversations. The conversations can be recorded for reference. Using the capability for media mashups (discussed later), teachers and facilitators can interject video and audio comments in the conversation.

Such cross-linguistic conversation apps help reduce speaker anxiety and contribute to increased fluency, enjoyment, and engagement. Virginia Commonwealth University, for example, uses these apps not only for language learning, but also in medicine, engineering, the sciences, art, and the humanities (Murphy-Judy & Quinlan, 2018).

Tutoring apps such as Duolingo offer online instruction in several languages, with structured listening, speaking, reading, and writing exercises. The program "italki" offers easy and economical interaction with live teachers. "Mixxer" offers interactions with native speakers who want to learn English and speak with others in their native language. "Extempore" is designed to provide speaking practice.

Practice in expression on a variety of topics is beneficial even when communicating in English. Learners unaccustomed to participating in challenging conversation need practice to move on to advanced reading and writing, where they will engage in higher cognitive tasks. Teachers can provide audio, video, or written feedback to the learner, based on learner needs and interests.

There are also media mashups – web pages or apps that integrate complementary elements from two or more sources. With GoReact, learners submit videos on which teachers and peers can pause and leave video feedback. For example, a conversation can be recorded on Zoom or Adobe Connect and reviewed for correct language and cultural appropriateness. VoiceThread allows threaded discussions using video, audio, and text for commentary about the content of asynchronous meetings. Padlet is an interactive web-page generator and mini-social media platform. Anonymous users can react to posts including video, audio, and text. Multiple participants can contribute, create, and respond.

Flipgrid allows teachers, learners, and families to create topics for the asynchronous posting of videos and commentary. Participants can post reflections, talk about books, explain their reasoning, voice opinions on current events, and more. Additionally, users can show what they mean and know, and respondents can provide a video commentary or elaboration asynchronously so that time zones and location are not inhibiting factors. Flipgrid also provides for global online exchange and is an excellent vehicle for practicing online collaboration and multicultural learning.

17.3 Toward Transformation

The direct encounter has generally been considered the best means to cause a change in values as it often brings with it a disorienting dilemma (Mezirow, 1990a, 1990b) that shakes a belief system and must be resolved, with the resolution typically being a transformation, or change, in values or worldview. Information technology can provide rich virtual opportunities to encounter such a disorienting dilemma, just as in real life. For example, readily available headgear can be worn by learners to enable their virtual attendance at functions (or simulated functions) as wide-ranging as a jazz festival, a Pashtun jirga, or a conference at long distance. Such hardware allows people to talk to those attending as the event is going on.

Robotic devices such as the Double Robotics 2 robot, outfitted with a camera and computer, can move from place to place while being controlled virtually. It can turn toward speakers and allow those who cannot attend to virtually participate. These telepresence robots are at work at about 400 US institutions, including Duke University, Virginia Tech, the University of Utah, and the University of West Florida. They are at work in public schools to allow disabled students to connect. In Alaska, school principals "walk the halls" in multiple and difficult-to-access locations (Goodman, 2017). These robots can provide a voice and a face in any encounter anywhere.

Tools for synchronous and asynchronous communication are now available almost everywhere and at any time. These tools move users into an Internet with unlimited resources for individual and collective learning – and potential transformation. YouTube brings users almost any aspect of the humanities, sciences, language, and the arts. Users can see the past and present, and obtain visions of the future through a connected world. Downes (2005) and Siemens (2005), in a very optimistic look at the future, prophesied a world of myriad learning opportunities assessed through artificial intelligence, leading, hopefully, to cheap, effective education for all. Virtual reality and augmented reality in the content of courses provide language learners with a wide range of immersive experiences that can ultimately lead to transformation (Griffith, 2019).

17.4 Conclusion

Opportunity exists to exploit the need of people to communicate. People can form online communities of practice, inquiry, even wisdom. In this manner, they can fulfill the vision of Martin Buber (1923/1958) in his work *Ich und Du* (*I and thou*), where all learn what works from each other and fashion a world culture best able to deal with challenges and chances. Future technology – more sophisticated gamification, more cross-culturally accurate representation in artificial technology, and greater networking capacity across continents – is likely to produce increased opportunities for transformative education. This will be not only in quantity, but also in approximating the Mezirowan "shaking of beliefs" that often accompanies real encounters on foreign soil and, ultimately, through transformation, creates a bilingual, bicultural person.

Looking into the future requires considering that the generation beyond the current Generation Z will be even more tied into technology as a mode of working and learning. Generation Z, being the first generation to grow up with full reliance on technology in nearly all aspects of life, has shown us that technology users view and approach life differently from nonusers (typical of previous generations). Given this different view, Generation Z learners are most likely to engage in transformative learning through gamification and the introduction of social-emotional learning strategies into programs and environments (Bovarie & Kroth, 2001; Snyder-Renfro, 2019). These opportunities provide seamless integration between the autonomous and the collaborative.

Language professionals must recognize the need to mesh newer and more interactive technologies to diversify instruction according to learner social, emotional, and cognitive needs. Technology provides the means to lead the learner to the transformative "water" and increase the likelihood of drinking it. Developing the emotional need to learn will be the basis for learners to go beyond subject to a place where the acquired language becomes an integral element of being and part of the foundation of a transformed life.

DISCUSSION QUESTIONS

1. Reflecting on the five planes of stimulus appraisal as factors in learner motivation with respect to language, what are the positive and negative elements of grading systems as a means to transform language learners?
2. Discuss ways in which technology contributes to transformative language learning.
3. Select a language or cultural skill exhibited by the transformed language learner and describe the environment or context that you would create to facilitate that transformation.

18

Transformation of Learners' Meaning-Making Repertoires through Classroom Instruction

Erin Kearney

Foreign language education (FLED) is a complex enterprise, and the potential for transformation of all kinds is great. While transformation may emerge naturally in the process of learning a new language, foreign language educators can create conditions for transformation in their classrooms and, in doing so more intentionally, play a significant role in realizing the potential and the promise of FLED.

While other changes are certainly possible for foreign language learners (e.g., growing communicative competence, deepening self- and other awareness, gaining greater access to and expanded participation in speech communities, exploring new social identity options, etc.), expanding the ability to make meaning lies at the core of what it means to learn a new language. Describing learner transformation as an expansion of meaning-making repertoires aligns with theoretical shifts occurring in the discipline, including movement toward an ecological-semiotic view of FLED and greater emphasis on both teacher and learner agency. From this perspective, beyond communicative or intercultural competence, we might articulate the goal of FLED as learners' "semiotic empowerment." Seeing FLED and learner transformation in these terms reflects substantial conceptual shifts in the field. These shifts are in line with the tenets of transformative learning theory (Mezirow, 1996, 2000; Taylor, 2008), especially its emphasis on meaning structures, frames of reference, and perspective transformation as key components of adult learning. While conceptualized as "arguably a rare occurrence" (Taylor, 2008, p. 18), perspective transformation "leads to 'a more fully developed (more functional) frame of reference ... one that is more (a) inclusive, (b) differentiating, (c) permeable, (d) critically reflective, and (e) integrative of experience' (Mezirow, 1996, p. 163). A perspective transformation occurs either through a series of cumulative transformed meaning schemes or as a result of an acute personal or social crisis" (Taylor, 2008, p. 18). In the foreign language classroom, regular opportunities that are deliberately planned by educators to raise awareness around learners' existing meaning schemes, to consider unfamiliar ones associated with the languages that they are studying, and to expand these personalized meaning schemes in new ways are supportive of the change that we often envision when we discuss the transformative potential of FLED but have trouble pinpointing in more precise terms. Alongside shifting theoretical currents, fostering transformative language learning and teaching (TLLT) and facilitating the transformation of learners' meaning-making repertoires in classrooms requires close examination of instructional practices, with an eye to identifying transformative moments and processes. When these are discerned through rigorous and systematic analyses of instructional practice, we have bases from which to draw illustrative examples of what it looks like when learners' meaning-making repertoires expand and what educators have done to foster such expansion.

18.1 Learners' Meaning-Making Repertoires and Language Education Processes Facilitating Semiotic Empowerment

That meaning matters in FLED is not a novel assertion; however, the way in which we conceive of "meaning" has evolved. Whereas "negotiation of meaning" in scholarship on instructed second language acquisition and in models of communicative language teaching generally refers to the way in which interlocutors seek to find common linguistic ground and achieve mutual understanding as they engage in information exchange (e.g., Ellis, 2003), semiotic views of language, language use, and language learning recognize that negotiation of meaning has inherently symbolic, not merely referential or propositional, dimensions.

In an ecological-semiotic view, language does not have fixed meanings; therefore, learning a new language does not involve the acquisition of a static code that maps set meanings to forms. Rather, the meaning of linguistic forms is in their potentials and instantiations (Halliday, 1978). Form–meaning connections are conventionalized through use and lead to overlap in individual language users' communicative repertoires (Rymes, 2014), making it so that we create and draw on shared systems of meaning and understand each other to some degree. Yet, the possibility always exists to use language forms (broadly conceived to include sounds, words, and syntactic constructions, as well as metaphors, genres, common narratives, etc.) in novel ways at any moment of language use. We can and sometimes do imbue forms with novel or unconventional meanings, and in all cases, even when we draw on largely conventional meanings, the instantiation of a form in a particular utterance or text represents a unique, situated meaning. For example, while users of English often share some common meanings related to the phrase "the American dream" and may find themselves thinking of similar images (white picket fences, doing better than one's parents, etc.), less common associations or wholly novel usages are possible, as in the editorial cartoon depicted in Figure 18.1, which draws on conventional meanings while fashioning new ones. Along with the image and a set of unconventional associations – credit card

Figure 18.1 The American pipe dream. This figure illustrates how the meaning of a phrase is subverted and recast.
Source: Keefe (2012).

debt, student loans, underemployment, and a retreating home as a mirage – the meaning of the phrase is subverted and recast.

In Van Lier's (2004) and others' (Kearney, 2016; Kramsch, 2002, 2006, 2009; Kramsch & Zhang, 2018) theorizing, learning a new language, then, entails the discovery and exploration of linguistic forms for their referential and symbolic meanings as realized in particular texts and situations of use, as well as across speakers/writers, perspectives, time, and cultures. It also involves developing the ability to leverage these forms to make one's own intended meanings and consequently to exercise one's agency and build semiotic empowerment. As Matthiesson (2009, p. 223) summarizes:

> When people learn languages, they build up their own personalized meaning potentials as part of the collective meaning potential that constitutes the languages, and they build up these personal potentials by gradually expanding their own registerial repertoires – their own shares in the collective meaning potential. As they expand their own registerial repertoires, they can take on roles in a growing range of contexts, becoming semiotically more empowered and versatile.

Matthiesson recognizes that language forms in the shared system of use have meaning potentials but emphasizes that language users have meaning potentials as well, both latent in their unique personalized, individual communicative and symbolic repertoires, and instantiated and ripe for expansion at every instance of language use. As Kramsch (2014, p. 301) explains:

> While many aspects of language use (e.g., academic language, high-end newspapers and TV discussions, public political speeches, canonical works of literature) abide by the norms of standard grammar and conventional genres, many uses of language in everyday life (e.g., online chats, marketing pitches, personal blogs and emails, conversational exchanges) are characterized by pragmatic unpredictability, semiotic uncertainty, and a commodification of language that inject additional layers of meaning into the supposedly stable signifiers of the dictionary and the predictable norms of conventional genres.... Globalization puts pressure on educators to diversify their teaching of language rules and conventions at the microlevel of age, gender, social class, and ethnicity and to teach what the diverse forms mean.

Kramsch (2006) similarly emphasizes the significance of today's language learners understanding processes of meaning-making and gaining facility with manipulating forms and meanings as they develop what she calls "symbolic competence." These theories put learners in the position to seize speakerhood and to express and assert themselves via the new forms and meaning potentials that they add to their existing repertoires. Notably, they accord language learners a power that is uncommon in our normal thinking and theorizing of language learning: the power to transform themselves and the very meaning-making systems that they are learning.

Educators, assuredly, have a significant role to play in the expansion of learners' meaning-making repertoires. Growth of the individual learner's personalized meaning-making repertoire depends on the conditions that teachers create for such expansion, the mindsets that they adopt, and the instructional practices that they engage in. Specifically, teachers increase their students' opportunity for semiotic engagement and empowerment when they highlight relevant symbolic forms and scaffold explorations of situated and broader meaning potentials. When they provide students with opportunities to deploy and possibly reshape conventional meanings, teachers open the door to stretching meaning-making repertoires.

18.2 Profiles in Learner Transformation toward Semiotic Empowerment

Examples of the ways in which educators and learners achieve semiotic engagement and build semiotic empowerment through their classroom interactions are needed to clarify the processes through which transformation can take place. The classroom excerpts presented in the following profile two learner transformations toward greater semiotic empowerment. These excerpts and analyses are drawn from micro-ethnographic studies of two very different FLED contexts: a university-level, content-based French course (Kearney, 2008b, 2012, 2016); and a pre-school program focused on developing multilingual awareness through exposure to new languages (Kearney & Ahn, 2014; Kearney & Barbour, 2015). Each profile highlights learner processes that mark growing semiotic empowerment and teacher practices that support these. Consequently, they begin to illustrate the range of teaching and learning interactions that are likely to expand learners' meaning-making repertoires, and, more broadly, to contribute to a more transformative FLED.

18.2.1 Profile 1: Sydney and Emilie

Sydney[1] was a student in an intermediate-level, university French course. Her instructor, Emilie, was intent on "catching students in a web of meanings" (interview) through an overarching global simulation project and her classroom instruction. The global simulation was organized around an extended out-of-class writing assignment, through which students were asked to author in weekly installments the stories of fictional but historically credible characters that experienced the Second World War in France. During class time, Emilie facilitated interactions aimed at developing students' ability to identify relevant symbolic forms (words, phrases, images, common cultural narratives, etc.) and to hypothesize about and analyze their meanings when used in particular visual and written texts. In this way, Emilie's instruction built up students' meaning-making repertoires by explicitly signaling relevant forms and providing opportunities for students to create meaningful associations around these. This routine practice of identifying and analyzing symbolic forms across a range of textual instantiations allowed students to experience and explore the multiplicity of perspectives that forms could be marshaled to express, and created an environment in which learners could construct a network of cultural and symbolic meanings, which they then drew on to express their characters' experiences and perspectives in the writing project.

In Excerpt 1 (see Figure 18.2), we get a glimpse at Sydney's initial attempts to make meaning around a text in Emilie's class. In this case, a propaganda poster depicting Maréchal Pétain at the start of the war was the basis for Sydney's halting interpretation. Figure 18.2 depicts what Sidney said after Emilie asked the class what they saw in the image's background and a few students offered the one-word responses of "ruin" and "chaos."

---

[1] All proper names cited in this chapter are pseudonyms.

24	Sydney:	la couleur de um le ciel derrière um Pétain c'est uh très
25		noir et um maréchal Pétain c'est um très clair c'est
26		blanche et um les couleurs de le um de le (2.2) de uh je
27		ne sais pas le scène
28	Emilie:	mm-hm
29	Sydney:	avant uh Pétain c'est très clair
30	Emilie:	ouais vous avez tout un un contraste clair obscur et ce qui
31		est obscur est derrière (1.8) d'accord c'est (0.6) donc
32		physiquement c'est derrière ça veut dire c'est derrière
33		moi c'est de l'histoire (0.4) la ruine de la France c'est
34		derrière moi moi je suis nous allons devant nous allons
35		vers le futur donc là à droite c'est la nuit concrètement
36		c'est quelle période de la guerre ça (0.8) avec les tanks

	Sydney:	the color of um the sky behind um Pétain it is uh very dark and um Maréchal Pétain it is um very light it's white and um the colors of the um of the (2.2) of um I don't know the scene
	Emilie:	mm-hm
	Sydney:	before uh Pétain it is very light
	Emilie:	yeah you have a a whole light-dark contrast and what is dark is behind (1.8) ok it is (0.6) so physically it is behind that means it is behind me it is history (0.4) the ruin of France is behind me me I am we are moving forward we are going toward the future so there on the right it's night concretely it is which period of the war that (0.8) with the tanks

Figure 18.2 Excerpt 1: What do you see in the background? This figure illustrates the use of literal and concrete vocabulary to hint at symbolic and figurative meaning.

In this short example, we see Sydney using the linguistic resources that she has at her disposal (vocabulary for literally and concretely describing features of the image) to hint at a more symbolic and figurative meaning, which Emilie recasts more fluently and analytically in the subsequent interactional turn.

Through such textual analyses, Emilie not only pointed out symbolic forms and made interactional space for students to analyze, interpret, and hypothesize about potential meanings, but also engaged in the discursive repositioning of her students as diverse speaking and hearing subjects. Linguistically, she shifted pronoun usage (transforming students sitting in a US classroom into French citizens of all kinds) and used tense in particular ways (bringing historical events into the immediate moment by using present tense verbs). In doing so, she routinely created conditions for robust teaching and learning interactions, during which students were repositioned as others, acquainted with relevant symbolic forms, and asked to interpret and create spoken and written texts from those new vantage points and perspectives. In her intentional curricular planning and then in her deliberate sequencing of classroom moments to engage students semiotically, Emilie created an iterative cycle that ultimately supported the transformation of students' abilities to interpret meaning in French.

Interviews with students reveal that Emilie's approach developed metalinguistic and semiotic awareness, transforming students' meaning-making repertoires in terms of their ability to interpret meaning in a variety of texts and to generate meaning in their own written and spoken productions (Kearney, 2008a). Students talked in interviews about the many opportunities for "perspective-taking" that arose from the design of Emilie's curriculum and instruction. Sydney described the impact of the global simulation and the writing of fictional memoirs from her invented character's point of view as accessing states of mind – "[having] to go into [French people's] minds" – and as an immersive experience – "being plunged into history." She reported coming away from the course with a deeper understanding of the French "cultural psyche" and further noted that she was cognizant that reading a limited number of texts on a topic did not reveal the richness and multiplicity of meanings and perspectives associated with historical events; in her words, reading just a few texts did not tell "the full story" of history. However, Emilie's approach instilled a sense of semiotic relativity in learners, who, like Sydney, came to see that although users of the French language may employ similar forms to talk about the Second World War, how they use them in context and how they are interpreted by particular audiences makes for substantial as well as subtle differences in meaning. Sydney experienced the transformative potential of FLED in this class largely through the perspective-taking that was built into Emilie's pedagogy. Whereas she reported having felt in previous language learning experiences as though she was learning how to use language to speak "like a polite tourist," in Emilie's class, she became comfortable using French, in particular, newly learned forms and narrative writing, "to discover things [and] explore new options."

18.2.2 Profile 2: Mikayla and Mina

In an entirely different context, preschoolers participated in a program intended to introduce children to new languages and to develop multilingual awareness. In this program, language partners – students from the local university who spoke languages other than English – visited a classroom twice a week, taught simple language lessons during whole-group instructional time, and then engaged in dialogue with children about languages in more spontaneous ways during free-play portions of the schedule. The goal of the program was not to cultivate substantial communicative proficiency in the young children, but rather to provide meaningful and curiosity-provoking experiences with language and opportunities to talk about and use language that might prompt the development of multilingual awareness, or the awareness that diverse languages exist in the world and that they offer alternative means for construing and expressing everything in it, including ourselves.

One of the preschool classrooms had a Korean-speaking language partner who visited the three and four year olds. During a free-play part of the class, the interaction in Excerpt 2 (see Figure 18.3) unfolded. What it illustrates is that even in classrooms where developing communicative proficiency is not a goal and immersion in a new language and universe of meanings is not taking place, semiotic engagement and empowerment can still occur. In this case, exposure to language difference and the space for dialoguing about that difference resulted in a remarkable interaction. The three-year-old Mikayla approached her language partner, Mina, pencil in hand and proposed they write their names (see Figure 18.3).

This encounter reflects a negotiation of meaning between Mikayla and Mina that is symbolic in nature. Together, they explored and negotiated what it means to write one's name and spell it in a "normal" way, with the little girl first positing English script as "regular" and Korean script, implicitly, as "irregular." The language partner makes several instructional moves in this excerpt to create conditions for semiotic engagement and ultimately Mikayla's movement toward semiotic empowerment. First, she draws attention to a meaningful symbolic form – the script system used to write in Korean, which is a wholly different available alternative for writing one's name. She also scaffolds discussion of the semiotic and linguistic options (the script systems) as equally viable and valuable options. After first calling Korean script "weird," perhaps articulating what she thought the child's reaction to the linguistic difference might be, Mina quickly asserts that writing her name in Korean script is "her regular name." Mina is arguably successful in convincing the little girl of the value of this alternative as, at the end of the interaction, Mikayla wants to try the new script option herself. She takes initiative and seeks the forms and skills she will need to write her name in Korean script. In turning to Mina to ask "How?," we see the seeds of her semiotic empowerment bear initial fruit: a child pursuing the symbolic resources that she needs to make the meanings she intends.

These classroom interactions illustrate some ways in which teachers can draw their students into meaningful semiotic engagements and how learners' personalized meaning-making potentials can consequently expand. There are, of course, many more ways of doing this, and documenting these many possibilities merits our attention in further research. The preceding examples show particular meaning-making processes in the classroom and help us to theorize, research, and practice a more transformative FLED. In Emilie's classroom especially, we see reframing as classroom participants are repositioned in discourse as historical actors of varying perspectives and

01	S1:	now can I write your name how what's your name
02		((gets a piece of paper and puts it on the table))
03	Mina:	oh my my name?
04	S1:	in Korean
05	Mina:	in Korean
06	S1:	yep
07	Mina:	((S1 leans forward as Mina writes her name)) *Min* (pause) I have square in my name
08		that's weird ((points to a part of her name)) *Min* (pause) *A* (pause)
09	S1:	you got that in your name
10	Mina:	*Mina* that's my name
11	S1:	how spell your regular name?
12	Mina:	my regular name? this is my regular name
13	S1:	((stares at Mina for a while))
14	Mina:	*Mina*
15	S1:	I'm gonna sh- ((takes Mina's pencil)) how do you sp- ((slides paper closer to write on it))
16		I show you how to write my first name and then you can write what name you
17		((unintelligible))
18	Ms. Lane:	do you remember her name (pause) *Mina*
19	S1:	*Mina* ((writes her own name on the paper, under Mina's name, then taps on Mina's arm
20		who is looking at other children)) look it ((spells name letter by letter))
21	Mina:	Mikayla
22	S1:	can you write can you write my name in Korean? ((smiles at Mina))
23	Mina:	sure
24	S1:	S ((starts to spell out her name for Mina using English alphabet))
25	Mina:	((writes S1's name in Korean on paper)) 학생의 이름 oh that's your name
26		*Mikayla*
((lines omitted – Mina helps Mikayla ask the Korean graduate student filming the interaction her name in Korean))		
46	Mina:	*Jung-Hee* oh I see *Jung-Hee* ((writes the graduate student's name on the paper))
47	S1:	in Korean now ((smiles at Mina))
48	Mina:	yeah that's Korean *Jung-Hee* her name is *Jung-Hee*
49	S1:	((shows the paper to Mina)) ((unintelligible)) lemme write um uh (pause) my name's
50		((looks at Mina, who was looking away for a moment)) in Korean ((taps on Mina's arm))
51		(pause) how
52	Mina:	your name?
53	S1:	no my name in Korean how do this

Figure 18.3 Excerpt 2: What does it mean to write your name? This figure illustrates a negotiation of meaning that is symbolic in nature.

experiences, we see students connecting forms to meaning potentials and building networks of meaningful associations as Emilie prepares them for and leads them through the interpretation of a range of visual and written texts, and we see the way in which she makes space for students to realize meaning potentials through language use, both in classroom talk and through their writing. In the case of Mina and Mikayla, notably different script systems are reframed as both potentially "normal" ways of writing one's name. At the core, these learners of language are gaining access to and gaining experience with new meaning structures. In transformative language learning and teaching (TLLT), these processes can serve to shift, temporarily or in more enduring ways, our habits of mind and our points of view – what theorists of transformative learning posit as the building blocks of perspective transformation (Taylor, 2008).

18.3 Conclusion

Classroom-based research shows that curricular and instructional practices encouraging engagement with meaning potentials and the realization of individual learners' meaning-making potentials help achieve a fuller potential of the FLED classroom. Yet, orthodoxies persist in our profession, including models of language teaching that privilege communicative but not symbolic dimensions of language, visions of the learner that are largely passive, and conceptions of the goals of FLED that remain relatively instrumental and transactional, as opposed to humanistic, individually fulfilling, and empowering. Kearney (2016, p. 3) has written that we need "a transformative foreign language education" with a pedagogy that aims to "spur change in learners' worldview," but we also need paradigm change in the discipline itself (Kearney, 2019), toward more meaning-oriented, ecological-semiotic approaches.

It is in viewing language learning as an engagement with meaning potentials and a stretching of semiotic repertoires that we begin to more adequately capture what language education stands to do for individual learners and broader communities. While we often speak of developing communicative competence and cultivating intercultural competence in learners as our central goals, we can define and enact educational practices that recast languages education as movement toward semiotic engagement and empowerment.

DISCUSSION QUESTIONS

1. What questions can language educators ask themselves when planning for instruction aimed at the transformation of learners' meaning-making repertoires?
2. Identify a culturally symbolic form associated with the language you teach, as well as several instances of its use. How does each instance of use illustrate an instantiation of meaning potential? In what ways do the various instances of use that you have chosen reflect differences in meaning?
3. What is your own definition of semiotic empowerment? What does semiotic empowerment mean for the language learners that you know or teach?

19

Language Learner Autonomy and Transformative Classroom Practice

David Little

The concept of learner autonomy was first introduced to second language (L2) education at the end of the 1970s, when Henri Holec's (1979; cited here as Holec, 1981 [1979]) report, *Autonomy and foreign language learning*, was published under the aegis of the Council of Europe's Committee for Out-of-School Education. The committee promoted adult education as "an instrument for arousing an increasing sense of awareness and liberation in man" (Janne, 1977, p. 5), and the ethos of its major adult education project had much in common with the contemporaneous work of Paulo Freire. The project insisted that adult education should not resemble school, which generally "leaves a memory of frustration or even defeat" (Janne, 1977, p. 19); instead, it should draw on learners' personal experience (Janne, 1977, p. 20), supporting them in self-management (Janne, 1977, p. 27) and the kind of group work that makes possible the "interpersonal dialectical dialogue" that supports "self-learning" (Janne, 1977, p. 53). The same features characterize Freire's (1970) "problem-posing education." Accordingly, the concept of learner autonomy that Holec introduced to adult L2 learning came freighted with the ethos and goals of transformative education.

This chapter is concerned with the evolution of our understanding of language learner autonomy under the impact of transformative classroom practice. It begins by summarizing Holec's definition of the concept, and then describes an approach to teaching and learning that sought to operationalize that definition, though with two added features: the use of the target language for all classroom communication; and a strong emphasis on collaborative learning. This gave the concept of language learner autonomy explanatory power: learners acquire L2 proficiency when their agency is channeled through the target language. The chapter then turns to inclusive education, describing an approach to the integration of immigrant pupils that engages their agency by encouraging them to use their home languages in the classroom. This enables them to develop a capacity for agentive behavior in English and Irish with the cognitive support that their home language provides. The chapter concludes by briefly associating the two learning environments described with the concept of plurilingualism as defined in the *Common European Framework of Reference for Languages* (Council of Europe, 2001).

19.1 Holec's Definition of the Autonomous Learner

In his 1979 report, Holec defines learner autonomy as "the ability to take charge of one's own learning," which means being responsible for "all the decisions concerning all aspects of this learning": "[D]etermining the objectives; defining the contents and progressions; selecting methods and techniques to be used; monitoring the procedure of acquisition properly speaking (rhythm, time, place, etc.); evaluating what has been acquired" (Holec, 1981 [1979], p. 3). According to Holec, the ability to take charge of one's own learning is "not inborn but must be acquired either by 'natural' means or (as most often happens) by formal learning" (Holec, 1981 [1979], p. 3). The Council of Europe's adult education project argued that learner self-management results in a new relationship between the learner and existing knowledge, and transforms the way in which knowledge is acquired (Janne, 1977, p. 24). Similarly, Holec (1981 [1979], p. 21) proposed that when learners take charge of their learning, "objective, universal knowledge is ... replaced by subjective, individual knowledge": "[T]he learner is no longer faced with an 'independent' reality ... to which he cannot but give way, but with a reality which he himself constructs and dominates."

However, there is one vital respect in which Holec does not follow the adult education project. As we have seen, the project viewed learning as an interactive process, assigning a central role to group work, which generates "interpersonal dialectical dialogue." By contrast, Holec's autonomous learner thinks and acts in and for themselves; there is no obvious sense in which they belong to a learning community. This may have its origins in an essentially monologic understanding of cognition and learning; it may also reflect the fact that Holec's chief practical concern was with self-access language learning that made use of non-interactive technologies: the language laboratory, supplemented by video recording and playback. Whatever its source, Holec's monologic version of the autonomous learner lives on in university language centers that promote blended and self-access language learning and in educational systems that expect learners to become autonomous without the benefit of pedagogical intervention.

19.2 Toward a Dialogic Understanding of Language Learner Autonomy

If we associate learner autonomy exclusively with organizational and cognitive control of the learning process, the following question arises: how can learner autonomy explain success specifically in L2 learning? The answer to this question was provided by the outstandingly successful classroom practice that emerged in Denmark and other Nordic countries in the 1970s. The paradigm case is the classroom of Leni Dam, who taught English in a Danish middle school (*Folkeskole*) for more than three decades (see Dam, 1995; Little et al., 2017). Within the framework provided by the official curriculum, Dam required her learners to fulfill Holec's definition of the autonomous learner: to decide on their own learning targets; choose materials and activities; and regularly evaluate the learning process and its outcomes. However, her approach differed from Holec's in two essentials. First, whereas Holec said nothing about the role of spontaneous target language use in L2 learning, in Dam's classroom, the target language was the preferred medium of communication from the very beginning. As it was used to plan, monitor, and evaluate learning, her learners developed a proficiency that was metacognitive as well as communicative. Second, Dam's version of learner autonomy was strongly interactive. Her learners pursued individual learning agendas in interaction with the learning agendas of their peers and as part of the larger learning agenda of the class. They exercised and developed their autonomy not as independent agents, but as interdependent active members of a collaborative learning community, that is, their autonomy was socially embedded and dialogically constituted. When added to Holec's foundational definition, these two features provide an understanding of *language* learner autonomy that has explanatory power. It claims that optimal L2 development is achieved when, from the beginning, the target language is the principal channel of the learners' agency, that is, the communicative and metacognitive medium through which, individually and collaboratively, they plan, execute, monitor, and evaluate their own learning.

Two techniques make it possible to use the target language in this way, even with beginners. First, the teacher scaffolds their learners' target language use in a multitude of ways and shows them how to build scaffolds for one another in group work. Second, they establish a symbiotic relation between speaking and writing: written prompts support speaking and speaking helps to generate written text. Learners are not expected to develop autonomous learning skills *ex nihilo*; rather, the teacher imposes a fixed structure on lessons (teacher time–learner time–together time [Little et al., 2017, pp. 80–82]), proposes and models learning activities, and frames the life of the classroom in reflective, evaluative talk.

The principal tools of learning are logbooks and posters. Learners use logbooks (plain exercise books) to record each lesson, make a note of new words and phrases they have learnt, plan project work, write the short texts they produce individually, and evaluate the learning process and its outcomes at regular intervals. Posters, a regular feature of "teacher time," are created by the teacher in interaction with the class. They are used to respond to the needs that arise from learning plans (e.g., in the early stages, "words we need," "useful sentences," etc.) and to capture discussion of the learning experience (characteristics of "a good talk" or "good group work," reasons for learning English, ways of learning

English, etc.). In keeping with the collaborative ethos and interactive dynamic of language learner autonomy, all learning activities begin in dialogue between the teacher and their learners or among learners working in groups. This includes self- and peer assessment and other forms of evaluation.

The learning activities pursued in Dam's classroom fall into two broad categories: analytic and creative. Analytic learning activities include the making of word cards, picture dominoes, and picture lotto to support the learning of language that the learners themselves judge relevant and important, while creative text production comprises stories, poems, plays, and projects of many different kinds. The strongly collaborative dynamic requires that learners share their learning materials and the texts they write with the rest of the class; in this way, each student contributes to the learning of their peers.

Little et al. (2017) provide a detailed description of Dam's approach, with many examples of learners' work; they also summarize the results of a four-year project that compared the learning achievement of one of Dam's classes with that of a class in a German gymnasium (the Danish learners consistently outperformed their German peers). Two examples will give some idea of the transformative achievement of Dam's autonomy classroom: the development of proficiency in English that is, at once, communicative and metacognitive, and bears testimony to the general educative power of autonomous language learning. At the end of their 4th year of learning English (three 45-minute lessons a week), Dam asked one of her classes how they would sum up their learning experience and achievement. Each learner was given a sheet of paper and had 15 minutes in which to compose a written answer to the question. Here are the (uncorrected) texts written by two 15-year-old learners:

> Most important is probably the way we have worked. That we were expected to and given the chance to decide ourselves what to do. That we worked independently.... And we have learned much more because we have worked with different things. In this way we could help each other because some of us had learned something and others had learned something else. It doesn't mean that we haven't had a teacher to help us. Because we have, and she has helped us. But the day she didn't have the time, we could manage on our own.

> I already make use of the fixed procedures from our diaries when trying to get something done at home. Then I make a list of what to do or remember the following day. That makes things much easier. I have also via English learned to start a conversation with a stranger and ask good questions. And I think that our "together" session has helped me to become better at listening to other people and to be interested in them. I feel that I have learned to believe in myself and to be independent. (Dam & Little, 1999, p. 134)

Dam first developed her approach in response to the official demand for "differentiation": the provision of an educational environment in which all learners could thrive according to their individual interests and abilities. She was strongly influenced by Douglas Barnes's (1976) book *From communication to curriculum*, which appeared in Danish translation in 1977. Barnes was especially concerned with the role played by exploratory talk, or thinking aloud, in bringing "school knowledge" (curriculum content) into fruitful contact with learners' "action knowledge" (the experiential knowledge, attitudes, and beliefs that are an important source of their capacity for autonomous behavior). Dam's learners necessarily drew on their action knowledge when deciding, for example, on the English words they needed to learn or the stories they wanted to write. By requiring them to take control, she ensured that their identity was invested in their learning; by making them responsible for planning, implementing, and evaluating their learning, she ensured that their emerging proficiency in English included a metacognitive dimension.

Barnes is recognized as one of the founders of dialogic pedagogy, which is an approach to teaching that emphasizes the importance of learners' contributions to reciprocal communication. Other contributors to dialogic theory have provided further illumination of the underlying processes of the autonomy classroom. For example, Vygotsky's (1987) argument that the capacity for discursive thinking (inner speech) is internalized from social speech via egocentric speech helped to explain how Dam's learners developed the ability to write sophisticated reflective texts like the examples cited earlier. Little et al. (2017) provide a full account of the theoretical underpinning of Dam's approach, which has been frequently cited but rarely replicated.

19.3 Language Learner Autonomy and Inclusive Education

The dialogic version of autonomous language learning can also have a transformative impact on learners with special educational needs. For example, Dam's classroom benefited Dennis, a young teenager with serious behavioral problems and learning difficulties (Little et al., 2017, pp. 162–171), and Susan, who became fluent in English despite suffering from severe dyslexia (Little et al., 2017, pp. 171–181). The emergent autonomy of the individual learner in a strongly supportive dialogic learning environment also helps to account for the success of the radical approach to educational inclusion adopted by Scoil Bhríde (Cailíní) (St Brigid's School for Girls), a girls' primary school in one of Dublin's western suburbs. The school has about 320 pupils: 80 percent are from immigrant families; between them, they have more than 50 home languages; and a high proportion of the immigrant pupils have little or no English when they start school at the age of four-and-a-half.

In many countries (including Ireland), some schools insist that immigrant pupils leave their home language at the school gate, the idea being that they should spend as much time as possible speaking, and therefore learning, the language of schooling. Scoil Bhríde has adopted a diametrically opposite policy. Recognizing that the language each pupil speaks at home is not only an essential part of her identity, but her principal cognitive tool and a major source of her capacity for autonomous behavior, the school encourages immigrant pupils to use their home languages for whatever purposes seem appropriate to them, inside as well as outside the classroom. In junior infant classes, four- and five-year-old immigrant pupils learn to count, add, and play action games in English, Irish (the obligatory second language of the curriculum), and their home languages. Furthermore, from the same early stage, they are invited to tell the rest of the class how they express key curriculum concepts in their home language. Sometimes they have to ask their parents for the words in question – days of the week, perhaps, or months of the year. As pupils move up the school, they are repeatedly invited to make linguistic comparisons between English, Irish, and their home language. In this way, their home language is always activated and their action knowledge, mostly acquired in their home language, is fully implicated in the educational process.

Immigrant pupils' home languages are mostly opaque to the teachers, the potential exceptions being the four European languages included in the Irish post-primary curriculum: French, German, Italian, and Spanish. Thus, in the oral communication of the classroom, home languages can fulfill three functions: they can be used in reciprocal communication with speakers of the same or a closely related language in pair or group work; they can be used for non-reciprocal purposes of display, for example, in counting or playing action games; and they can be used as a source of intuitive linguistic knowledge. However, Scoil Bhríde's approach does not stop here. With support from their parents, immigrant pupils transfer their gradually developing literacy skills from English and Irish to their home language, producing texts with the same thematic content in English, Irish, and their home language. This provides native-born Irish pupils with a strong motivation to adopt Irish as their "home language."

Scoil Bhríde's approach to the management of linguistic diversity produces high levels of age-appropriate plurilingual literacy, an unusually sophisticated degree of language awareness (Little & Kirwan, 2018a), an unusual enthusiasm for learning and using (speaking and writing) Irish, and the capacity to undertake ambitious autonomous learning projects with a linguistic focus from an early age. A class of seven year olds, for example, decided to translate the chorus of the song "It's a small world" into all the languages present in the class and used their time in the school yard to teach one another all the versions; they were then able to sing the chorus in 11 languages (it would have been 14, but three pupils were absent from school for the week in question). A 12-year-old pupil taught herself Spanish using two textbooks that she found in the school library and various internet resources; when the principal retired, the pupil wrote her a letter of good wishes that was half in Spanish and half in English.

Scoil Bhríde has no access to special resources; nevertheless, its pupils perform above the national average in the standardized tests of math and English that they take annually from 1st class (6+ years old) to 6th class (11+ years old). Little and Kirwan (2018b) provide an overview of Scoil Bhríde's language education policy and its implementation; Little and Kirwan (2019) is a book-length case study.

19.4 Conclusion

Since the publication of the *Common European Framework of Reference for Languages* (Council of Europe, 2001), the Council of Europe's work in language education has focused on the promotion of plurilingualism: the ability to communicate in two or more languages, at whatever level of proficiency. According to the *Common European Framework*, a plurilingual repertoire is underpinned by "a communicative competence to which all knowledge and experience of languages contributes and in which languages interrelate and interact" (Council of Europe, 2001, p. 4). By definition, the various languages in a plurilingual individual's repertoire are available for immediate, spontaneous use in relevant and appropriate contexts. Leni Dam's teenage learners of English and Scoil Bhríde's immigrant pupils are plurilingual in this sense: the language(s) they use outside school and the language(s) they are learning as well as using in school are equally part of their "everyday lived language" (García, 2017, p. 18).

In Dam's classroom, learners draw on their action knowledge to decide on learning targets and select learning materials and activities; in this way, their identity is implicated in their learning and the capacity for agentive behavior that they bring with them is fully engaged. They achieve high levels of communicative as well as metacognitive proficiency in English because their agency is channeled through the target language: English is the medium in which they plan, implement, monitor, and evaluate their own learning.

In Scoil Bhríde, immigrant pupils' action knowledge is activated and their identity implicated when they use their home languages in the classroom; they develop their capacity for agentive behavior in English and Irish partly with the cognitive support that their home languages provide. In turn, they transfer the literacy that they acquire at school, in English and Irish, to their home languages. If the Council of Europe's ideal of plurilingualism is to be realized in Europe's education systems, it is likely to be as a result of the more widespread adoption of transformative pedagogies that exploit and further develop the symbiotic relationship between learners' agency and the languages in their emerging repertoires.

DISCUSSION QUESTIONS

1. In what sense(s) are the examples of language education described in this chapter transformative? What is transformed, and in what ways?
2. Select any two textbooks that you have used as a language teacher or learner. How easy would it be to use them to support the dialogic pedagogy described in this chapter? From the perspective of learner autonomy, what are the textbooks' positive and negative features?
3. Think of the program of language teacher education that you contributed to or participated in most recently. What assumptions did it make about language learning and language teaching? List the ways in which its dynamic was (1) similar to and (2) different from the classroom dynamic described in this chapter.

20

Cognitive and Affective Transformations in Developing Bilingual and Bicultural Competence

Shannon Salyer and Betty Lou Leaver

Those who accompany students on their transformative learning journeys as bilingual/bicultural individuals will need to understand their students on a personal level, reaching deeply, at times, into areas of cognition and affect in order to provide the sophisticated, supportive coaching necessary for building linguistic and intercultural competence in a way that transcends traditional binary and dualistic models of thinking.[1] Coaching is essential if students are to learn how to manage the cognitive distortions and affective dissonances that can derail their language learning success. Students' abilities to self-identify and manage their own unhelpful responses in thinking and emotions will contribute to the development of the levels of learner autonomy required for recognizing, resolving, and moving beyond disorienting dilemmas. Recognizing cognitive distortions and affective dissonances for what they are establishes a degree of "sobriety" that is closely connected with self-awareness, empowerment, and the ability to make reasonable choices as autonomous learners (see Garza, this volume; Little, this volume; see also Wenden, 1991).

20.1 Cognitive Distortions

When acquiring a new concept, learners, sometimes inadvertently assisted by teachers or curriculum design, take heuristic shortcuts that lead them away from reality, rather than in its direction. Cognitive behavioralists label these short cuts *cognitive distortions*: ways of thinking that convince us that something contrary to fact is true, and therefore have detrimental effects on learning. Such instinctive, automatic-thinking fallacies, sometimes further reinforced by mismatches between learning styles, instructional programs, and appropriate learning strategies, can derail the learner's progress in becoming a bilingual/bicultural individual. Binary thinking and dysmorphic focus are two of several possible categories of cognitive distortions found among language learners.

---

[1] Here, the reference is to the Cartesian notion that the material and divisible brain and body are distinct from the immaterial and indivisible mind and soul but interact: *"Je pense, donc je suis [cogito ergo sum]"* (Descartes, 1668/2013).

20.1.1 Binary Thinking

Anyone who has studied a foreign language or been exposed to a foreign, émigré, or immigrant culture realizes that life is truly not binary. However, those whose only experience has been in a monolingual, monocultural environment may develop binary thinking, which is realized as expecting everything to be either "on" or "off." Examples of binary thinking include:

- all-or-nothing thinking;
- labeling;
- either/or thinking;
- right-or-wrong thinking;
- "us" versus "them" thinking (polarization); and
- black-or-white thinking.

This set of cognitive distortions is exemplified by learners who tend to think in oppositional categories. If their performance in the language falls short of perfect, they see it as a total disaster – and may even label themselves with a self-defeating epithet, such as "failure," which, in turn, often spirals downward with an increasing loss of self-esteem to the point that the label seems true. For example, if students mispronounce a word or do not correctly answer a question on a quiz, binary thinking causes them to believe that they are failing to learn the language, and, indeed, cannot learn the language. Trapped by binary thinking, otherwise good students may continue to magnify their shortcomings in the target language and study to the point of burnout. Similarly, high-achieving high school graduates may fare poorly in intensive foreign language courses because they aim for perfection – and second languages are rarely perfectly expressed.

The transformative language learning and teaching (TLLT) instructor/ mentor, recognizing binary thinking, helps learners identify their specific language learning challenges and make a plan for overcoming them. Ectenic learners,[2] who naturally focus on details and differences, have the easiest time

---

[2] Ectenic learning is one of two core dimensions, the other being synoptic learning, delineated by the E&L cognitive style construct (Ehrman & Leaver, 2002) as learning style continua. Validated at the Foreign Service Institute in 2002/2003 in a study of 1,300 students and since expanded to several thousand students and replicated in the USA and elsewhere, the E&L cognitive style construct establishes ten subscales of these two dimensions. Synoptic learners see the world as a whole, process through osmosis (i.e., unconsciously), and easily tolerate ambiguity; their learning styles encompass synthesis (assembling new ideas from pieces of information), impulsivity, leveling (noticing similarities among objects), preference for induction (figuring out rules from the examples), and thinking in concrete and analogic (metaphoric) terms. Ectenic learners see the world as composed of pieces, process consciously, and experience considerable discomfort with ambiguity; their learning styles include analysis (disassembling ideas into their components), reflectivity (thinking before acting), sharpening

in doing this, though perhaps the hardest time in escaping their binary thinking because of a need for clarity that languages rarely accommodate. For their counterparts, the synoptic learners, who are focused nearly exclusively on the big picture, the TLLT mentor may suggest more appropriate learning strategies or have the learners produce Venn diagrams that distinguish the black, the white, and, in the intersection, the grey, including the roles of perspective-taking or semiotic perspective that can make non-binary-thinking cultures more accessible to English-speaking learners.

Presented with disorienting dilemmas, learners unaware of their own binary thinking can encounter slowdowns in the acquisition of biculturalism, while nonetheless forging ahead with building bilingualism. In Arab countries, for example, *yes* can mean *no*, both in language and in behavior. It is not atypical for an Arab, being polite, to say نعم (*naam, yes*) when they really have no intention of undertaking a requested action, expecting the listener to interpret the response as politeness rather than as agreement or assent. This can be a significant dilemma for the speaker of English, in that English has lesser dependence on context for interpreting meaning than Arabic. Study abroad programs in Arab countries that are transformative in nature coach learners in embracing the ambiguity of a high-context language (see Farraj, this volume).

20.1.2 Dysmorphic Focus

Dysmorphic focus occurs when learners fail to see a comprehensive whole and misinterpret a reality accordingly, much like the story of five blind men describing an elephant while each is touching a different part of the elephant's anatomy. In language learning, dysmorphic focus can lead to fossilization and the avoidance of difficult learning situations or linguistic expressions, and most typically occurs through:

- selective abstraction (drawing a conclusion based on only one or two of several factors);
- overgeneralization (applying a conclusion or result too broadly);
- jumping to conclusions (making an affective assumption in the absence of logic);

(noticing differences among objects), preference for deduction (learn the rule, then practice with examples), and thinking in abstract and digital (non-metaphoric) terms. Synoptic learners handle high-context languages, such as Arabic, with relative ease; ectenic learners tend to do best with low-context languages, such as French or Spanish. Synoptic and ectenic learners have been found to differ in the learning strategies that they use, the speed of acquisition, the balance between accuracy and fluency, and the paths that they take to the highest levels of proficiency (Ehrman & Leaver, 2002).

- magnification (assuming one negative detail overwhelms everything else);
- minimization (assuming that important but difficult-to-master details do not matter); and
- filtration (discounting positive information).

Learners will often selectively abstract a negative experience and overgeneralize it: "You never taught us that" or "You always favor [someone else]." Similarly, learners who have done well in some aspects of the language, such as vocabulary acquisition, may filter out their positive experience when encountering difficulties with another aspect of language, such as structure. As the thinking is unbalanced, dysmorphic focus can swing between extremes of magnification (e.g., being convinced that a bad accent means an inability to learn the language) and minimization (assuming that accent does not matter).

All too often, learners are unaware of this kind of dysmorphic thinking. Fortunately, the TLLT teacher has the ability to address dysmorphic thinking in ways not available to the sage-on-the-stage teacher. For example, in the process of establishing contracts with learners for focusing on specific and personally preferred aspects of the language and culture (Knowles, 1986), the TLLT teacher has the opportunity to interview learners. Information gleaned during the interview, as well as during diagnostic assessment[3] and dynamic testing[4] (typical of TLLT programs such as those at US government institutions), may uncover elements of dysmorphic focus. These data provide a starting point for a contract discussion.

The attuned teacher can also discern the discounting of positive experiences by learners and help them refocus. For example, in an open-architecture[5] Czech language classroom at the Defense Language Institute Foreign Language Center (DLIFLC), the teacher overheard students complaining that they had learned nothing all week because they had not been given vocabulary lists and grammar exercises like their peers in a parallel textbook-controlled class. Therefore, at the end of the day on Friday, the teacher asked learners to list anything at all

---

[3] At the Defense Language Institute Foreign Language Center (DLIFLC), for example, diagnostic assessment (a term that has been used in widely different ways in second language [L2] and English as a second language [ESL] teaching) consists of probing students for their current language proficiency level, determining their learning style preferences (generally using the E&L cognitive style construct [Ehrman & Leaver, 2002]), and recording demographic information that might shed light on language learning difficulties (Cohen, 2014).

[4] At the DLIFLC, dynamic testing (also called dynamic assessment in some circles) is part of the diagnostic assessment and probes for the learner's zone of proximal development (Vygotsky, 1978/2013, 1987), that is, the identification of those language features that the students are most ready to learn.

[5] For a definition and description of open architecture curricular design (OACD), see Campbell (this volume).

that they had learned that week: the learners filled up a large blackboard three times – and from then on considered that they were the lucky ones, telling a journalist who visited the class that they felt guilty because they had an easier learning experience yet learned more than their peers in traditional classes (Duri, 1992).

What the Czech teacher did in this case was to help students reframe[6] their understanding of their language learning experience. Instead of focusing on *memorized knowledge*, in reframing the question, these students focused on their osmotically learned language based on their *ability to use* it.

20.2 Affective Dissonance

Separately from *cognitive* distortions, affective dissonance, that is, impairments of the *emotional* aspects of language learning, can undermine learning and deprive students of the resiliency they need to make the most of their learning time, especially in study abroad situations. Resiliency supports self-actualization, feelings of self-efficacy, a sense of self-esteem, and the ability to interact more confidently with the social, especially the foreign, environment (Carter, 2015), which are key components in resolving disorienting dilemmas. Emotional reasoning and self-absorption are just two examples of several categories of affective dissonance.

20.2.1 Emotional Reasoning

Emotional reasoning, as opposed to rational, logical, or critical reasoning, relies on feelings rather than facts.[7] Examples of emotional reasoning include:

- negation of reality (assuming that negative feelings reflect a negative reality);
- confusion of self-perception and other perception; and
- low emotional intelligence.[8]

---

[6] Reframing is an outgrowth from cognitive restructuring (Beck, 1979; Rogers, 1969/1986), a technique used in cognitive therapy to turn negative thoughts into positive ones. Reframing is used outside clinical settings to put a conception, belief, thought, or perception into a new "frame," or, in other words, to look at something in a different light. In language classrooms, reframing can be used to reset the expectations students have of themselves and programs, better understand the local population in study abroad programs, or resolve a disorienting dilemma.

[7] Oxford (this volume) describes the intersection of cognition, emotion, and TLLT.

[8] The psychosocial construct of emotional intelligence (Goleman, 1995) refers to the capacity to be aware of, control, and express one's emotions, and to handle interpersonal relationships judiciously and empathetically. Cross-culturally, high emotional intelligence is expressed by the acceptance of differences in values and beliefs, and the ability to integrate these into an emergent, transformed, bicultural personality.

Emotional reasoning deprives students of the ability to distinguish between fact and fiction, and between their own emotions and the emotions of others, as well as to regulate their own moods, concerns, and fears. These characteristics, in turn, inhibit the development of biculturalism (Carter, 2015).

Critical thinking activities, which are a typical way of dealing with disorienting dilemmas in transformative classrooms, can help students reorient their approach from emotion to logic (see Crane & Sosulski, this volume). Similarly, student counseling activities – focused on revealing the sources of students' difficulties in language acquisition and informed by a diagnostic assessment of styles, strategies, and proficiency – can be easily incorporated into TLLT programs (Ehrman, 1996).

20.2.2 Self-Absorption

Self-absorption occurs when learners cannot get past thinking only about themselves. The stances taken can be of either an offensive (even self-destructive) or a defensive nature. At a minimum, they involve using one's own standards and can include:

- self-imposed standards;
- personalization;
- defensive mechanisms;
- blaming; and
- projection.

- When language learning turns emotional – which, given language learning anxieties, it very often does – learners often demonstrate extremes in behavior. Some students become despondent because they feel that they can never measure up to self-imposed standards, typically blaming themselves for any failure. Others prioritize self-interest above group interest and can become hostile if they feel that a teacher is not being fair to them. What motivates them to become hostile is a complex set of self-defense mechanisms (Takys Sapountzis, personal communication, May 1987). Learners generally do not find their way out of the labyrinth of self-absorption without the help of a teacher/mentor, who has at least two important tools to deploy: first, empathy allows the mentor to perceive and elucidate the learner's internal frames of reference; and, second, reframing allows the student to adjust or change those internal frames of reference.[9]

---

[9] Rogers (1995) posted three core conditions for a mentor to be able to assist a learner in changing an internal frame of reference: (1) congruence (genuineness); (2) accurate empathy; and (3) a nonjudgmental stance.

20.3 Navigating the Cultural Borderland and Matters of Diversity

The territory between the native culture and the foreign culture has been called the "cultural borderland" (Dunlop, 1999), which bicultural persons must ultimately traverse, including crossing the *fault line* between the two cultures and moving into a *third space* of critical thinking and dialogic interaction (Bhaba, 1994), where the other and the self intertwine in a form of hybridization, or what has been referred to in this volume as the "bilingual/ bicultural personality." To cross these borderlands successfully and live as a hybrid critical thinker in the third space requires a deeper understanding of the learner on a cognitive and affective basis than is required in non-TLLT classrooms – and greater discussion than the limited length of this chapter permits.

In an attempt to summarize the large number of individualized and unique variables necessary for successful TLLT, especially at upper levels of bilingual competence and deeper levels of bicultural competence, the following list is proposed for further investigation and potential incorporation into TLLT programs:

1. A new look at the development of bilingualism and biculturalism, perhaps even a new definition, emanating from moving into the third space, where cultures mesh, transformations are metanoic, and thinking is critical and capable of resolving disorienting dilemmas.

2. A way to help learners successfully translate where concepts and words do not match, understanding that "the map is not the territory" and "the word is not the thing" (Korzybski, 1995) – or "the menu is not the meal" (Watts, 1999). The smooth integration into another culture relies upon understanding that one word (such as *home*) in English and the same word in Russian (*дом*) do not conjure up the same image (or signal the same mental model) in both cultures.

3. An exploration of ego boundaries (Hartmann, 1944/1964), in which individuals with thick boundaries are less receptive to ideas from another culture and individuals with more permeable, thin boundaries more readily embrace cultural differences. Linguistically related to these personality boundaries is tolerance of ambiguity, the lack of which impedes learners' ability to acquire high-context languages and blend into high-context cultures readily.

4. The knowledge of learning strategies, their relationship to learning styles, and the ways in which to help students expand their strategy repertoire for creating style flexibility and having more learning tools available, as well

as a way to help students more fully understand and incorporate human learning principles into their approaches to language study.

5. Insight into personality types, either Jungian (Myers & Myers, 1995; Jung, 1921) or Socionic (Filatova, 2009), how they influence individual learners, and the relationship between the learner and the teacher/mentor and peers, such that within any assembled visible classroom, another, invisible, classroom exists (Dabbs & Leaver, 2019; Ehrman & Dörnyei, 1998) in which the interpersonal dynamics among members of a class play out on a subconscious battleground in which less compatible personality types can create unspoken (or overtly articulated) dysfunction. One example of dozens of possibilities is the presence of two or more Extroverted (E), Intuitive (N), Thinking (T), Judger (J) (ENTJ) personality types,[10] each unconsciously striving for implicit (or explicit) leadership of the classroom.[11]

6. Further uncovering attributes of the invisible classroom beyond covert personality conflicts to include cognitive styles, demographics, learning histories, competing goals, out-of-class liaisons and conflicts, and other characteristics of significance in maintaining a functional classroom (Dabbs & Leaver, 2019), and beyond uncovering, coaching students to develop their own individualized study plans that accommodate their learning preferences and learning histories.

20.4 Conclusion

Understanding and helping students to address the cognitive distortions and affective dissonance that can otherwise derail their language learning goals is essential for successful teaching. Unfortunately, little research has been undertaken to date in identifying the psychosocial barriers to learner achievement in bilingualism and biculturalism. As TLLT becomes more pervasive, the necessity for expanding the study of linguistically related cognition and affect beyond the areas of distortion and dissonance to include all seven conceptual areas of potential insight proposed earlier will become apparent. Such research may well mirror findings of previous work in adult education, as identified by Oxford (this volume), both cognitive-analytic

[10] Each personality variable can conflict with its opposite when that personality is shared by a minority of the learners in a given class. Dabbs and Leaver (2019) lay out possible scenarios for each Jungian personality type.

[11] According to Keirsey and Bates (1987), the ENTJ is a natural leader who will vie with others (including a teacher) to be in charge. A TLLT mentor, aware of this indirectly expressed conflict, will design small-group activities that allow natural leaders to lead, natural followers to follow, and natural nurturers to support.

(Mezirow, 1990a) and emotional-integrative (Dirkx, 2012), with the aim of transforming how we teach as we proceed to work toward helping language learners become self-transformative as globally conscious lifelong learners.

DISCUSSION QUESTIONS

1. Consider the characteristics of less successful students in any of the classes that you are teaching. Could any of them be dealing with cognitive distortions? How would you find out? What would you do about it? How could you help the whole class manage their cognitive distortions?
2. Have students revisit a past assignment and reflect on how much easier this assignment is now that they are further along in their studies. Have them identify and discuss why this assignment was challenging and why it is easier. This reflection and discussion allows learners to see personal gains and hear the strategies employed by the most successful students.
3. Reflect on your own language learning. When did you experience effective coaching or mentoring that helped you overcome a cognitive distortion? Is there a particular cultural experience that you can replicate for your students? How can you mentor and coach the most successful students so that they continue to grow?

PART VI

Faculty Development

21

Incremental Drivers of Transformative Learning among World Language Preservice Teachers

Martha Nyikos

This year-long study investigated the specific ways in which teacher candidates perceive, frame, and process their own transformations as they grow into their roles as teachers. It investigates the type of transformations to which preservice teacher candidates (PSTs) aspire and later lay claim, while working through two methods courses, three microteachings, and 80 hours of field experience. This study addresses the sources, dilemmas, and critical drivers of change in PSTs' self-concept as they strive toward their aspirational teacher selves through reflections on readings, discussions, planning, and the implementation of lessons, and, most significantly, through repair and peer co-construction of their performance in post-teaching critiquing sessions.

21.1 Background

As Freeman and Johnson (1998) note, preservice teachers are not blank slates as they enter teacher education programs. They have goals and images of what type of teacher they aspire to become and are also knowledgeable of many potential pitfalls, having observed and critically evaluated the instructional practices of their former teachers (Labaree, 2004; Lortie, 1975). These preconceived conceptualizations regarding best teaching practices serve as a powerful influence on their reception and interpretation of key pedagogical issues such as the primacy of oral speech, learner-centered classrooms, and fostering communicative competence. These, in turn, impact the ways in which they see their own roles in the classroom and the instructional practices that they consider most effective (Johnson, 1996), though are frequently not in line with current thinking and practice (see Lyman-Hager et al., this volume).

Expanding the parameters of PST conceptualizations and pedagogical beliefs is the basis of a constructivist approach (Bruner, 1990; Vygotsky, 1978/2013), whereby PSTs are challenged to ever greater precision in defining and shaping their pedagogic knowledge base. These complex processes demand a safe, supportive learning community, where members are united in the stresses and challenges of incorporating standards of the profession and research-based best practices into their teaching. In order to encourage critical analysis, the successful completion of courses is dependent on the active social sharing of beliefs and reactions to best practices, as well as deeper reflections on a number of key issues. Self-assessment and robust assistance in shaping one another's planning, implementation, and improvement of teaching is another vital component.

Yet, even with assignments designed to elicit expansions in pedagogic understandings, the ability to "construe a new or revised interpretation of the meaning of one's experiences in order to guide future action" is elusive (Mezirow, 1996, p. 162). Frequently repeated concrete examples, experiential data, accountability, and repairs to lessons in peer cooperative sessions do not guarantee substantive changes in perception, beliefs, or practices that manifest themselves in subsequent teaching demonstrations.[1]

Transformative learning to effect change in future language teachers can best be explored through multiple means to capture the incremental shifts in perceptions and views reported by PSTs themselves. In this study, preservice teachers were asked to rely upon past and ongoing teaching experiences (Lortie, 1975) to discover, unpack, and critically analyze their own core beliefs regarding the principal cognitive and affective dimensions that directly impact the strategies that they employ to optimize their teaching of a new language. By closely scrutinizing critical reflection as a tool for reaching transformation (Akbari, 2007; Farrell, 2009, 2015; Mezirow, 1990a), the difficulty in shifting paradigms (see Leaver, this volume) and the strong hold of previous learning experiences become evident (see Lyman-Hager et al., this volume). The deep divide between the acceptance of a pedagogic or language learning strategy and the factors that intervene and cancel out the consistent implementation of those strategies in lesson planning and classroom teaching is brought into sharp relief for PSTs in this way. One assignment used to capture early aspirations included the PSTs' initial essays, in which they enumerate their goals for the methods courses for world language teachers. PSTs were asked to describe the qualities and pedagogic practices of their aspirational teacher selves, linking them, in turn, to specific experiences and individuals. Responses to these questions revealed PSTs' pedagogic knowledge base and their interpretation of the approaches, methods, and strategies that they considered to be a good fit with their beliefs about best practices.

---

[1] Salyer and Leaver (this volume) suggest that cognitive distortions and affective dissonance disrupt the ability to transform in these ways and, in effect, derail potentially successful learning experiences.

21.2 **Method**

Using a constructivist lens to trace and analyze teacher candidates' evolving understandings of their practices, the research questions included:

1. Which factors are the predominant drivers of transformation among preservice world language teachers?
2. How do PSTs identify, reflect on, and describe their pedagogic/linguistic stances and transformations?
3. Which push factors need to be implemented by teacher educators to effectuate transformative practices?

Participants comprised 21 preservice world language education majors (predominantly late-term juniors and seniors) at a large university. The PSTs were enrolled in a sequence of two world language standards-based methods courses – one focused on K-6 and one on 6–12 teaching. This program follows American Council on the Teaching of Foreign Languages (ACTFL) teacher competencies related to second language acquisition (SLA), methods of language teaching, and student assessment, and is accredited through the Council for the Accreditation of Educator Preparation(CAEP)/ACTFL.

Data sources include microteaching video transcripts, peer feedback (spontaneous and structured), preservice teachers' written reflections on their microteaching videos (guided by questions), four teaching essays, and an end-of-course self-report on PSTs' three sources of perceived change or transformation in their teaching journey. Data derived from these sources were thematically analyzed using an iterative process (Creswell, 2007/2013) to seek answers to the research questions posed by this study.

21.3 **Procedures**

21.3.1 **Focal Assignments: Microteaching, Peer Feedback, Reflections**

Language teacher educators focus much attention on teacher reflection as a key means of promoting teacher candidate insights on learning (Akbari, 2007; Borg, 2006, 2012). Through multiple, structured reflective assignments, PSTs were guided toward uncovering their thinking and insights about teaching, and their beliefs regarding the ways in which their potential students learn. Yet, chasms divide PSTs' specific goals and insights about effective language teaching from their actual implementation as documented in the focal assignments that served as the key data sources for this study.

21.3.2 Microteaching and the Co-construction of Changes/Repairs

During three assigned microteaching presentations, PSTs took on two roles:

1. participating fully as "students," pushing PSTs to consider the strategy needs of the learner; and
2. maintaining pedagogic metacognitive critical awareness as teachers.

This dual role, with its two very different perspectives, was challenging and took practice to implement effectively. After the initial microteachings, the peer cohort responses consisted mainly of very general, amorphous comments of praise: "You did really great – that was interesting." As a teacher trainer, it became necessary to spell out specific guidelines for the debriefing sessions:

1. undergird all praise with specific references to lesson components or teacher behaviors/actions, for example, providing a learning strategy; and
2. prepare to provide a minimum of two ideas, techniques, formative assessments, spurs to student oral production, or student challenges that will enhance and help repair or augment the lesson.

This affirmative co-constructive paradigm for the feedback sessions evolved over time as PSTs were challenged to be more critical and exacting in what they shared. They were encouraged to treat the lesson plan in an objective fashion – separate from its implementer. It proved to be far easier for the PSTs to express needed repairs to the lesson plan, slowly transitioning to critiquing its implementation. Over time, an evolving collegiality defined the social-constructivist stance toward one another of the PST group profiled here.

Each PST completed three video-recorded microteachings of 20 minutes each during two semesters with their PST peers as their students. This data source was analyzed to gauge the extent to which the theoretical and practical course information had been put into practice over time. Growth in the self-assured delivery of lessons was also evaluated. Each required microteaching lesson was immediately followed by peer-led intensive debriefing sessions, which were also recorded, transcribed, and analyzed. Subsequently, the presenting PST submitted written lesson repairs on the basis of oral peer feedback and their peers' written personalized critique for the "teacher's" further consideration and written reflections. Data from these recordings, reflections, and repairs served as the main data source reported here.

Written reflections and video transcripts were analyzed closely to identify the emerging categories of pedagogical knowledge and transformation. The qualitative data analysis was done in four stages, using open coding to discern the major categories and then axial coding to further analyze one of the major categories – transformative learning – into subcategories. The PSTs' self-identified pivotal changes in viewpoints and beliefs regarding their teacher identity and pedagogic practices fell into three subcategories:

1. personal/conceptual: cognitive apprenticeship, disorienting dilemmas (e.g., explicit versus implicit teaching);
2. social/cultural: impacts of peer and cooperating teacher critiques/advice (e.g., comprehensibility of lessons); and
3. emotional/affective: risk-taking (e.g., solo microteaching).

21.4 Results

While many pivots toward transformation were made, resistance factors also persisted.[2] Following the first post-microteaching oral peer debriefing, the expectation was that repairs would mirror what had been discussed. While this was largely true, preservice teachers needed guidance to resolve many unaddressed repairs and to be pushed toward greater specificity and variety in doing so through dialogic exchange with the teacher-trainer. Although PST "teachers" had seemingly comprehended the areas of need discussed in class, changes in the lesson plan and their reflections showed that the depth of reconceptualization needed for actionable changes to the lesson plans – let alone their implementation – had been insufficient.

A few PSTs resisted the requirement to repair past lesson plans, choosing rather to begin planning their next microteaching. This impatience to move forward rather than to revisit past performances was evident from how seldom students accessed their past teaching videos. Recorded lessons were available to PSTs throughout the course, yet most PSTs watched their microteaching once or only partially, relying on their memory to repair their lessons and write their reflections. In subsequent microteaching lessons, it became apparent that several PSTs did not implement the repairs that they had written or acted on the feedback on specifically addressed aspects of lesson planning and execution, believing that they had absorbed the critiques sufficiently without needing to "dwell on them."

21.4.1 Evidence from Reflections

After the second microteaching, there was some evidence of incorporation and an expansion in the conceptualization of some pedagogic steps. There was a

---

[2] This phenomenon does not adhere only to teachers in the US. Cleret (this volume) reports a parallel situation at the War College in the French Ministry of Defense, where she supervises the English language program and managed resistance through compromise, as do Sifakis and Kordia (2019) in their preservice and in-service work with English language teachers in Greece.

modicum of increase in the quality of those aspects of the lesson plans that had undergone "repairs"; however, this was more evident in the thoughtful insights shared in reflections. PST teachers commented on:

1. aspects of their plan/implementation that were omitted (i.e., a cultural component, the ongoing performance assessment of outcomes);
2. aspects that were not sufficiently delimited in either time or content (i.e., presenting the entire conjugation of an irregular verb rather than focusing on oral practice of the first- and second-person singular);
3. aspects of the lesson that were ineffectually implemented (i.e., the shaping of pronunciation, supplying rather than eliciting oral speech, comprehension checked in the aggregate, more teacher talk than student talk); and
4. reasons for poor time management (i.e., the poor pacing of activities, the inefficient modeling of tasks).

After making changes to the original lesson plan, the importance of those adjustments was pondered in the reflections. These revealed the strong hold of habit and of familiar pre-existing images of teaching (Lortie, 1975), which caused PSTs to struggle against reverting to a traditional bifurcation of the class to teacher presentation followed by pair work. The concern expressed in many of the reflections was finding a good fit with their aspirational teacher persona and the more assertive ways introduced to build linguistic competence. While PSTs accepted in theory the need to maximize the productive use of language, their dilemma was in demanding what they framed as tedious repetition or stressful assessment to measure whether students had achieved the lesson's stated goals. The issue of "putting students on the spot" surfaced repeatedly during peer debriefings. Following one microteaching, several PSTs stated that they hated to single students out, preferring to ask for volunteers. While they admitted that the silent students may not be comprehending the material, they felt that it was critical to refrain from embarrassing students.

21.5 Discussion

What emerges from the discussions, written reflections, debriefings, and repairs is a strong undercurrent of belief: if the teacher is likable and connects with students in the affective domain, the PST's love of language and culture will transfer, leading to achievement and agency. As PSTs reflect on approaches and techniques that suit their conceptualization of their teacher role and identity, they often mention teacher likability ("being perceived as the 'fun' teacher") and its direct link to language learning. This belief was quite resistant to change or even small pivots in perspective, and was central to the rejection of classroom practices that were perceived as commanding or demanding in favor of practices seen as inviting and enticing.

In their reflections and end-of-course self-reports on three sources of perceived change or transformation in their teaching journey, PSTs identified and described pivotal and transformative experiences, which fell into three major subcategories.

21.5.1 Personal/Conceptual

PSTs who mentioned impactful changes in their thinking in this category described them as a deeper understanding of the value of or need for building their pedagogic skill in particular areas. While their belief in the primacy of oral speech in the language classroom had been greatly strengthened, they profiled their continuing dilemma in eliciting student voice, and their struggle to move away from habitual paradigms for the teacher–student use of the target language.

21.5.2 Sociocultural

Personally impactful shifts in pedagogical beliefs and self-perception fell most often into this category. PSTs identified smaller and larger pivots in their thinking as well as changes that they tagged as transformative (see Crane & Sosulski, this volume). PSTs reported their surprise regarding the unexpected constructive impact of peer critiques regarding a wide variety of issues in their microteaching debriefing sessions, including the comprehensibility of lessons, the creative formulation of lesson structures, and the teaching of learning strategies. Clarity and self-confidence gleaned from peer PSTs' feedback, substantive support with lesson planning, revisions, and empathetic dialogue were mentioned frequently.

Finding one's personal teaching style within the aspirational teacher self was a major driver in seeking synergy between the demands of the profession and what works for each individual PST. These realizations, identified by PSTs as pivotal and even transformational, came indirectly through the need to "put themselves out there" during actual teaching. Although teaching was the anvil, pivots were forged in the cauldron of constructive criticism, productive debates, and peer affirmation. It was in the immediacy and perceived safety of post-microteaching debriefings that PSTs felt they had experienced changes in their perspectives, stances, and self-conceptualizations. In the heightened emotional state immediately after teaching, the time to process and reflect on positives and negatives in an honest forum with similarly invested, empathetic colleagues created the conditions for pivots and shifts in perspectives and lesson instrumentation. PSTs expressed gratitude for the self-discovery facilitated by peer appraisal.

21.5.3 Emotional/Affective

Responses on the final reflection regarding risk-taking (e.g., solo microteaching) evidenced growth in self-confidence each time PSTs taught. Standing in front of a group of peers tested both their skill and resolve, rewarding them with the conviction that they were competent to engage learners effectively. Even if the microteaching demonstration had not gone well in the eyes of the PST, their growing self-efficacy and discipline in having faced the challenge, especially in front of peers, was described as pivotal.

21.5.4 Incremental Drivers of Transformation among PSTs

The practical demands of attaining the competency and requisite skills to align with their ideal *aspirational teacher selves* is the most potent driver of transformative learning. However, these transformations, as reported by PSTs, are best described as a series of smaller pivots, that is, an accumulation of insights and changes in PSTs' conceptualizations resulting in reorientations, shifts, and expansions in perception and practices (see Crane & Sosulski, this volume). Significantly, those identified by the PSTs as pivotal all have a socio-emotional component associated with their growing sense of competency and confidence (see Oxford, this volume). The dominant concern expressed by the majority of PST teachers is how they wish to be perceived – both by themselves and their future students and superiors. The most oft-repeated adjectives are "competent," "caring," and "confident."

Push factors by teacher educators to effectuate transformative practices might include facilitation toward greater specificity and concrete examples in discussions, post-teaching repairs, and reflection on underlying beliefs related to practices in PSTs' teaching. In order to maximize the possibility of pivotal changes in planning and implementation, push factors could include greater accountability through awarding repair points for PSTs who address missing components, coupled with incentives to provide specific, substantive strategies and techniques during post-microteaching with presenters.

Changes in perspective and changes in the beliefs constituting their pedagogic knowledge base were described by the majority of teacher candidates as small, incremental pivots or formative experiences rather than transformations. Rarely did preservice teachers characterize a change in perception that they described as transformative. Smaller and larger pivots were the norm; PST teachers were generally hesitant to describe changes in their thinking as rising to the level of a transformation.

21.6 Conclusion

Preservice teachers can be nudged toward transformations through the use of features and approaches based on constructivist and social cognitive theory. As a general group, PSTs frame the changes in their beliefs more conservatively as expansions or pivots, rather than full 360 revolutions or transformations. Methods and techniques that "work," that is, creative approaches that "make sense" to them or that PSTs perceive as enriching their skill set to teach a linguistic feature or to incorporate cultural dimensions into the lesson, still need to align with their core pedagogic beliefs and aspirational self-images. These beliefs are amalgamated and tightly intertwined with PSTs' projected aspirational conception of their optimal teacher selves, which lie at the heart of each socio-emotional shift at pivotal points identified by the PSTs as meaningful. In their reflections, preservice teachers perceive that they "own" those pivotal experiences, which have strong emotional components and directly impact their evolving sense of their teaching competence and style. The most frequently identified pivotal moments are connected with those that bolster self-confidence and are strongly tied to their social peer group's input, which was ascribed greater significance than the more policy-oriented feedback received in post-teaching debriefings.

The role of the teacher educator is one of moving aspects of more effective teaching into PSTs' immediate consciousness amid peer support and in the context of the very immediate moment of the teaching performance (rather than future teaching), and guiding future teachers through necessary pivots toward their aspirational selves. When done in increments, the PST uptake is substantive and potentially transformative.

DISCUSSION QUESTIONS

1. A major disorienting dilemma reported by PSTs is the tension between their wish to put students at ease juxtaposed with the need to challenge them to step outside their comfort zones (particularly in oral language production) in order to achieve a high level of measurable outcomes. What specific strategies can be given to PSTs to enable them to develop optimal challenge and reward structures to achieve their pedagogic goals?
2. As teacher educators, what are some ways in which we might capitalize on the finding that PSTs' positive socio-emotional peer relationships had the

greatest impact on changing pedagogic beliefs and practices? How can these social bonds be best utilized when PSTs encounter disorienting dilemmas that might foster the positive transformation of perspective?

3. One of the most powerful shifts in PSTs' pedagogic understanding is an orientation toward the needs of the learner for the sufficient and explicit modeling of content and strategies. How can we more effectively introduce PSTs to high-leverage teaching practices such as the simultaneous modeling of task instructions with the illustration of the target language to be produced?

22

Transformative Aspects of Teacher Education and Training for Preservice Instructors of Chinese and Japanese

Cornelius C. Kubler

To prepare to teach English-speaking learners "truly foreign languages" such as Chinese and Japanese,[1] preservice instructors[2] of these languages must in a number of ways transform their thought and behavior as regards language and culture generally, and language learning and language teaching specifically. To some extent, this is true for all instructors of Chinese and Japanese but it is especially critical for native-speaking instructors who grew up in Asia, who now make up the majority of preservice and in-service instructors of these languages.

These native-speaking instructors are not blank slates when they begin teacher education and training programs; they have been influenced by their learning of their native language, their learning of English and other foreign languages, and the education that they received in their native countries. Without doubt, there is much of value in what they bring to the table. However, since the process by which they learned their native language differs from the process by which their English-speaking students will be learning Chinese or Japanese, these instructors often need to transform in basic ways how they view language learning and language instruction. Moreover, some of them may have already taught Chinese or Japanese as a second or foreign language for a period of time. These instructors' preconceived notions regarding education and language teaching tend to have a strong impact on their reception, interpretation, and implementation of a number of key instructional and professional issues.

22.1 Examples of Issues Requiring Transformative Learning

Discussed in the following are a number of basic issues typically requiring the transformation of thinking and behavior on the part of preservice instructors

---

[1] The term "truly foreign languages" was coined by Eleanor H. Jorden to refer to languages that are not cognate with English linguistically or culturally (Jorden & Walton, 1987).

[2] In this chapter, the term "preservice instructor" refers primarily to instructors who are being trained to teach native English-speaking adults at American colleges, universities, and government language schools.

of Chinese and Japanese because these issues do not exist or do not exist in the same way in Chinese and Japanese society. The following section includes common examples and is not meant to be comprehensive.

22.1.1 The US Educational System and Classroom Culture

The US educational system and classroom culture differ greatly from China, Taiwan, or Japan. New teachers from East Asia must learn about the relationships at US educational institutions among the classroom instructor, department head, dean, and school president – and whom to contact when about which kinds of issues (Kubler, 2006). There are also classroom management issues with which new instructors need to become familiar, including how to handle learners who misbehave or are chronically absent or late. Another important question is that of student–teacher boundaries, for example, is it acceptable for students to address teachers by their first name or for teachers to attend parties with students?

In the USA, certain questions to students, especially if asked in a public setting, would ordinarily be inappropriate, for example, asking if students are on financial aid or how much their family earns, or questions regarding politics, religion, and sexual orientation. There are numerous other aspects of US classroom culture that will surprise new instructors from Asia, for example, in many US classrooms, students may leave the classroom to go to the bathroom without asking for permission from the instructor.

22.1.2 The Role of the Teacher

In East Asia, education has been a very teacher-centered and teaching-centered process for thousands of years. However, learner-centered and learning-centered foreign language programs have been shown to be more effective (Nunan, 1988). Instructors certainly play an important role in facilitating and managing the learners' learning but it is the learners who are at the center of the enterprise and bear the responsibility for learning.

Instead of serving as a disseminator of knowledge, as is typical in East Asian cultures, an effective teacher of Chinese or Japanese as a second or foreign language serves as the designer of the curriculum and facilitator of instruction. Instead of lecturing, they generally find it more effective to set up situations where learners interact with each other in the target language to accomplish tasks with observable outcomes, with the instructor critiquing and mentoring as needed. In transformative language learning and teaching (TLLT), the role of teacher largely transforms to that of counselor or guide, who helps learners identify learning needs and then assists them in attaining their communicative goals. The ultimate goal is to help learners better understand both others and themselves.

22.1.3 Act–Fact Distinction

For most adult foreign language learners, the most effective method of language learning consists of large amounts of language practice and use (termed "Act") combined with smaller amounts of analysis and explanation (termed "Fact") about pronunciation, grammar, word choice, society, and culture (Jorden & Walton, 1987). Act and Fact are presented at separate times in the curriculum; during Act, only the target language is used, while during Fact, English may be used, albeit minimally.

The Act–Fact distinction is related to other dichotomies with which preservice instructors need to become familiar, including training versus education, language acquisition versus language learning, and experiential learning versus academic learning. The recently much-cited model of the "flipped classroom,"[3] where the instructor does not present new information, but rather facilitates the practice and use of language with which learners have already familiarized themselves prior to coming to class, represents one way of implementing Act and Fact.

22.1.4 The Primacy of Spoken Language

When they think back to how they learned their native language, preservice instructors from China or Japan typically remember learning reading and writing in school, where there is great emphasis on learning the Chinese characters, but they tend to forget that when they began reading and writing, they could already speak their native language, which they learned naturally at home. Moreover, in both Chinese and Japanese societies, the written language – think Chinese calligraphy – is accorded deep respect. Thus, it seems strange to some of them that in basic-level Chinese and Japanese classrooms in the USA, training in the oral skills should receive priority and be seen as the foundation for reading and writing.

In both Chinese and Japanese, the division between the registers of the spoken language and the written language is particularly large, which has implications for the point in the curriculum where Chinese characters are

---

[3] Contrary to the impression of many, the flipped classroom model is actually not new, but has been implemented in various ways (e.g., through textbooks, phonograph records, open-reel tapes, cassette tapes, and computers) at US government language training institutions since the 1950s.

introduced, as well as the manner in which reading and writing are taught. At the basic level, oral and written skills are best taught from separate but related materials; as oral skills are easier to acquire and, for most learners, more immediately useful, priority should be devoted to speaking and listening comprehension (Kubler, 2001; Kubler, 2006). The learning of written skills proceeds more efficiently if learners study for reading and writing only words that they have previously learned for speaking and listening comprehension. In this approach, learners already know the pronunciation, meaning, and usage of a word, and need only learn its written representation, which substantially lightens the learning load.

22.1.5 Transcription Systems

Since the Chinese characters used in Chinese and Japanese are difficult to write and do not indicate pronunciation in a systematic and consistent manner, it can be useful to employ transcription systems (such as Hanyu Pinyin for Chinese or Kunreisiki Romanization for Japanese) at the beginning stages of language learning. It is important to realize that transcription does not equal pronunciation; transcription is nothing more than written symbols designed to remind one, in a rough manner, of the sounds that should already be stored in the brain. Pronunciation can only be learned from native speakers or audio recordings. Learners should be introduced to the sounds of a language before they encounter transcription (Jorden & Walton, 1987; Kubler, 2006).

22.1.6 Writing Systems

Contrary to the impressions of most native speakers, the Chinese writing system is a mixed system, consisting of not only simplified and traditional characters, but also alternate characters, Arabic numerals, the uppercase and lowercase letters of the Roman alphabet, mathematical symbols, other special symbols, punctuation, and a transcription system such as Pinyin or Zhuyin (Kubler, 2017). The Japanese writing system is similarly a mixed system, consisting of numerous components. To make matters even more complex, in the writing systems of both of these languages, there are different handwritten and printed versions of many characters, in an assortment of different font styles, with the option of formatting the text either vertically or horizontally.

Learners need practice in reading texts that are representative of all of this possible variation. Chinese characters should always be taught in context. When selecting characters to be learned, the frequency of occurrence should be taken into consideration, with some characters taught for both production and recognition, and others taught for recognition only.

22.1.7 Culture

Language is a part of culture. Language is so deeply intertwined with the particular culture in which it is used that language instruction should always be immersed in a cultural context. Although this is true of all languages, it is especially critical in the case of Chinese and Japanese, which differ so greatly from English linguistically and culturally (Jorden & Walton, 1987; Kubler, 2006).

Varying kinds of culture exist: behavioral, informational, and achievement culture (Hammerly, 1982). These should be taught using the target language in and outside the classroom, at different times and in differing ways, depending on the level of the learners. In the beginning language classroom, the focus should be on learning the language in its behavioral cultural context.

As pointed out by Fischer and Garza (this volume), educational technology can be transformative and alter a learner's worldview since it allows us to bring culture into the classroom and provide learners with almost unlimited access to cultural materials. Educational technology can also enable both teachers and learners to make more efficient use of time by moving certain kinds of language learning tasks out of the classroom and freeing up valuable classroom time for those interactive learning activities that require a "live" instructor.

22.1.8 Curriculum

As discussed by Campbell (this volume), open architecture curriculum design (OACD) can enable instructors to more efficiently meet the learning needs of their students. Under such a system, learner input can be used to adjust the curriculum and focus of each lesson as needed since, in many cases, learners may be clearer than their instructors about their current and future language needs. Such an approach is very different from the lecture- and textbook-based, inventory-centered curriculum to which most East Asian teachers are accustomed.

Rather than orthodox works of literature, reading passages can be chosen from newspapers, advertisements, emails, and text messages, and may include larger social and global questions. The use of authentic materials, both oral and written, can give learners exposure to language as used in the real world and provide them with opportunities to develop strategies for discovering the meaning of unfamiliar material. Depending on learner needs, the curriculum may include modules on language for specific purposes, for example, business Chinese, Chinese for diplomats, Japanese for healthcare professionals, and so on.

22.1.9 Lifelong Language Learning

The concept of lifelong language learning (Walker & McGinnis, 1995), in a succession of different learning environments, including but not limited to the classroom, is novel for many new East Asian instructors. For example, learners might begin their study of a language in one course at a US university, then take part in a study abroad program in Asia, then continue in another course at a different US institution, and finally learn and use the language on their own for a number of years in Asia or the US.

A long-term outlook is essential if learners are truly to attain professional levels of proficiency in difficult languages. A successful language course emphasizes teaching learners how to learn and helping them develop into self-reliant, lifelong language learners who are able to assume responsibility for their own learning (see Little, this volume; see also Wenden, 1991).

22.1.10 Other Issues

There are many other issues and concepts with which preservice instructors of Chinese and Japanese need to become familiar. They include but are not limited to: the concept of communicative competence (as opposed to inventory-based approaches such as character counting or word counting); modes of communication (interpersonal, interpretive, and presentational); interactive versus noninteractive listening; intensive versus extensive reading; different motivations for language study; learning styles; and assessment systems.

22.2 Implementing the Needed Transformations

Training programs for preservice teachers face the challenge of transforming teachers so that the teachers can, in turn, transform their students. Now that we have identified important issues for which transformative learning is typically required, how do we go about convincing preservice teachers to change? According to Mezirow (1991), "disorienting dilemmas" are needed to shake learners' belief systems and cause them to transform their thought and, most crucially, their behavior. Based on the author's experience at a number of different training programs for preservice teachers of Chinese and Japanese, there follows a list of several types of activities that can serve as "disorienting dilemmas."

22.2.1 Acquisition of Relevant Knowledge

Dissemination and careful study of information about the key issues listed earlier is one useful way to facilitate transformations in preservice instructors' ways of thinking and behaving. Readings, lectures, and class discussions about these topics can ensure that preservice instructors acquire the requisite knowledge.

22.2.2 Discussion of Preservice Instructors' Language Learning and Study Abroad Experiences

Discussion of the successes and failures of preservice instructors' own language learning is another useful way to promote transformative thought and action. As Davidson et al. (this volume) have pointed out, study and residence abroad can itself be transformative, especially when supported by opportunities for reflection and discussion. Therefore, preservice instructors would do well to discuss "disorienting dilemmas" experienced during their own study, work, and daily life in the US and other countries.

22.2.3 Observation of Classes in Familiar and Unfamiliar Languages Taught by Master Teachers

According to a well-known Chinese proverb, 百聞不如一見 Bǎi wén bù rú yí jiàn ("Hearing about something one hundred times is not as good as seeing it once") or, to cite a similar English proverb, "Seeing is believing." Preservice instructors would benefit from observing language classes taught by master teachers. These observations could include both languages with which the preservice instructors are familiar and unfamiliar languages since observers tend to notice different phenomena when observing in these two types of situations. After the class observations, there should be a discussion of what has been observed both with and without the master teacher present.

22.2.4 Taking a Course in an Unfamiliar Language Taught by a Master Teacher

Even better than observing a class is taking a course in a completely unfamiliar language taught by a master teacher. This could be for just a few hours but would preferably be for several weeks or longer. Such an experience has value on multiple levels, including: observing effective learning and teaching in action; understanding the challenges and pressures that language learners face; and, of course, encountering yet another "disorienting dilemma."

22.2.5 Demonstration Teaching

One of the best ways to learn is by doing. As Confucius is quoted in the *Analects*: 學而時習之，不亦樂乎？ Xué ér shí xí zhī, bú yì lè hū? ("To learn something and at the appropriate time to put it into practice, is this not a pleasure?"). A strong teacher education and training program provides trainees with ample opportunities for practice and demonstration teaching, including

video-recording the demonstration class for the preservice instructors to view
and critique later. Watching a video of one's own teaching can, by itself, be a
most disorienting dilemma!

The demonstration teaching should also be observed by a master teacher,
who can critique and discuss it with the preservice instructors afterwards.
Before that critique, the preservice teachers should try to critique and reflect
on their own teaching, based on criteria that have been discussed beforehand.
When scheduling the demonstration teaching for the preservice instructors,
it is usually best to begin with fairly short segments consisting of one or two
specific learning activities, which can be a portion of a longer class taught by
the regular instructor. Over several weeks, one can gradually build up to an
entire class period.

22.3 Conclusion

As we have seen, there are a number of important issues that can drive the
transformation of thought and behavior in preservice instructors of Chinese
and Japanese. Through the activities and "disorienting dilemmas" described
earlier, many preservice teachers are able to successfully change their outlook
and adjust their teaching. However, even after participating in these activities,
it may prove difficult or impossible for some to transform their thinking and
behavior.

Whether an individual instructor is willing or able to be transformed
ultimately depends on the individual. In some programs with which the
author has been associated, a few preservice instructors have openly rejected
unfamiliar ways of teaching, while others have sometimes "gone through
the motions" without really believing in the underlying principles or being
convinced of the value of what they were doing. It is not possible to transform
every new teacher. However, if given the appropriate training and allowed
sufficient time to reflect on and discuss their training experiences, the
majority of preservice instructors are able to effect transformations in their
thinking and behavior so that they are able, in turn, to transform their own
students.[4]

---

[4] The views expressed in this chapter are based on the author's experience in educating and
training language and culture instructors in: the Chinese and Japanese sections at the Foreign
Service Institute, US Department of State; the MA in Teaching of Chinese Program at
Middlebury College; and the Alliance for Language Learning and Educational Exchange
(ALLEX) Chinese and Japanese Teacher Training Institute.

DISCUSSION QUESTIONS

1. The examples cited in this chapter of issues requiring the transformation of thinking and behavior on the part of new Chinese and Japanese language instructors reflect certain assumptions about effective language learning and teaching. List several of those assumptions. Do you agree with these assumptions? Why or why not?

2. If you have learned or taught Chinese or Japanese in the past, give examples of issues where your views and practices have changed over time. Why did you make these changes?

3. Interview several instructors of Chinese or Japanese about changes in their views and practices concerning language teaching since they first began teaching.

PART VII

Assessment

23

Identifying and Evaluating Transformative Learning in the Language Classroom

Cori Crane and Michael J. Sosulski

Learning another language is a complex and enriching process. However, language learners do not always immediately recognize the profound learning outcomes – such as a deepened understanding about others and oneself – that often emerge through the experience. Johnson (2015, p. 93), who studied "Bella," a college student enrolled in a first-semester Spanish course, describes how learners and educators can have very different perspectives on the learning process:

> [W]hen I asked Bella what she had learned in her Spanish class, she described her progress in terms of learning to speak. I have pored over her learning journals and interview transcripts and I know that she was also learning about cultural and linguistic differences, about connections between her own life and the target culture and about what it takes to learn a language. Yet, Bella herself did not recognize these experiences as learning.

Despite Bella (and her fellow students) consistently seeing "*learning* Spanish as synonymous with *speaking* Spanish" (Johnson, 2015, p. 93, emphases in original), Johnson observed rich, multifaceted learning among the students that went beyond traditional interpersonal communication skills. While the learners here viewed their work primarily through a skills-based, instrumental lens, Johnson adopted a *transformative learning* approach that afforded her a view of student learning as deep, complex, and meaningful. Most notably, she valued the ways in which the students' "frames of reference" (Mezirow, 1991) about the course material and themselves had changed. How to help language learners to recognize and appreciate such perspective-shifting moments is the focus of this chapter. Employing the holistic model of transformative learning, our discussion looks specifically at how reflective practice – considered a cornerstone of perspective transformation – can be used to foster and assess shifts in one's meaning perspective.

23.1 Understanding Transformative Learning

Despite a range of diverse theories that serve to explain how transformative learning happens (see Oxford, this volume), general consensus in the scholarship points to perspective transformation as a core goal (Cranton & Taylor, 2012;

Kasworm & Bowles, 2012; see also Leaver, this volume). Indeed, a shift in perspective – and what an individual then does with their transformed meaning perspective – sets transformative learning apart from other types of learning that focus on developing deeper understanding (Brookfield, 2000; Cranton & Taylor, 2012).

Mezirow's (2000) list of ten non-sequential processes pertaining to perspective transformation continues to be the most influential theoretical model in shaping the field's understanding of the transformative experiences of adult learners, and has served as a foundation for studies that have sought to track the presence and process of transformative learning in individuals (Boyer et al., 2006, reviewed in Snyder, 2008; King, 2004; Kitchenham, 2006; Stansberry & Kymes, 2007). In the model, a catalyzing event, or *disorienting dilemma*, conflicts with and creates discomfort in one's current meaning perspective. Through a series of events that follow involving critical reflection, dialogue with others, and intended and actual actions, this dilemma can lead one to re-examine existing assumptions and thereby expand and alter one's frames of reference.

By recognizing students' personal dilemmas as potential "pedagogical entry points" (Lange, 2004, p. 129, cited in Taylor, 2009, p. 6), instructors interested in fostering transformative learning are positioned to anticipate difficult, complex topics and activities in their pedagogies that may nudge students toward shifting perspectives in developmentally appropriate ways. For assessment, understanding where in one's pedagogy such learning opportunities lie is an important first step to understanding how transformative learning can be evaluated.

The pathway toward perspective transformation is not always linear, clear, or complete – a factor that complicates how one goes about evaluation. Moreover, individuals often require time to process their own resistance and change their attitudes when confronted with new meaning perspectives (Featherston & Kelly, 2007). The highly individualized, context-dependent, and variable hallmarks of perspective transformation explain why assessing such learning is challenging and why many transformative learning scholars question evaluating transformative learning as an appropriate goal. Although Mezirow's ten processes of perspective transformation have been successfully applied to coding and tracking transformative learning in adult learners (see, e.g., King, this volume; see also Kitchenham, 2006; Stansberry & Kymes, 2007), the danger persists that such research may overly rely on outcome (whether transformative learning occurred) at the expense of the more pertinent question of process (what transformative learning looks like) (Snyder, 2008).

Cranton and Hoggan's (2012) review of commonly used instruments for evaluating transformative learning (e.g., self-evaluation, interviews, narratives, observations, surveys, checklists, and journals) highlights tools designed to track the process of perspective-shifting as learners develop understanding about themselves, often through self-report or follow-up reflection. Determining appropriate tools depends on how one defines transformative learning, which aspects of the theory one wishes to prioritize, and what purpose assessment ultimately serves. While interviews, observations, and checklists may be appropriate tools to measure development towards perspective transformation over time, for program-wide assessment (e.g., student learning outcomes), transformative pedagogies in the classroom typically employ self-report, often in the form of journal or narrative writing, to support and evaluate the skills that underlie the ability to transform one's meaning perspective, namely, critical reflection on one's assumptions.

23.2 Structured Reflection for Transformative Learning

Transformative pedagogies create intentional spaces for learners to critically reflect on incremental changes in their own perspectives as they become aware of and question their frames of reference vis-a-vis key course concepts (Kiely, 2005; Slavich & Zimbardo, 2012; Snyder, 2008). In the language classroom, consciousness-raising activities involving dialogue and extended reflective time have been found to contribute to perspective transformation (Johnson, 2015; Johnson & Mullins Nelson, 2010; King, 2000). As a formative assessment tool, written structured reflection allows instructors to evaluate learners' critical reflection abilities as learners practice articulating and interrogating their assumptions about central course concepts (Crane, 2018; Sosulski, 2013). In the following, we describe how multiple, interconnected guided reflection opportunities help language learners to engage their frames of reference.

Drawing on transformative learning research on study abroad experiences (Anderson & Cunningham, 2010; Cunningham, 2010; Cunningham & Grossman, 2009), this model of structured reflection encourages learners to connect three broad areas of knowledge: (1) "assumptions held"; (2) "theories/concepts known"; and (3) "experiences encountered" (Cunningham, 2010, p. 25). Each reflection prompt guides students to consider moments when these different ways of knowing are similar or when they contrast or even conflict, setting up opportunities for perspective transformation. A first prompt asks students to articulate their initial assumptions, while a second, acting as a type of "secondary reflection" (Moon, 2006, p. 112), directs students to revisit their first reflections and examine their assumptions. In this way, the prompts build on each other, encouraging students to notice small changes in their perspectives that naturally occur as part of the language learning process. What does success look like in this evaluative scheme, and how does an instructor discern good reflective writing from poor attempts that are less likely to lead to transformation of one's meaning perspective?

23.2.1 Evaluating Structured Reflection

The evaluation rubric presented in Table 23.1 assesses learners' written reflections across five criteria: completeness; specificity; engagement with course material; connection-making; and clarity.

This rubric highlights the type of engagement proposed in Cunningham's (2010) triangular model of structured reflection described earlier and reflects common criteria in assessing student journal writing (see, e.g., Moon, 2006). Importantly, perspective-shifting itself is not a criterion for evaluation; rather, active student engagement in the reflection process is prioritized.

To illustrate how the rubric and individual reflection prompts (see Table 23.2) work in tandem, more and less successful learner reflections are examined. Examples come from first-semester German courses (spring and fall 2014) at a state university located in the Southwest US, in which students responded in English to three to four prompts over the course of the semester. Due to space constraints, only excerpts from the student reflections are presented.

23.2.2 Prompt One: Articulating Assumptions

We begin by looking at examples from the first reflection prompt that beginning German learners completed one week into the semester. In the first of two prompt questions, students were asked to identify assumptions that they held about the German language and explain where and how these ideas developed. Here, learners were not expected to engage with the course's content material, but rather to articulate a baseline understanding that they could refer back to in later reflections. As such, a rich, detailed first reflection gives learners substantive material to work with and reflect on later. The extent to which students demonstrate an ability to think deeply about their understandings becomes a key criterion in evaluating their reflections.

The following example represents a strong response to this first prompt, which calls for a descriptive account of students' beliefs:

> Before joining German class, I did not have many assumptions about the language or know much about it. The few facts I knew about the German language came from TV shows, movies and readings. From Inglorious Basterds [sic] and Band of Brothers I learned that Germans count differently on their fingers. From reading books like *The Book Thief* and watching

Table 23.1 Structured reflection evaluation rubric

	A	B	C	D
Overall assessment	A strong reflection (an "A" paper) addresses the questions in the prompt in rich detail and with specific examples, engages thoughtfully with the class material,[a] and makes connections between learning in and outside of the classroom			
Completeness	Addresses questions in prompt fully and with rich detail	Addresses questions in prompt adequately with some detail; some points may require further elaboration	Addresses questions adequately but minimally, with little detail	Does not address questions adequately; no detail given
Specificity (as contrasted with vagueness)	Provides specific examples to illustrate and/or support ideas discussed	Provides some examples to illustrate and/or support ideas discussed but may be underspecified	Examples provided are vague and need specification	No examples are given to illustrate or support ideas
Engagement with class material	Responds to class material thoughtfully and critically (e.g., dialogues with and asks questions of material, attempts at synthesizing materials, etc.)	Responds to class material with some thought but response may lack critical awareness	Draws minimally on class material	Does not draw on class material
Connection-making	Makes rich connections between learning in the classroom and experiences outside class (including from traveling, previous coursework and study, personal connections, media and entertainment sources)	Makes some connections between learning in the classroom and outside experiences, though may require further elaboration	Makes few substantive connections between learning in the classroom and outside experiences; more elaboration needed	Makes no connections between learning in the classroom and outside experiences
General writing and awareness of audience	Writes very clearly and shows evidence of writing for an external audience	Writes clearly most of the time, though some mechanics may distract and lead the reader to question the meaning of a passage	Writes clearly only some of the time and shows little awareness of an audience	Does not write clearly (i.e., conceptually randomized writing); shows no evidence of writing for an external audience

Note. [a] For certain reflections, students may not be asked to engage with specific class material. This is likely to be the case for the first reflection.

Requires effortless reading and understanding of ideas ⇔ considerable effort required by reader to follow the flow of ideas

Table 23.2 Structured reflection prompts one and two

Prompt one: Learning German	Prompt two: Interrogating assumptions about learning German
This is a writing exercise in which you use the mode of reflection to think about your experiences and what they mean to you. We call this "structured reflection" because the idea is to focus carefully on a couple of specific aspects of your experience, with the goal of learning from them.	In the last reflection, you were asked to identify and describe your assumptions and understandings of the German language and consider your personal language learning goals when it comes to German. In this reflection, you will be engaging with these assumptions and looking deeper into your developing understanding of the German language.
Please write two paragraphs based upon your personal experience.	Please take one (or two) assumptions that you identified in your first reflection about the German language or the learning of German, and consider how you might respond to – or even challenge – these assumptions now that you have been studying German intensively for a month. What new insights are you seeing? Are there certain experiences from the course (e.g., through coursework, class discussion, homework, etc.) that have shifted your initial perspective(s)? Are you seeing connections to experiences outside of your German class that are providing new understandings about the German language or the learning of it?
The German language: Before you joined this class, what assumptions or notions about the German language did you have? Where and how did these ideas develop?	
Personal language learning goals: What do you hope to learn and do with the German language by taking this course? What do you envision the learning process looking like for you? Do you have strategies that you think could help you in learning German? Do you have questions that you would like to pursue?	

movies and documentaries that involved the German language I learned a few German words and came to recognize the harsh/strong, for lack of better words, German accent. One of the few things I knew for sure before taking this class was that German is a base language for English. I learned this fact in one of my Spanish classes when we learned about language origins. One of my old co-workers is fluent in German and has spent lots of time in Germany. He told me that many Germans know English however they do not like to speak it. I am a huge F. C. Bayern fan and enjoy watching them in their interviews, which, for the most part, are in German, so I have come to pick up a few terms. (Journal 1, fall 2014)

This reflection can be considered successful for several reasons. The writer addresses the prompt fully and with rich detail and connects their specific understandings to a diverse range of experiences with German – from media and entertainment, to prior coursework and individual people. Of course, not all students will have a wealth of prior, direct experiences with the language to draw on for such a reflection; what matters at this stage is that students describe one or two prior assumptions, regardless of origin, in ample detail.

By contrast, a second response to the same prompt represents a weaker reflection, with discussion marked by vague language, blanket statements, and minimal detail:

> Before I joined my German class I had the assumptions that German was really entertaining and cool to listen to but most definitely a challenging language to conquer. My dad is fluent in German and my family has traveled in and around Germany countless times, so the German culture is not completely foreign to me. (Journal 1, fall 2014)

The information presented remains on a surface level, which is all the more remarkable given the student's previous experiences with the language and culture that could have been elaborated. While the rubric does not address text length, the relative brevity already indicates the likelihood of a shallow treatment of the prompt. Feedback to this student might therefore include questions that probe detail behind the statements: What do you find entertaining or cool about German? Can you think of specific moments, for example, from your travels in Germany? What do you find challenging about the language? I'm curious, how might one "conquer" a language? Are there other relationships to learning a language that one can have? Such formative assessment encourages learners to acknowledge their taken-for-granted assumptions, thereby preparing them for further reflection work, as seen in the next prompt.

23.2.3 Prompt Two: Interrogating Assumptions

The second prompt asks learners to interrogate at least one assumption that they had described in their first reflection. The following two examples show common features of weaker reflective writing. In the following example, a learner boldly states that their earlier assumptions remain unchanged:

> After being exposed to more than a month to [sic] German I have come to a few conclusions. None of my original ideas have changed; I like German and always have especially after my obsession with WWII grew. However, I have found out how difficult it is to get the gender right in nouns. (Journal 2, spring 2014)

The concern here is not the assertion itself, but rather the lack of deeper engagement with the original assumptions and continued reliance on vague generalizations at the expense of detailed examples (For example, what does the student continue to like about German?). Follow-up questions to nudge students toward this thinking include: What were your original ideas again? Did anything from the course so far (or elsewhere) confirm or expand your assumptions and understandings about German?

A common pitfall in reflective writing is misinterpreting such assignments as primarily content summaries of what one has learned in class. In the following example, a learner sidesteps the main task, that is, questioning assumptions, and instead presents a list of language and cultural points that they have learned:

> I have learned the conjugations of many verbs such as Heißen, Sein, Sprechen, Wohnen, Essen, Lese, Machen, Finden.... Some of these verbs are alike with [sic] English verbs helping me to acquire a better understanding of certain verbs. I have learned more about German history and culture such as the creation of euro, the story of Otto Von Bismarck, Oktoberfest, and main holidays like Mardi Gras, Christmas Eve, Christmas, and German Unity Day that is related with the fall of the Berlin Wall that reunited Germany as a whole. (Journal 2, fall 2014)

Without further exploration of what this self-assessment means for the learner and their understandings of studying German, the student misses the opportunity to look more deeply into their frame of reference. In responding, the instructor can ask the student to make themselves more visible in the piece and include affective responses: Were you surprised to see the connections between English and German? How do these connections help you in your learning of German? Has your learning about the culture and history of the German-speaking world changed some of your initial ideas about the language? If so, how?

A more successful realization of this task shows how this second prompt can provide students with an opportunity to reconsider initial assumptions in light of course learning. Table 23.3 depicts the different reflection moves that a learner employs in re-evaluating their previously stated assumption that German is a harsh language, a popular view among novice learners of German (Crane, 2018).

We see that this student addresses the prompt fully, provides rich detail (particularly in thinking about childhood experiences with the grandmother), gives examples to illustrate different viewpoints, and connects experiences both in and outside class with their previous assumptions. From the standpoint of perspective-shifting, the tool of structured reflection provided a framework within which the student was able to see German differently. Instead of viewing the language as noise, the learner adopted a view of language as meaningful

Table 23.3 Successful reflection moves

[...] Another assumption I mentioned in the first reflection is that German sounds harsh. This view was formed from hearing my grandmother's German exclamations as a kid. Although this assumption was based on a first-hand experience, I have begun to think otherwise.	**Identifying and questioning validity of the assumption's source**
After learning German for a month, I don't find the language to be as harsh as I once did. A reason for this is that I have been hearing the whole language rather than just exclamations. My grandmother always spoke in English (else no one would have understood her!) When she would insert a German exclamation, the different sounds didn't sound right, sandwiched between English phrases.	**Questioning and re-evaluating original assumption**
Now that I hear full sentences and paragraphs, I have begun to appreciate the different sounds found in the language. I watched the film, *Das Kalte Herz* ["*The cold heart*"], and I was totally used to German sounds by the end of it. After four days of German per week, I have come accustomed to hearing the throaty noises that appear in the language. I think that once I learned and accepted these different sounds, I lost the view that German is harsh.	**Reflecting on previous assumption in light of current learning**

Source: Journal 2, spring 2014.

discourse. This type of reflection represents the sort of emergent reflective writing found in later stages of Hatton and Smith's (1995) model, which treats development as movement from pure description to greater reflection on experience through an increasingly multifaceted contextualized lens.

The preceding examples share a view of assessment that prioritizes the learner's individual journey and level of engagement. Through cumulative steps guided by prompts and questions, students are afforded the opportunity to reframe their meaning perspectives. Given the longitudinal, complex, and often nonlinear nature of transformative learning, it is unlikely that complete perspective transformation will occur over a course or semester. For this reason, the focus of evaluation in structured reflection must remain on the discrete steps required to transform one's meaning perspective over time: examining assumptions; comparing and contrasting new course concepts with one's prior beliefs; and processing one's life experiences in light of new learning and prior beliefs.

23.3 Conclusion

Assessing for transformative learning encourages educators to consider the nature of perspective transformation, as well as the diverse transformative learning affordances found in their pedagogies and curricula that may promote dissonance and deep reflection. As teachers view their practice through a transformative learning lens, they are better able to help their students do the same.

The overall goal of structured reflection is to trigger metacognition in students through the use of reflective writing. The tools and methods of assessment, like the rubric shared earlier, therefore seek to identify and evaluate perceptible signs of the metacognitive process taking place, rather than the presence or absence of a fully transformed perspective. It is noteworthy that, as with Johnson's student, Bella, some students do not evince a conscious awareness of perspective-shifting, despite having participated successfully in the course in many other ways. This type of cognitive development occurs over time and is aided by an assessment practice aimed at identifying and rewarding self-observation and connection-making, which are the building blocks of a transformed meaning perspective.

DISCUSSION QUESTIONS

1. In this chapter, we saw how structured reflection prompts can encourage learners to express and question their assumptions about the target culture. What kinds of assumptions do *you* think your learners might have about the language that you teach? Where do *your* assumptions about their assumptions come from? (The advanced move: Ask your students about their assumptions, e.g., in a reflection prompt, and compare their responses to your own assumptions. Were any of your own ideas about your learners' ideas challenged?)

2. A common question that emerges for language teachers when contemplating the use of reflection in the classroom is the choice of language: Should students reflect in the target language, their first language, or a combination of both? Consider the pros and cons of reflecting in different languages.

3. The prompts in this chapter focus students' attention on their relationship to the target language and its cultures. What other themes could be explored in structured reflection prompts for beginning second language learners, especially for learners who may have few experiences with the target language to draw on in their reflections? What would these first and second prompts look like?

24

Testing and Transformative Language Learning
Ray Clifford

Both the definition of *transformative education* offered in this volume and the definition of *transformative teaching* offered by Slavich and Zimbardo (2012) agree that the goals of transformative learning go beyond the acquisition of knowledge and include personal development. Slavich and Zimbardo (2012, p. 597) posit that transformative teaching may be applied at any level of instruction but add that our understanding is still limited in this area: "Exactly how transformational teaching[1] is represented at these different levels of instruction, however, remains an open question. It seems reasonable to hypothesize that the amount of structure that is required to realize transformational teaching goals will differ in a significant way across different levels of instruction."

24.1 Outcomes at Different Levels of Transformative Learning

If we treat "levels of instruction" as generic terms related to progressive stages of learning rather than levels in an educational system, there is a body of related educational research that may inform our thinking – and even shed light on how we might reasonably determine appropriate combinations of learning and personal development. Anderson et al. (2001) consolidated subsequent research findings and updated Bloom's taxonomy of cognitive learning, which was originally published in 1956. Their revision modified the original, unidimensional "Bloom's taxonomy" into a two-dimensional scale. One dimension contains a hierarchy of types of *knowledge* that begin at the factual level and progress to the metacognitive level. The second dimension describes categories of *cognitive development* that progress from rote memorization to higher-order cognitive behaviors. From a transformative perspective, it seems

---

[1] The terms "transformative" and "transformational" have been used interchangeably in the literature to date, including by Mezirow himself. In this volume, the editors have chosen to abide by the use of one consistent term, and the one that has been most commonly used in recent years: *transformative*.

Table 24.1 Bloom's revised taxonomy

		Remember	Understand	Apply	Analyze	Evaluate	Create
Knowledge dimension	Metacognitive						
	Procedural						
	Conceptual						
	Factual						

justifiable to relabel this cognitive-development dimension as the personal-development dimension. The resulting two-dimensional model is depicted in Table 24.1.

Anderson et al. (2001) give examples of instructional outcomes for each level of each dimension. Theoretically, each of the 24 interaction cells in the matrix in Table 24.2 could be a valid instructional outcome; however, it is not often that one is expected to combine rote learning with creative cognitive processes, and metacognitive strategies are developed, not memorized.

Table 24.2 shows the same matrix depicted in Table 24.1 but with the commonly co-occurring interactions of knowledge and cognitive behaviors combined into three categories. From left to right, these commonly occurring interaction nodes are labeled in ascending order: *direct application, near transfer,* and *far transfer.* A brief description of each of these types of learning follows.

Table 24.2 Three common combinations of types of knowledge and levels of cognition

		Remember	Understand	Apply	Analyze	Evaluate	Create
Knowledge dimension	Metacognitive					Far transfer	
	Procedural						
	Conceptual			Near transfer			
	Factual	Direct application					

With *direct application* learning, students:

- memorize and practice specific responses;
- focus on the content of a specific course, textbook, or curriculum; and
- learn only what is taught.

With *near-transfer* learning, students:

- go beyond rote responses and use rehearsed and semi-rehearsed responses;
- focus on a specific set of tasks within a limited number of communicative settings and respond within those domains; and
- apply what they learn within a range of familiar, predictable settings.

With *far-transfer* learning, students:

- develop the ability to transfer what is learned from one context to another;
- acquire the knowledge and skills needed to respond spontaneously to new, unknown, or unpredictable situations; and
- learn how to continue learning and to become independent learners.

24.2 Relating These Three Levels of Learning with Levels of Affective Experiences

In the article "From ordinary to extraordinary: A framework of experience types," Duerden et al. (2018) describe three levels of experience: memorable, meaningful, and transformative. These three types of experiences are clearly among the "attitudinal and behavioral changes that instructors can reasonably pursue during a course" (Slavich & Zimbardo, 2012 p. 597). In brief:

- At the *memorable* level, there is an emotional experience, which makes the experience memorable, but no insights are gained.
- At the *meaningful* level, the emotional experience leads to new insights or understanding.
- At the *transformative* level there is an emotional experience with insights and that combination leads to reflection and a change in attitude and/or behavior.

As Duerden et al. point out, each of these three types of extraordinary learning experiences can be either positive or negative. In fact, they suggest that negative experiences are often the most impactful and instrumental in motivating transformative learning.

Planning for and providing memorable, meaningful, and transformative experiences is challenging in any educational domain but teachers attempting to do so in language courses must also consider the communication capabilities of their students. Learners with direct application second language (L2) abilities are still communicating from a personal, "me" perspective. They can certainly have emotional experiences, but because of their limited L2 abilities, insights will more likely be gained through supplementary first language (L1) activities.

Learners with near-transfer skills will have some emerging abilities that allow them to recognize and adjust to the reactions of others. They can use those emerging L2 skills to gain insights from their emotional experiences and have meaningful experiences. However, they will not yet have developed the language skills necessary to work through a reflection process in their L2. Therefore, L1 activities should be provided to help these learners turn meaningful experiences into transformative experiences.

Learners with far-transfer skills will have the L2 skills needed to analyze, reflect on, and turn meaningful experiences into transformative changes in their attitudes and behaviors. For this level of learners, transformative learning activities can be conducted in their L2 (as well as in their L1).

24.3 The Testing Dimensions of Instructional Environments

Whether language testing supports or detracts from transformative teaching and learning is dependent on the learning environment, and the learning environment is determined by interactions among three instructional components: knowledge content, learner behaviors, and outcomes assessment. Each of these components is multidimensional and includes a continuum of options.

Using the three commonly occurring interactions of direct application, near transfer, and far transfer provides a rational way of merging testing and assessment considerations into the three-stage model of transformative education. Fortuitously, these learning categories have parallel assessment categories: achievement testing, performance testing, and proficiency testing. Unfortunately, these three terms are often used interchangeably, resulting in statements like "He has achieved a high level of proficiency," and "She performed well on that achievement test." Semantic confusion is further heightened by the reality that tests are sometimes categorized by their purposes rather than their content. As a result, the same test may be called a "placement test" or a "diagnostic test" depending on how it is being used. For the purpose of this discussion, we offer the following descriptions of three main types of language tests.

Language achievement tests measure:

- practiced, memorized responses;
- the acquisition of what was taught; and
- the content of a specific textbook or curriculum.

Language performance tests measure:

- rehearsed and semi-rehearsed responses;
- one's ability to respond in constrained, familiar, and predictable settings; and
- the transfer of learning to similar situations.

Language proficiency tests measure:

- whether skills are transferable to new tasks;
- spontaneous, unrehearsed abilities; and
- the general ability to accomplish tasks across a wide variety of real-world settings.

When instructional outcomes and assessment procedures are aligned within the categories of direct application, near transfer, and far transfer, a plethora of interacting variables are reduced to three contrasting constellations – and with that understandable model, we can explore how testing choices can support or detract from transformative learning.

24.4 The Instructional Impact of Testing and Assessment Practices

The desired learning outcomes of a course or instructional program are usually labeled "desired learning outcomes," "student learning outcomes," or simply "learning outcomes." Such learning outcomes can be the basis for establishing what transformative learning calls a "shared vision" of course expectations; however, students do not yet have those abilities, so they seldom understand the complete meaning of those stated outcomes. Instead, it is the testing procedures used in the course that provide the operational models that define for students the "real" objectives of a course or instructional program. In fact, the impact of testing practices is so great that tests can undermine a teacher's efforts to implement transformative learning. In formal learning environments, the tests or assessment methods used are such powerful influences that they determine *de facto* the students' knowledge and behavior goals.

Learners, especially adult learners, do not want to waste their time studying what is not going to be "needed," and tests typically define what is going to be "needed." The question "Is that going to be on the test?" is a common refrain in school settings. As a result, tests can have a negative or a positive wash-back effect on transformative learning.

Testing has a *negative* impact when not aligned with the desired learning outcomes. This misalignment happens when, for instance:

- educational goals are reduced to those that are most easily measured;
- multiple choice tests are given in language courses that have the stated goal of improving speaking skills; and
- grammar tests are used as a measure of general language proficiency.

Testing has a *positive* impact whenever the tests are aligned with the desired learning outcomes. This alignment allows tests to:

- clarify teacher expectations;
- reinforce shared course objectives;
- inform teaching and learning practices; and
- provide useful models of mastery experiences.

24.5 Aligning Tests to a Shared Vision of the Desired Learner Outcomes

Instructional goals and testing are aligned when:

- achievement tests are used to assess the direct application of low-level knowledge;
- performance tests are used to assess the near transfer of rehearsed abilities in familiar settings; and
- proficiency tests are used to assess learners' far transfer of unrehearsed, internalized abilities across a range of real-world abilities.

The careful alignment of teaching and testing is too often ignored, and when they are not aligned, learning will suffer. When learning suffers, teachers' efforts to create a transformative learning environment are set back or even stymied. Two contrasting examples may suffice to demonstrate the need for assessment practices that are aligned with teachers' instructional practices.

Example 1

The teacher of a beginning language class recognizes the need for students to build a repertoire of memorized greetings, but then the teacher uses (or is forced to use) tests of general language proficiency to measure the students' learning. The results are highly predictable. The learners will not be prepared for the tests, they will fail, and their motivation will be reduced.

Example 2

The teacher of an advanced language course has established learning outcomes expressed in terms of *can-do statements* and has negotiated a shared vision for the course based on those real-world communication requirements. Then, because of limited time or department policy, achievement tests are administered that focus on discrete vocabulary and grammar points. The students may do well on the test, but they will see that the test was less demanding than they had anticipated. As a result, the students will adjust their learning to match the level of the tests. Motivation and the disposition to pursue higher-order learning and related behaviors will be reduced.

24.6 A Systemic Flaw That Hinders Transformative Teaching

There is a major systemic flaw within most institutional instructional systems – a flaw that is hindering the implementation of transformative learning. Testing is a part of that systemic flaw.

What is this systemic obstacle that hinders transformative education? The obstacle is an educational philosophy that conflicts with the goals of transformative education. Whereas the goals of transformative education are individualized and expansive, the general trend in instructional institutions has been to make the curriculum, teaching, and testing practices increasingly collective and reductive. In a section titled "The limitations of formative assessment," Popham (2008, p. 121) points out how standardized tests and state-mandated content standards are unworkable and are being ignored. This reality is largely the result of the instructional systems design (ISD) procedures that are applied by curriculum developers.

Typically, the application of ISD has four stages. The first step in the ISD process is often referred to as the *front-end analysis*, where a study is done to determine the communication needs that the learners will encounter in real-world settings. At this early stage, learner needs and desired learning outcomes are collectively determined for all future learners. In the second step of the ISD process, curriculum developers review the identified array of communication needs and (because of space limitations) select a subset of those communicative interactions for inclusion in a textbook. In the third ISD step, teachers use the resulting textbook to organize their teaching, at which point they invariably find that there is too much material to cover during the available instructional time. The teachers' prevalent coping strategy for dealing with limited class time is to limit the depth of their teaching so that they can present as much of the material in the textbook as possible within the time available.

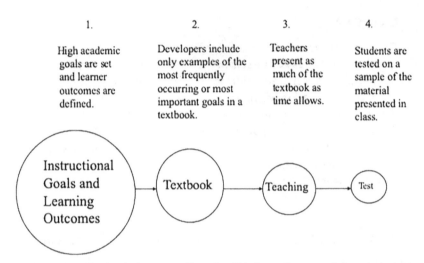

1.

High academic goals are set and learner outcomes are defined.

2.

Developers include only examples of the most frequently occurring or most important goals in a textbook.

3.

Teachers present as much of the textbook as time allows.

4.

Students are tested on a sample of the material presented in class.

Figure 24.1 Reduction in the scope of learning. This figure illustrates that curriculum, instruction, and testing practices can reduce the scope of learning.

A further reduction in the scope of instruction occurs when the students are tested. As pointed out earlier, for students, it is the tests that define the "real" learning outcomes of a course. Since the time available for testing is only a fraction of the time devoted to teaching, the scope of learning is further reduced to those items "that will be on the test." Figure 24.1 depicts this step-wise reduction in learning.

To maintain an expansive view of learning and create an environment where learners are striving to enhance their learning, teachers must consciously work to counteract the institutionalized pressures that otherwise result in a step-by-step reduction in learning opportunities – a reduction that shrinks both the quantity of the knowledge that can be acquired and the development of students' cognitive abilities.

Figure 24.2 attempts to show how teachers can overcome reductionist educational practices by linking both the examples in the textbook and the items included in tests back to the more expansive, real-world communication tasks that are of interest to individual learners. Given the time constraints in most instructional programs, transformative teaching will only be possible if teachers resist the pressure to "cover" the entire textbook at the direct application skill level, and instead devote more time to teaching near- and far-transfer skills. Of course, these near- and far-transfer abilities must also be regularly assessed (in a formative way with personalized feedback) to motivate the students and to provide them with models and mastery experiences.

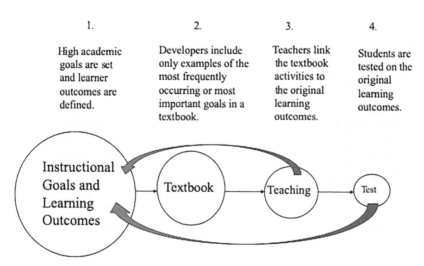

Figure 24.2 Re-expansion of the scope of learning. This figure illustrates that "good" teaching (reinforced by "good testing") can re-expand the scope of learning.

Applying this open curriculum syllabus (Clifford, 1988) requires changing the role of the textbook. Instead of the textbook serving as the entirety of the course, it can be used as a springboard or starting point for instruction. Changing the perceived role of the textbook will also change the role of the teacher from a presenter of information to a facilitator of individual learning. In this more flexible instructional environment, teachers will be freed to individualize learning and motivate learners to strive for higher-order communicative abilities – and there will be more time to implement transformative teaching (see Figure 24.2).

24.7 Integrating Assessment into Transformative Language Teaching

Slavich and Zimbardo (2012, p. 597) describe the following six transformative teaching activities as *core methods*:

1. establishing shared vision for the course;
2. providing modeling and mastery experiences;
3. challenging and encourage students;
4. personalizing attention and feedback;
5. creating experiential lessons; and
6. promoting preflection and reflection.

Each of these elements can be made more effective through the use of assessment procedures that are aligned with transformative teaching practices. Further, if nonaligned assessment procedures are permitted, then those nonalignments are likely to reduce or even nullify teachers' attempts to implement transformative practices. Of particular importance is building programs that include testing practices that go beyond low-level direct application items and assess near-transfer and eventually far-transfer behaviors. It is transferable learning that provides operational manifestations of the shared vision of outcomes and mastery experiences that make learning intellectually challenging and promote a lifelong view of the educational process.

Obviously, testing is not the only component of the instructional process that can derail attempts to create a transformative learning environment. However, tests can have an inordinate impact on learning – and yet that impact is too often overlooked.

24.8 Conclusion

Transformative teaching and learning can be made more effective through the use of assessment procedures that are carefully aligned with one's instructional goals. If nonaligned assessment procedures are used, then those nonalignments will reduce, or even nullify, teachers' attempts to implement transformative practices. If time constraints are incentivizing the coverage of textbook content over more meaningful forms of learning, or if external pressures are forcing a reliance on easily scored, direct application testing procedures, then those misalignments can sabotage teachers' efforts to implement transformative learning activities.

Finally, it is also important to maintain alignment between the students' second language abilities and the learning activities, such as the analysis and reflection tasks that are essential components of transformative learning. Transformative instructional strategies for beginning students are most effective when implemented in the students' first language.[2]

DISCUSSION QUESTIONS

1. Do testing practices have an impact on transformative learning? Have you seen evidence that testing practices influence the study practices of learners? Which kinds of assessment practices best support transformative learning?

---

[2] This conclusion is based on extensive personal experience with a wide range of languages and proficiency levels, as well as extrapolated from many of the chapters in this volume.

2. How should a teacher reconcile conflicts between the breadth or depth of a course's expected learning outcomes and the limited time available for learning? Would it be better for the students to develop far-transfer abilities in a fewer number of objectives, or would it be better for the students to develop a wider range of direct application skills? How should teachers respond when they perceive that their students' rate of learning is not keeping up with the prescribed pace of instruction?

3. How should teachers prepare students for the reality that some transformative experiences will be negative? What can a teacher do to prepare students to learn from negative experiences? Would it be ethical for teachers to deliberately design instructional activities where students are likely to have negative but impactful learning experiences?

25

Assessing Students in a Transformative Learning Program

Jeff King

Assessment of *transformative learning* carries unique challenges due to key aspects of the transformative experience that are often difficult for faculty to recognize and for learners to communicate. Additionally, there is an affective component frequently involved in the struggles prompted by disorienting dilemmas and the subsequent perspective shifts that accommodate students' new ways of making sense of self, others, and the world.

This is not to say that assessing transformative learning must always remain a slippery construct. There are ways to track and measure student progress across an arc of development in beyond-disciplinary and life skills and mindsets that are hallmarks of good employees, entrepreneurs, artists, citizens, and family members – humans that are, in short, creators, not just consumers. However, faculty must generally be trained in this process because such skills as creating good reflective prompts and spotting individual learners' idiosyncratic expressions as they attempt to articulate felt shifts of worldview are not typically developed while earning the graduate degree/entrance ticket for application to the professoriate.

Across five years of institution-wide work, the University of Central Oklahoma (UCO) in the US has met the challenge of eliciting and assessing transformative learning. Lessons learned and specific, replicable processes and tools are shared in this chapter.

25.1 Challenges in Assessing Transformative Learning

Jack Mezirow is frequently named as transformative learning's foundational theorist (e.g., Hoggan et al., 2017; Kitchenham, 2015; Swartz & Sprow, 2010). Mezirow referred to critical reflection as a key component in transformative learning (Taylor, 2017) because learners' reflections on disorienting dilemmas are what help them expand their worldviews or think differently (Mezirow, 2006). This internal change was characterized nicely by Patricia Cranton (1998, p. 192), herself a major writer and researcher in the field, when she said that transformative learning happens when we are "led to reflect on and question something we previously took for granted and thereby change our views or perspectives."

These experiences, then, are often internal shifts in learners' perspectives. The internal nature of this process means that learners could have the transformation that comes, for example, in understanding that merely speaking a world language is wholly insufficient to relate to others in a different country but may not necessarily exhibit observable or measurable changes in the classroom demonstrating this new understanding.

Longitudinal observation of such learners within a foreign environment where they gain this transformative understanding and therefore change their actions and interactions might yield a valid assessment but logistical constraints are obvious, especially when trying to assess learners' world language (L2) acquisition in the classroom where there exists a fundamental transformative learning challenge: Can you recognize such a shift when you see it, and if it is an internal shift, how do you "see" it?

Further, even if there is not an obvious transformative learning-defined perspective shift/expansion, there may be valuable growth presaging the better integration of key understandings – something that serves to push learners forward to the transformative threshold (Snyder, 2008, p. 177). This is valuable information to collect as learners progress in the class and across the curriculum.

The preceding and remaining discussions in this chapter relate to assessing learners' internal shifts and changes or expansions in perspective, not to L2 proficiency development, for which there are already scales in existence. Processes to help measure learners' progress toward transformative realizations are important in L2 education because mere fluency is but part of understanding and communicating with people who speak a world language. Acquiring the transformative understanding that the way in which people in a culture act and communicate derives from multiple forces acting upon common humanity must link with an empathetic realization that can then undergird interactions with native speakers.

Due to the internal nature of any transformation, learners' written or other responses to reflective prompts are often used to assess transformative learning (Fullerton, 2010, p. 41) because this allows faculty to consider learners' reflective artifacts. These artifacts provide something tangible to help gauge learners' progress toward transformation. Such artifacts constitute self-reports, but a body of research indicates that these can be useful in assessing transformation (e.g., Brock, 2009; Guce, 2017), and Mezirow (1990b) himself puts forward critical reflection as the triggering process for transformative learning. However, having multiple ways to measure is recommended, both as good assessment practice in general (Huba & Freed, 2000; Maki, 2010; Rundle, 2016) as well as within L2 (Ghahari & Farokhnia, 2017), and to ensure that learners do not simply provide in reflections what they think instructors want to see as evidence of transformation (Featherston & Kelly, 2007, p. 266).

However, there is little doubt that reflecting on one's learning experiences helps improve outcomes beyond merely engaging in the experience (McGuire, 2015). As Di Stefano, Gino, Pisano, and Staats (2014, p. 30) state: "[W]e find that individuals who are given time to reflect on a task outperform those who are given the same amount of time to practice with the same task."

While challenges in assessing transformative language learning and teaching (TLLT) within L2 are perhaps many, the challenges inimical to TLLT are that the change process is internal and that transformation is often a longitudinal process that includes progress along the way toward a transformative understanding. A specific challenge in TLLT assessment is that the classroom is an artificial environment for gauging important student realizations. At UCO, the general transformative learning operationalization within the curriculum and co-curriculum includes multiple assessment points, student critical reflection, the rubrics-based assessment of progress toward transformative shifts, and student journaling within study abroad environments as mechanisms to prompt for perspective shifts about world language and culture as a necessary but insufficient component in appreciating and working within a foreign country.

UCO began including transformative learning in its mission with the 2008/2009 academic year. *Learning reconsidered* and *Learning reconsidered 2* (Keeling, 2004, 2006) were important resources for the president's cabinet in identifying transformative learning as the appropriate characterization of a UCO education along with campus-wide discussions. However, unique to UCO was the determination of specific categories within which student success initiatives and engagement occurred. These six categories became UCO's central six tenets: discipline knowledge; global and cultural competencies; health and wellness; leadership; research, creative, and scholarly activities; and service learning and civic engagement.

UCO began work in February 2012 on the student transformative learning record (STLR) process as its formal operationalization of transformative learning. An operational definition was therefore needed. UCO's became: transformative learning (1) develops learners' beyond-disciplinary skills and (2) expands learners' perspectives of their relationships to self, others, community, and environment (for extensive information, see UCO's STLR site: http://stlr.uco.edu/).

STLR enables faculty and staff to design, track, and assess activities in both the curriculum and the co-curriculum to help learners achieve transformative realizations within an authentically assessed, evidence- and badge-based environment built around student progress toward transformative realizations in each of the beyond-disciplinary central tenets. (Discipline knowledge progress is tracked via grades and the academic transcript, not via STLR activity.)

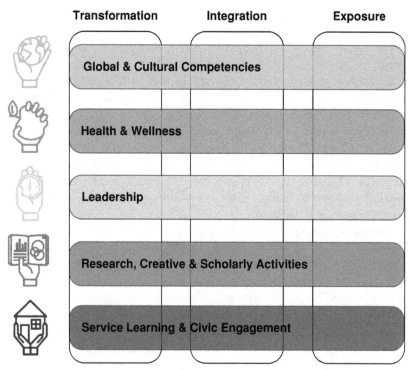

Transformation   Integration   Exposure

Global & Cultural Competencies

Health & Wellness

Leadership

Research, Creative & Scholarly Activities

Service Learning & Civic Engagement

Figure 25.1 STLR achievement badge levels. This figure illustrates the levels of achievement possible in student reflective artifacts as assessed using STLR rubrics in each tenet, ranging from the lowest assessment (exposure) to the highest (transformation).

The badge levels of achievement are named "exposure," "integration," and "transformation" (see Figure 25.1).

On the curricular side, one or more of the tenets are associated with at least one existing assignment in a class. Learners complete the assignment as usual but faculty also require a reflective artifact that becomes part of the assignment but that is assessed only using the STLR rubrics. The rest of the assignment is graded as usual. From the outset, UCO wanted to minimize work for already busy faculty; "STLRizing" a class does not involve creating a new assignment (unless that is something that the instructor chooses to do).

As an example, a statistics teacher has been using the textbook's data set for the central limit theorem homework assignment. To STLRize the assignment, learners could instead use a data set from the (OECD) Organization for Economic Cooperation and Development or similar website identifying distances from villages in certain regions to the nearest potable water. The instructor adds a global and cultural competencies reflective prompt to the assignment requiring learners to reflect on the reality of the nearest source of drinkable water in some parts of the world being an hour's walk away.

For most learners, that realization may prompt nothing more than awareness (they were "exposed" to the concept). For some, they may connect the reality to a greater awareness of living conditions in other parts of the world because they read a certain book in a literature class (they begin "integrating" and connecting). For some learners, the assignment might prompt a transformative realization leading to a life of service working with the disadvantaged.

In this example, the instructor adapted an existing assignment to a tenet; they were not asked to create an entirely new activity. Knowing how to do this successfully happens because UCO faculty are trained in STLRizing classes (including L2 classes), assessing learner outcomes with the STLR rubrics, how to create effective prompts, and so on.

No matter the assigned badge level rating of the reflection, UCO's "STLR Snapshot" captures the information. The Snapshot is both formative and summative for learners because they have access to it to "take a snapshot" of their progress toward beyond-disciplinary development. The Snapshot sits alongside the STLR mobile app badge achievement dashboard as a formative-summative tool. The Snapshot is summative when used for job interviews, for instance, and regardless of what learners choose to show on their Snapshots, everything has been vetted by university faculty or staff, with each Snapshot version carrying the registrar's imprint (see Figure 25.2).

Many of the world language sections at UCO have assignments associated with the global and cultural competencies tenet. Some L2 departments have adopted common STLR-tagged assignments across all sections of a course.

STLR training presupposes neither faculty familiarity with rubrics nor that faculty know how to write good reflective prompts, so these are key focuses in the training. Both training topics illustrate how STLR training is part of professional development, and UCO's STLR trainers work closely with the teaching center.

Assessment challenges, then, are that assessing internal shifts is inherently difficult, faculty are not trained in how to elicit statements and artifacts that demonstrate progress toward transformative understandings, and faculty may not know how to use rubrics. Additionally, one as-yet-unmentioned challenge is how to use the learning management system (LMS) to track and record this activity. STLR training addresses all of this.

25.2 Faculty Training in Transformative Learning Assessment

UCO's faculty training for how to assess transformative learning occurs in two three-hour segments. The first segment focuses on transformative learning's

Buddy Broncho
*00001234
****-**-1254
01/30/2017

STUDENT
TRANSFORMATIVE
LEARNING
RECORD

University of Central Oklahoma
100 North University Drive
Edmond, OK 73034

The purpose of this record is to provide a visual representation of this student's achievement in the University of Central Oklahoma's (UCO) Tenets of Transformative Learning.
This student's educational experience at UCO has resulted in achievements at the exposure, integration or transformation level as indicated below.
See the key on the back of this document for short descriptions of what these levels of learning indicate with regard to student knowledge and experience.
These experiences have been assessed and validated by trained faculty and professional staff members at the University of Central Oklahoma.

Leadership

Transformation
Integration
Exposure

1/4
4

▶ Organizational Comm. Capstone – Capstone Project/Reflection – Spring 2016 - Transformation
▶ Fundamentals of Speech – Passions Speech Reflection – Fall 2012 - Integration
▶ Conflict and Negotiation in Org – Case Study Reflection – Fall 2014 – Integration
▶ Corporate Training/Consulting – Training Design Artifact – Fall 2014 – Integration
▶ Interviewing Practices – Mock Interview – Spring 2016 - Integration
▶ Internship: Recruiting, Event Planning, and Marketing Strategies – Fall 2015 – Exposure
▶ Ted x UCO – Event Participant – Fall 2015 - Exposure

Service Learning and Civic Engagement

Transformation
Integration
Exposure

2/3
4

▶ Integrated Knowledge Portfolio Project (IKPP) - Fall 2015 – Transformation
▶ Internship: Recruiting, Event Planning, and Marketing Strategies – Fall 2015 – Transformation
▶ Success Central – Service Learning Activity Reflection Paper – Fall 2012 - Integration
▶ MLK Day of Service – Event Participant - Spring 2016 - Exposure

Research Creative and Scholarly Activities

Transformation
Integration
Exposure

1/3
10

▶ Intro to Organizational Comm. – Reflection Paper – Summer 2014 – Transformation
▶ Specialized Publications – Research Project Paper – Fall 2014 – Integration
▶ Media Production – Media Artifact – Fall 2015 – Integration
▶ Major Quest – Event Participant – Fall 2015 - Exposure
▶ General Biology – The Decline of Bees Film – Spring 2013 - Exposure
▶ LA Symposium – Event Participant – Spring 2016 - Exposure
▶ Internship: Recruiting, Event Planning, and Marketing Strategies – Fall 2015 - Exposure

Figure 25.2 STLR. This figure illustrates how one page of a student's STLR Snapshot might look, showing how they have arranged and arrayed STLR assignments and activities in which they have engaged along with the assessment for each regarding three of the five tenets shown on this page of their Snapshot: leadership; service learning & civic engagement; and research, creative, and scholarly activities.

theoretical underpinnings, a broad overview of how STLR at UCO works, creating good prompts to elicit student reflections, STLR rubrics, and badge levels to indicate achievement, and includes time spent assessing real-world STLR assignments and discussing the actual ratings given. The second segment focuses on work at the computer to set up STLR assignments and to record assessments within the LMS course shell. In this second segment, faculty are able to adapt an existing assignment with an STLR component and arrange everything in the course shell for an upcoming class.

STLR training drills down into creating good reflective prompts, which is not a skill set that most faculty possess. The training also offloads as much of the how-to-push-the-buttons-in-the-LMS aspect as possible to short, just-in-time, and on-demand video clips, thereby minimizing the amount of training time devoted to "doing STLR" within the LMS.

STLR training adapts to other institutions' cultures and missions, as demonstrated at other institutions that have "STLRized." STLR was built to be scalable, replicable, platform-agnostic, and free, with both two- and four-year institutions successfully adopting and adapting STLR.

One reason for STLR's success is the faculty training in how to assess transformative experiences. That reason holds for any institution focused on learner success and positively impacting learners' lives. While "success" might be couched for some faculty simply in terms of high grades achieved by learners, that is a reductionist approach focused on course content (see Clifford, this volume). However, faculty knowing that they have changed learners' lives – and possessing the proof – is something that generally happens only by accident in the absence of an intentional focus plus a supportive process to create this type of learner change.

Multiple UCO faculty have expressed the sentiment that "STLR helps me know better the impact I'm having on my students." Grades generally do not do this. STLR expands faculty's focus to consider the ways in which assignments and activities can impact learners in positive ways beyond simply learning course content.

25.3 Operationalizing Transformative Learning Assessment

Helping faculty learn to authentically assess STLR artifacts using the STLR rubrics is key to UCO's curricular implementation of STLR. Rubrics for the beyond-disciplinary tenets are built on the Association of American Colleges and Universities' Valid Assessment of Learning in Undergraduate Education (VALUE) rubrics (Rhodes, 2010), and then faculty can customize tenet rubrics to particular assignments. Two UCO world language instructors explained their personal take on the differences among STLR's badge-level ratings as they have learned to work with reflective artifacts: exposure, integration, and transformation.

25.3.1 Exposure

Learners demonstrate simple understanding that two cultures may differ in how they meet certain needs (safety, education, community life, food, etc.)

but that the human needs themselves are the same in both cultures, while external circumstances outside of the population's control may dictate how the needs are met differently (dictatorships, extreme poverty or affluence, etc.). Examining current events is a good tactic to illustrate the commonality of needs and reactions thereto. Being judgmental about the L2 culture is a sure sign of no advancement beyond exposure.

25.3.2 Integration

Learners actively and voluntarily participate in L2 and different-culture activities in order to "live" as nearly as possible within the other culture and in a way that is closer to real-world experience than classroom or structured experiences (e.g., hosting international students and speaking the language with them, or visiting areas of the city where the language is native and used in shops and restaurants) (regarding transformation and study abroad, see later).

25.3.3 Transformation

Both instructors agreed that many UCO students will struggle to reach transformation in L2 because of the monocultures from which they come (e.g., homogeneous small-town Oklahoma or underrepresented subculture environments). Study abroad experiences can prompt transformation but the experience must include good reflective prompts that elicit more than mere observation ("tourist experience") and more than mere interaction with native speakers (even if that interaction requires good L2 skills). What must occur is a felt realization that the culture is merely idiosyncratic compared to their own culture and is worthy of complete embrace while learning the expression of shared humanity.

Study abroad can be the triggering event that prompts transformative realizations, these instructors say (see also Davidson et al., this volume). The odds increase with good reflective prompts and when faculty leading the experience abroad arrange interactions with native speakers that enable a depth of exchange that allows for things like conversations about personal histories and the kinds of storytelling that elicit emotion around shared human experience.

25.4 Assessing Transformative Learning Assessment: Signals of Success or Failure

An early worry in UCO's STLR rollout was faculty inter-rater reliability concerning rubrics usage. Randomly spot-checking transformation-level ratings each term to ensure fidelity to rubrics continues to show faculty hewing closely to the rubrics. Faculty have welcomed this small "look over their shoulders," saying that such spot-checking is helpful because rubrics-based assessment is so new to so many of them. UCO has also had outside raters read through random, assessed reflective narratives; those raters note strong adherence to the rubrics.

Another concern was whether some faculty might "give out transformation-level ratings like candy" since there was no effect on the grade of the assignment, and because such injudicious STLR assessments might be easier than explaining an exposure-level rating to a perfectionist student. However, faculty stuck to their rubrics. One L2 example is as follows. An instructor led a group of students on a Guatemala study tour that included living and working with local populations to build a library. Some students' artifacts (journal entries kept throughout and after the trip) were assessed at integration level. Those students asked the instructor: "How could we have lived with these people and helped them build a library and not have gotten 'transformation'?" The instructor used the rubrics to explain the rating; the students understood, accepted the decision, and, in the process, learned more about transformative engagement.

Transformation-level assessments comprise 9–12 percent of badge-level assessments each term. The largest percentage of transformation-level assessments come from capstone classes. Regarding L2 instruction, UCO has so far seen study abroad yielding a higher number of transformation ratings than occurs in L2 classroom instruction.

Two other strong indicators that the assessment of STLR artifacts (as well as the entire STLR process) is successful concern improvements in retention and grade point averages associated with STLR. Figure 25.3 shows the retention/improvement story.

25.5 Concluding Thoughts, Recommendations, and Exciting Future Research

The STLR process develops beyond-disciplinary skills, mindsets, and motivations, many of which are crucial for L2 learners wishing to function well in world cultures. A graphic visualization of STLR's overall development of beyond-disciplinary skills appears in Figure 25.4.

STLR activity builds toward "twenty-first century work and life skills" on the map. For L2, the stops on the lines named, "able to collaborate," "cultural awareness," "political and organizational acumen," "communication skills," and others certainly represent the kind of beyond-disciplinary competencies that L2 faculty must help students to achieve for them to succeed in world cultures.

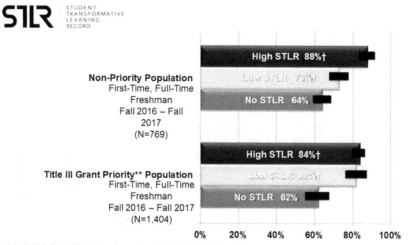

SΠR STUDENT
TRANSFORMATIVE
LEARNING
RECORD

High STLR 88%†

Non-Priority Population
First-Time, Full-Time
Freshman
Fall 2016 – Fall
2017
(N=769)

Low STLR 73%†

No STLR 64%

High STLR 84%†

Title III Grant Priority** Population
First-Time, Full-Time
Freshman
Fall 2016 – Fall 2017
(N=1,404)

Low STLR 82%†

No STLR 62%

0%   20%   40%   60%   80%   100%

† An ANOVA Test indicated results are statistically significant at p<.001
*Includes confidence intervals at 95%.
**Priority Population Definition: Low socio-economic status, first generation, underrepresented minorities. "Low STLR": Engaged only through attending STLR-tagged events and automatically assigned lowest level of achievement ("exposure"); "High STLR": Created a learning artifact assessed using STLR rubrics.

Figure 25.3 Cohort 2-first year student achievement measure (SAM) retention. This figure illustrates retention rates for learners with a high STLR, low STLR, and no STLR, correlated with the type of population: non-priority and priority (low socioeconomic status, first generation, and underrepresented minorities).

Exciting upcoming research concerns adapting artificial intelligence (AI) algorithms to scan reflective narratives to search for linguistic signifiers that correlate to transformation. With over 24,000 of these artifacts already collected and assessed at UCO, the AI will be able to teach itself quickly by learning from humans' assessments of the narratives. In the world of L2 instruction, it would be exciting to, for example, discover how L2 speakers' expressions that correlate with transformation might differ from those of native speakers.

Transformative understandings can spontaneously break through into consciousness in L2 classes but UCO's experience indicates that the likelihood that this will happen increases with the intentional design of reflective practice, the assessment of students' reflective artifacts, and a process allowing learners to see their progress toward personal transformation. Whereas L2 course content will include things like conjugations, vocabulary, and so on, it is the beyond-content realizations that support comfort within and appreciation for other cultures to the degree that allows for the non-judgmental, human-to-human connections needed for students to truly be in a country outside their native land.

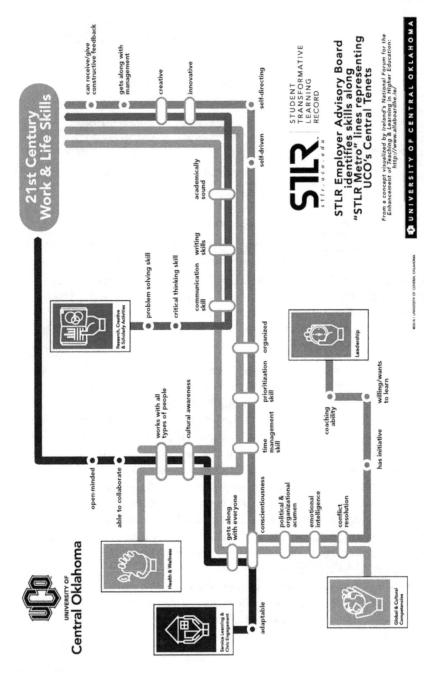

Figure 25.4 Twenty-first century work and life skills. This figure illustrates the skills needed for and developed by learning and experiential activities in the areas of: leadership; service learning and civic engagement; research, creative, and scholarly activities; global and cultural competencies; and health and wellness.

DISCUSSION QUESTIONS

1. What means other than STLR exist within educational institutions to prompt transformative learning? As transformative learning is commonly studied as part of adult and continuing education curricula in higher education, there are surely other ways that have been proposed to operationalize transformative learning on campus. What are some of them, and are they successful in helping language learners have transformative realizations about successful communication in world languages?

2. Writing good prompts for student reflection can be challenging. As the reflection is meant to elicit students' self-examination of the impact that the activity or assignment has had on their own lives and relationships, if you were asked to write three prompts to elicit student reflection about using L2 when communicating with residents during study abroad, how would you word those three questions?

3. Consider your own personal history to identify a time when you, to paraphrase transformative learning researcher and theorist Patricia Cranton, "reflected on and questioned something you previously took for granted and thereby changed your views or perspectives." Knowing that you had such a shift in perspective, what would have been a good reflective prompt to elicit your self-knowledge about the shift?

References

3RP (Regional Refugee and Resilience Plan) (2015). *In response to the Syrian crisis.* Retrieved from www.3rpsyriacrisis.org/wp-content/uploads/2015/01/3RP-Report Overview.pdf.

Abarbanel, J. (2019). *For study abroad professionals, supporting resilience in transition. A guide for conversations with students about emotional health.* Unpublished document, College of Literature, Science, and Arts at the University of Michigan, MI.

Abraham, A. (2018). *Lack of diversity in studying abroad.* Retrieved from https://diverseeducation.com/article/134254/.

Abrami, P., Bernard, R., Borokhovski, E., Wade, A., Surkes, M., Tamim, R., & Zhang, D. (2008). Instructional interventions affecting critical thinking skills and dispositions: A Stage 1 meta-analysis. *Review of Educational Research, 78*(4), 1102–1134.

ACCJC (Accrediting Commission for Community and Junior Colleges of the Western Association of Schools and Colleges). (2014). *Accreditation Standards* (adopted June 2014). Retrieved from https://accjc.org/wp-content/uploads/Accreditation-Standards_-Adopted-June-2014.pdf.

Achiume, E. T. (2013). Beyond prejudice. Structural xenophobic discrimination against refugees. *Georgetown Journal of International Law, 45*, 323.

ACTFL (American Council on the Teaching of Foreign Languages). (1986). *ACTFL proficiency guidelines.* Yonkers: ACTFL.

Adair-Hauck, B. & Donato, R. (2016). The PACE model: A story-based approach to meaning and form for standards-based language learning. *French Review, 76*(2), 265–276.

Akbari, R. (2007). Reflections on reflection: A critical appraisal of reflective practices in L2 teacher education. *System: An International Journal of Educational Technology and Applied Linguistics, 35*(2), 192–220.

American Academy of Arts & Sciences. (2017). *America's languages: Investing in language education for the 21st century.* A report of the Commission on Language Learning. Retrieved from www.amacad.org/publication/americas-languages-investing-language-education-21st-century.

Anderson, C. & Cunningham, K. (2010). Culture, religion, and nationality: Developing ethnographic skills and reflective practices connected to study abroad. In E. Brewer & K. Cunningham (eds.), *Integrating study abroad into the curriculum: Theory and practice across the disciplines* (pp. 63–84). Sterling: Stylus Publishing.

Anderson, K. (2014). Transformative learning and spirituality. In M. Kroth & P. Cranton (eds.), *Stories of transformative learning* (pp. 77–88). Rotterdam: Sense Publishers.

Anderson, L., Krathwohl, D., Airasian, P., Cruikshank, K., Mayer, R., Pintrich, P., Raths, J., & Wittrock, M. (eds.). (2001). *A taxonomy for learning, teaching, and assessing: A revision of Bloom's taxonomy of educational objectives* (Complete ed.). New York: Longman.

Angulo, S. (2010). *Trading cultures, transforming lives: Positive change during study abroad.* Saarbrücken: VDM Verlag Dr. Müller.

Arce, J. (2000). Developing voices: Transformative education in a first-grade two-way Spanish immersion classroom: A participatory study. *Bilingual Research Journal, 24*(3), 249–260.

Arnold, J. & Murphey, T. (eds.). (2013). *Meaningful action: Earl Stevick's influence on language teaching.* New York: Cambridge University Press.

Aubrey, R. (2019). Strategies for differentiation from the ACTFL National Language Teacher of the Year's classroom. Paper presented at the 2019 Conference of the American Association of Teachers of Spanish and Portuguese, San Diego, CA.

Bailin, S. & Siegel, H. (2003). Critical thinking. In N. Blake, P. Smeyers, R. Smith, & P. Standish (eds.), *The Blackwell guide to the philosophy of education* (pp. 181–193). Oxford: Blackwell.

Bain, S. & Spring, M. (2017). Creating collaborative communities through online cafés. In D. Murphy & K. Evans-Romaine (eds.), *Exploring the US language flagship program: Professional competence in a second language by graduation* (pp. 116–136). Bristol: Multilingual Matters.

Bandura, A. (1977). Self-efficacy: Toward a unifying theory of behavioral change. *Psychological Review, 84*(2), 191–215.

Barnes, D. (1976). *From communication to curriculum.* Harmondsworth: Penguin.

Bass, R. & Elmendorf, H. (2010). *What are social pedagogies?* Retrieved from https://blogs.commons.georgetown.edu/bassr/social-pedagogies/.

Bass, R. & Elmendorf, H. (2011). *Designing for difficulty: Social pedagogies as a framework for course design.* Teagle Foundation White Paper.

Bass, R. & Elmendorf, H. (2012). *Designing for difficulty: Social pedagogies as a framework for course design.* Teagle Foundation White Paper.

Bateman, B. & Lago, B. (n.d.). *Methods of language teaching.* Retrieved from https://hlr.byu.edu/methods/content/communicative.html.

Baumgartner, L. (2012). Mezirow's theory of transformative learning from 1975 to present. In E. Taylor & P. Cranton (eds.), *The handbook of transformative learning* (pp. 99–115). San Francisco: Jossey-Bass.

Beck, A. (1979). *Cognitive therapy and the emotional disorders.* New York: Plume.

Beitman, B. (2009). Brains seek patterns in coincidences. *Psychiatric Annals, 39*(5), 255–264.

Bennett, J. & Bennett, M. (2004). Developing intercultural sensitivity: An integrative approach to global and domestic diversity. In D. Landis, J. Bennett, & M. Bennett (eds.), *Handbook of intercultural training* (3rd ed., pp. 147–165). Thousand Oaks: Sage.

Bennett, M. (1993). Towards ethnorelativism: A developmental model of intercultural sensitivity. In R. Paige (ed.), *Education for the intercultural experience* (pp. 21–71). Yarmouth: Intercultural Press.

Bennett, M. (2004). Becoming interculturally competent. In J. Wurzel (ed.), *Toward multiculturalism: A reader in multicultural education* (2nd ed., pp. 62–77). Newton: Intercultural Resource Corporation.

Benson, P. (2011). Language learning and teaching beyond the classroom: An introduction to the field. In P. Benson & H. Reinders (eds.), *Beyond the language classroom* (pp. 7–16). New York: Palgrave Macmillan.

Benson, P. & Reinders, H. (2011). *Beyond the language classroom*. New York: Palgrave Macmillan.

Benson, P., Barkhuizen, G., & Bodycott, P. (2012). Study abroad and the development of second language identities. *Applied Linguistics Review, 3*(1), 173–193.

Bernhardt, E. (1983). Testing foreign language reading comprehension: The immediate recall protocol. *Die Unterrichtspraxis, 16*, 27–33.

Bhaba, H. K. (1994). *The location of culture*. London: Routledge.

Bhugra, D. & Becker, M. (2005). Migration, cultural bereavement and cultural identity. *World Psychiatry, 4*(1), 18.

Block, D. (2003). *The social turn in second language acquisition*. Washington, DC: Georgetown University Press.

Blommaert, J. (2010). *The sociolinguistics of globalization*. Cambridge: Cambridge University Press.

Blommaert, J. (2013). *Ethnography, superdiversity and linguistic landscapes: Chronicles of complexity*. Bristol: Multilingual Matters.

Blommaert, J. & Rampton, B. (2011a). Language and superdiversity. *Diversities, 13*(2). Retrieved from www.unesco.org/shs/diversities/vol13/issue2/art1.

Blommaert, J. & Rampton, B. (2011b). Language and superdiversity. In K. Arnaud, J. Blommaert, B. Rampton, & M. Spotti (eds.), *Language and superdiversity* (pp. 21–48). New York: Routledge.

Bloom, B. (ed.). (1956). *Taxonomy of educational objectives, Handbook I: Cognitive domain*. New York: David McKay.

Bonneuil, C. & Fressoz, J. B. (2015). *The shock of the Anthropocene*. London: Verso.

Borg, S. (2003). Teacher cognition in language teaching: A review of research on what language teachers think, know, believe, and do. *Language Teaching, 36*(2), 81–109.

Borg, S. (2006). *Teacher cognition and language education: Research and practice*. London: Continuum.

Borg, S. (2012). Current approaches to language teacher cognition research: A methodological analysis. In R. B. Burns (ed.), *Researching language teacher cognition and practice: International case studies* (pp. 11–29). Bristol: Multilingual Matters.

Bovarie, P. & Kroth, M. (2001). *Transforming work: The five keys to achieving trust, commitment, and passion in the workplace.* Cambridge: Perseus Publishing.

Bowers, C. (2001). How language limits our understanding of environmental education. *Environmental Education Research, 7*(2), 141–151. DOI: 10.1080/13504620120043144.

Bowers, C. (2012). *The way forward: Educational reforms that focus on the cultural commons and the linguistic roots of the ecological/cultural crises.* Eugene: Eco-Justice Press.

Bown, J. (2006). Locus of learning and affective strategy use: Two factors affecting success in self-instructed language learning. *Foreign Language Annals, 39*(4), 640–659.

Boyd, R. (1991). The matrix model: A conceptual framework for small group analysis. In R. D. Boyd et al. (eds.), *Personal transformation in small groups: A Jungian perspective* (pp. 14–40). London: Routledge.

Boyd, R. & Dirkx, J. (1991). Methodology for the study of the development of consciousness in the small group. In R. D. Boyd et al. (eds.), *Personal transformation in small groups: A Jungian perspective* (pp. 14–40). London: Routledge.

Boyd, R. & Myers, J. (1988). Transformative education. *International Journal of Lifelong Education, 7*(4), 261–284.

Boyer, N., Maher, P., & Kirkman, S. (2006). Transformative learning in online settings. The use of self-direction, metacognition, and collaborative learning. *Journal of Transformative Education, 4*(4), 335–361.

Brock, S. (2009). Measuring the importance of precursor steps to transformative learning. *Adult Education Quarterly, 60*(2), 122–142. doi: 10.1177/0741713609333084.

Brookfield, S. (1987). *Developing critical thinkers: Challenging adults to explore alternative ways of thinking and acting.* San Francisco: Jossey-Bass.

Brookfield, S. (1990). *The skillful teacher: On technique, trust, and responsiveness in the classroom.* San Francisco: Jossey-Bass.

Brookfield, S. (1995). *Becoming a critically reflective teacher.* San Francisco: Jossey-Bass.

Brookfield, S. (2000). Transformative learning as ideology critique. In J. Mezirow et al. (eds.), *Learning as transformation: Critical perspectives on a theory in progress* (pp. 125–150). San Francisco: Jossey-Bass.

Brookfield, S. (2005). *The power of critical theory.* San Francisco: Jossey-Bass.

Brookfield, S. (2012). Critical theory and transformative learning. In E. Taylor & P. Cranton (eds.), *The handbook of transformative learning: Theory, research, and practice* (pp. 131–146). San Francisco: Jossey-Bass.

Brooks, A. (1989). *Critically reflective learning within a corporate context.* Unpublished doctoral dissertation, Teacher's College, Columbia University.

Brown, T., Balykhina, T., Talalakina, E., Bown, J., & Kurilenko, V. (2014). *Mastering Russian through global debate*. Washington, DC: Georgetown University Press.

Bruner, J. (1990). *Acts of meaning*. Cambridge: Harvard University Press.

Bruzos, A. (2017). Encuentros con el español: A case study of critical service learning in the Latino community. In S. Dubreil & S. Thorne (eds.), *Engaging the world: Social pedagogies and language learning* (pp. 37–63). AAUSC 2017 Volume. Boston: Cengage.

Buber, M. (1923/1958). *I and thou*. Translated by Ronald Gregor Smith (1958). New York: Scribner Classics.

Byram, M. (1997). *Teaching and assessing intercultural communicative competence*. Clevedon: Multilingual Matters.

Byram, M. & Wagner, M. (2018). Making a difference: Language teaching for intercultural dialogue. *Foreign Language Annals, 51*(1), 140–151.

Byrnes, H. (2011). Perspectives. *Modern Language Journal, 95*(2), 291.

Calleja, C. (2014). Jack Mezirow's conceptualisation of adult transformative learning: A review. *Journal of Adult and Continuing Education, 20*(1), 117–136. doi: 10.7227/JACE.20.18.

Campbell, C. & Sarac, B. (2017). The role of technology in language learning in the twenty-first century: Perspectives from academe, government, and the private sector. *Hispania, 100*(5, Centenary Issue), 77–84.

Canagarajah, S. (2014). In search of a new paradigm for teaching English as an international language. *TESOL Journal, 5*(4), 767–785.

Candy, P. (1991). *Self-direction for lifelong learning*. San Francisco: Jossey-Bass.

Capstick, T. & Delaney, M. (2016). *Language for resilience: The role of language in enhancing the resilience of Syrian refugees and host communities*. Report. British Council. Retrieved from www.britishcouncil.org/sites/default/files/language-for-resilience-report-en.pdf.

Carreira, M. & Chik, C. (2017). *Project-based learning for heritage language instruction*. Paper presented at the Tenth Annual Language Teacher Education Conference at UCLA, Los Angeles, CA.

Carter, M. (2015). *Exploring the relationship between study abroad and emotional intelligence*. Unpublished doctoral dissertation, University of Alabama, Birmingham, AL.

Catalano, T. & Hamann, E. (2016). Multilingual pedagogies and preservice teachers: Implementing "language as a resource" orientation in teacher education programs. *Bilingual Research Journal, 39*(3–4), 263–278.

Cazzell, M., Theriot, S., Blakey, J., & Sattler, M. (2014). Transformation of, in, and by learning in a service-learning faculty fellows program. *Journal of Service-Learning in Higher Education, 3*. Retrieved from www.citationmachine.net/apa/cite-a-journal/manual.

Charitos, S. & Van Deusen-Scholl, N. (2017). Engaging the city: Language, space, and identity in urban environments. In S. Dubreil & S. Thorne (eds.), *Engaging the world: Social pedagogies and language learning* (pp. 35–50). Eugene: AAUSC Press.

Chávez, A. F., Guido-DiBrito, F., & Mallory, S. (2003). Learning to value the "other": A framework of individual diversity development. *Journal of College Student Development, 44*(4), 453–469.

Cheon, S. (2018). Achieving a superior level of proficiency: Cbi, Korean film, and the five Cs. *Dialog on Language Instruction, 28*(1), 29–44.

Cleret, E. (2018). Transformation at the learner, teacher, and instruction levels: One teacher's story at the French War College. *Dialog on Language Instruction, 28*(1), 52–64.

Clevinger, J. (1993). *Exploring transformative learning: The identification and description of multiple cases among kidney transplant recipients.* Unpublished doctoral dissertation, The University of Tennessee, Knoxville, TN.

Clifford, Ray T. (1988). What you test is what you get: Open versus closed instructional systems. *Die Unterrichtspraxis, 21*(1), 37–40.

Cochrane, N. (1981). *The meanings that some adults derive from their personal withdrawal experiences: A dialogical inquiry.* Unpublished doctoral dissertation, University of Toronto, Toronto, Canada.

Coffman, P. (1989). *Inclusive language as a means of resisting hegemony in theological education: A phenomenology of transformation and empowerment of persons in adult higher education.* Unpublished doctoral dissertation, Northern Illinois University, DeKalb, IL.

Cohen, B. (2014). *Diagnostic assessment at the superior–distinguished threshold.* Virginia Beach: Villa Magna LLC Center.

Cohen, B. (2015). *Presentations about enhanced final learning objectives activities.* Presidio of Monterey: The Defense Language Institute Foreign Language Center.

Conchas, G. (2001). Structuring failure and success: Understanding the variability in Latino school engagement. *Harvard Educational Review, 71*(3), 475–505.

Conlon Perugini, D. (2017). *Core practices: Using authentic texts and resources.* Retrieved from www.kentuckyteacher.org/subjects/global-competency-world-languages/2017/06/core-practices-using-authentic-texts-and-resources/.

Conteh, J. & Meier, G. (eds.). (2014). *The multilingual turn in languages education: Opportunities and challenges.* Bristol: Multilingual Matters.

Corin, A. (1997). A course to convert Czech proficiency to proficiency in Croatian and Serbian. In S. Stryker & B. L. Leaver (eds.), *Content-based instruction in foreign language education: Models and methods* (pp. 78–104). Washington, DC: Georgetown University Press.

Corin, A. & Leaver, B. L. (2019). *Fields of the mind: History, theory, and application of cognitive field concepts to language learning.* Hollister: MSI Press.

Council of Europe (2001). *Common European Framework of Reference for Languages: Learning, teaching, assessment.* Cambridge: Cambridge University Press.

Crane, C. (2018). Making connections in beginning language instruction: Structured reflection and the World-Readiness Standards for Learning Languages. In P. Urlaub & J. Watzinger-Tharp (eds.), *The interconnected language curriculum: Critical transitions and interfaces in articulated K-16 contexts* (pp. 51–74). Boston: Heinle.

Crane, C., Fingerhuth, M., & Huenlich, D. (2018). "What makes this so complicated?" On the value of disorienting dilemmas in language instruction. In S. Dubreil & S. Thorne (eds.), *Engaging the world: Social pedagogies and language learning* (pp. 227–252). Boston: Heinle.

Cranton, P. (1994). *Understanding and promoting transformative learning.* San Francisco: Jossey-Bass.

Cranton, P. (1998). Transformative learning: Individual growth and development through critical reflection. In S. M. Scott, B. Spencer, & A. M. Thomas (eds.), *Learning for life: Canadian readings in adult education* (pp. 188–199). Toronto: Thompson Educational Publishing.

Cranton, P. (2001). *Becoming an authentic teacher in higher education.* Malabar: Krieger Publishing Company.

Cranton, P. & Hoggan, C. (2012). Evaluating transformative learning. In E. Taylor & P. Cranton (eds.), *The handbook of transformative learning. Theory, research, and practice* (pp. 520–535). San Francisco: Jossey-Bass.

Cranton, P. & Taylor, E. (2012). Transformative learning theory: Seeking a more unified theory. In E. Taylor and P. Cranton (eds.), *The handbook of transformative learning: Theory, research, and practice* (pp. 3–20). San Francisco: Jossey-Bass.

Creese, A. & Blackledge, A. (2010). Towards a linguistics of superdiversity. *Zeitschrift für Erziehungswissenschaft, 13*(4), 549–572.

Creswell, J. (2007/2013). *Qualitative inquiry and research design: Choosing among five approaches.* Thousand Oaks: Sage.

Cronin, M. (2016). *Eco-translation: Translation and ecology in the age of the Anthropocene.* London: Routledge.

Culham, T., Oxford, R., & Lin, J. (2018). Cultivating the ability of the heart: Educating through the pedagogy of love. In J. Miller et al. (eds.), *International handbook of holistic education.* New York: Routledge.

Cummins, J. (2019). *Biliteracy, empowerment, and transformative pedagogy.* Retrieved from www.researchgate.net/profile/Jim_Cummins5/publication/241492125_Biliteracy_Empowerment_and_Transformative_Pedagogy/links/0deec534e935756ca3000000.pdf.

Cunningham, K. (2010). Putting the anthropological toolkit to use in international and intercultural learning. *Practicing Anthropology, 32*(3), 23–26.

Cunningham, K. & Grossman, R. (2009). *Transformative learning: An epistemological study of Kalamazoo College student learning outcomes*. Paper presented at the 3rd National Conference on Innovations in the Scholarship of Teaching and Learning at Liberal Arts Colleges, Wabash College, Crawfordsville, IN.

Dababneh, R. (2018). The scenario-based syllabus for the post-basic Arabic program. *Dialog on Language Instruction*, *28*(1), 13–26.

Dabbs, L. & Leaver, B. L. (2019). *The invisible foreign language classroom: Bringing hidden dynamics to light for individual and group harmony and success*. Hollister: MSI Press.

Dam, L. (1995). *Learner autonomy 3: From theory to classroom practice*. Dublin: Authentik.

Dam, L. & Little, D. (1999). Autonomy in foreign language learning: From classroom practice to generalizable theory. In *JALT98 Proceedings. Focus on the classroom: Interpretations* (pp. 127–136). Tokyo: The Japan Association for Language Teaching.

D'Andrea, A. (1986). *Teachers and reflection: A description and analysis of the reflective process which teachers use in their experiential learning*. Unpublished doctoral dissertation, The University of Toronto, Canada.

Davidson, D. (2010). Study abroad: When, how long, and with what results? New data from the Russian front. *Foreign Language Annals*, *43*(1), 6–26.

Davidson, D. & Frank, V. (2012). The overseas component of the Language Flagship: Addressing learner needs within an acquisition-rich environment. *Journal of Chinese Teaching and Research in the U.S.: Special Issue for The Language Flagship*, *4*, 8–15.

Davidson, D. & Garas, N. (2018). *360 survey, conducted for the Flagship Culture Initiative*. Unpublished report.

Davidson, D. & Lekic, M. (2010). The overseas immersion setting as contextual variable in adult SLA: Learner behaviors associated with language gain to level-3 proficiency in Russian. *Russian Language Journal*, *60*, 55–78.

Davidson, D. & Lekic, M. (2012). Comparing heritage and non-heritage learning outcomes and target-language utilization in the overseas immersion context: A preliminary study of the Russian Flagship. *Russian Language Journal*, *62*, 47–78.

Davidson, D. & Shaw, J. (2019). A cross-linguistic and cross-skill perspective on L2 development in study abroad. In P. Winke & S. Gass (eds.), *Foreign language proficiency in higher education* (pp. 217–242). Educational Linguistics 37, Springer Nature Switzerland AG. doi: 10.1007/978-3-030-01006-5_12.

Deardorff, D. (2011). Intercultural competence in foreign language classrooms: A framework and implications for educators. In A. Witte & T. Harden (eds.), *Intercultural competence: Concepts, challenges, evaluations*. ISFLL 10. Bern: Peter Lang International Academic Publishers.

Dekutoski, C. G. (2011). *Mainstream teacher attitudes toward English language learners*. Dissertation, Wayne State University, MI.

Dempster, H. & Hargrave, K. (2017). *Understanding public attitudes towards refugees and migrants.* Working Paper 512. London: Overseas Development Institute.

Department of Defense. (2005). *Defense language transformation road map.* Retrieved from https://apps.dtic.mil/dtic/tr/fulltext/u2/b313370.pdf.

De Santis, P. & Willis, O. (2016). From Karamzin to Putin: Transformative learning in practice. *International Journal of Arts and Sciences, 9*(3), 65–74.

Descartes, R. (1668/2013). *Discours de la méthode pour bien conduire sa raison, et chercher la vérité dans les sciences.* New York: Hachette Livre.

Dewey, J. (1938/1997). *Experience and education.* New York: Free Press Reprint Edition (reprinted from 1938 Kappa Delta lecture).

Diducka, A., Sinclair, A. J., Hostetler, G., & Fitzpatrick, P. (2012). Transformative learning theory, public involvement, and natural resource and environmental management. *Journal of Environmental Planning and Management, 55*(10), 1311–1330.

DiRienzo, A. (2015). Email message to Christine Campbell, in which she cites C. Bonk & E. Koo (2014). *Adding some TEC-VARIETY: 100 activities for motivating and retaining learners online* (p. 283). Bloomington: Open World, 2014.

Dirkx, J. (1997). Nurturing soul in adult learning. In P. Cranton (ed.), *Transformative learning in action: Insights from practice* (pp. 79–88). San Francisco: Jossey-Bass.

Dirkx, J. (2001). The power of feelings: Emotion, imagination, and the construction of meaning in adult learning. In S. Merriam (ed.), *The new update on adult learning theory* (pp. 63–72). San Francisco: Jossey-Bass.

Dirkx, J. (2006). Engaging emotions in adult learning: A Jungian perspective on emotion and transformative learning. *New Directions for Adult and Continuing Education, 109,* 15–26.

Dirkx, J. (2008a). *Adult learning and the emotional self.* San Francisco: Jossey-Bass.

Dirkx, J. (2008b). The meaning and role of emotions in adult learning. *New Directions for Adult & Continuing Education, 120,* 1–96.

Dirkx, J. (2009). *Adult learning and the emotional self: New directions in adult and continuing education. No. 120.* New York: Wiley & Sons, Ltd./Jossey-Bass.

Dirkx, J. (2012). Nurturing soul work: A Jungian approach to transformative learning. In E. Taylor & P. Cranton (eds.), *The handbook of transformative learning* (pp. 116–130). San Francisco: Jossey-Bass.

Dirkx, J., Mezirow, J., & Cranton, P. (2006). Musings and reflections on the meaning, context, and process of transformative learning: A dialogue between John M. Dirkx and Jack Mezirow. *Journal of Transformative Education, 4*(2), 123–139. DOI: 10.1177/1541344606287503.

Di Stefano, G., Gino, F., Pisano, G., & Staats, B. (2014). Learning by thinking: Overcoming the bias for action through reflection. *Harvard Business School*

Working Paper Series 58(14-093). Retrieved from http://k12accountability.org/resources/For-Principals/Learning_Through_Reflection.pdf.

DLIFLC (Defense Language Institute Foreign Language Center). (2017). *Institutional self-evaluation report for educational quality and institutional effectiveness in support of reaffirmation of accreditation*. Retrieved from www.dliflc.edu/wp-content/uploads/2018/01/DLIFLC-Self-Study-December-2017_small.pdf.

DLIFLC. (2018). *General catalog 2017–2018*. Retrieved from www.dliflc.edu/wp-content/uploads/2016/12/GeneralCatalog_Online-Color_FY17-18.pdf.

DLNSEO (Defense Language and National Security Education Office). (2018). *National Security Education Program annual report*. Retrieved from https://nsep.gov/sites/default/files/NSEP%202018%20Annual%20Report%20%28web%29.pdf.

Donato, R. (1994). Collective scaffolding in second language learning. In J. Lantolf & G. Appel (eds.), *Vygotskian approaches to second language research* (pp. 33–56). Norwood: Ablex Publishing Corporation.

Dörnyei, Z. (2005). *The psychology of the language learner: Individual differences in second language acquisition*. London: Routledge.

Dörnyei, Z., Henry, A., & Muir, C. (2015). *Motivational currents in language learning: Frameworks for focused interventions*. London: Routledge.

Doughty, C. & Williams, J. (eds.). (1998). *Focus on form in second language acquisition*. New York: Cambridge University Press.

Downes, S. (2005). *An introduction to connective knowledge*. Blog post. Retrieved from www.downes.ca/cgi-bin/page.cgi?post=33034.

Dubreil, S. & Thorne, S. (2017). Introduction: Social pedagogies and entwining language with the world. In S. Dubreil & S. Thorne (eds.), *Engaging the world: Social pedagogies and language learning* (pp. 1–11). AAUSC 2017 Volume. Boston: Cengage.

Duerden, M., Lundberg, N., Ward, P., Taniguchi, S., Hill, B., Widmer, M., & Zabriskie, R. (2018). From ordinary to extraordinary: A framework of experience types. *Journal of Leisure Research*, 49(3–5), 196–216. DOI: 10.1080/00222216.2018.1528779.

Dunlop, R. (1999). Beyond dualism: Toward a dialogic negotiation of difference. *Canadian Journal of Education* 24(1), 57–69. Retrieved from www.jstor.org/stable/1585771?seq=1#page_scan_tab_contents.

Duri, J. (1992). Content-based instruction: Keeping DLI on the cutting edge. *The Globe*, 5, 4–5.

Ehrman, M. E. (1996). *Understanding second language learning difficulties*. Thousand Oaks: Sage.

Ehrman, M. E. (2002). The learner at the superior–distinguished threshold. In B. L. Leaver & B. S. Shekhtman (eds.), *Developing professional-level foreign language proficiency* (pp. 245–259). Cambridge: Cambridge University Press.

Ehrman, M. E. & Dörnyei, Z. (1998). *Interpersonal dynamics in second language acquisition: The visible and invisible classroom*. Thousand Oaks: Sage.

Ehrman, M. E. & Leaver, B. L. (2002). *The E&L cognitive construct.* Unpublished manuscript on file at the Library of Congress.

Ehrman, M. E., Leaver, B. L., & Oxford, R. L. (2003). A brief overview of individual differences in second language learning. *System, 31,* 313–330.

Eisenbruch, M. (1991). From post-traumatic stress disorder to cultural bereavement: Diagnosis of Southeast Asian refugees. *Social Science & Medicine, 33*(6), 673–680.

Ellis, R. (2003). *Task-based language learning and teaching.* Oxford: Oxford University Press.

Esch, E. (1996). Promoting learner autonomy: Criteria for the selection of appropriate methods. In R. Pemberton, S. Edward, W. Or, & H. Pierson (eds.), *Taking control: Autonomy in language learning* (pp. 35–48). Hong Kong: Hong Kong University Press.

Evans-Romaine, K., Goldberg, S., Kresin, S., & Galloway, V. (2020). Language and cultural learning through song: Three complementary contexts. In E. Dengub, I. Dubinina, & J. Merrill (eds.), *Art of teaching Russian* (pp. 231–253). Washington, DC: Georgetown University Press.

Farrell, T. (2009). Critical reflection in a TESL course: Mapping conceptual change. *ELT Journal, 63,* 221–229.

Farrell, T. (2015). *Promoting teacher reflection in second language education: A framework for TESOL professionals.* New York: Routledge.

Featherston, B. & Kelly, R. (2007). Conflict resolution and transformative pedagogy: A grounded theory research project on learning in higher education. *Journal of Transformative Education, 5*(3), 262–285.

Filatova, E. (2009). *Understanding the people around you.* Hollister: MSI Press.

Firth, A. & Wagner, J. (1997). On discourse, communication, and (some) fundamental concepts in SLA research. *The Modern Language Journal, 81*(3), 285–300.

Firth, A. & Wagner, J. (2007). Second/foreign language learning as a social accomplishment: Elaborations on reconceptualized SLA. *The Modern Language Journal, 91*(Focus Issue), 800–819.

Fleming, T. (2008). A secure base for adult learning: Attachment theory and adult education – The adult learner. *The Irish Journal of Adult Education, 25,* 33–53.

Fleming, T. (2019). Connected knowing in Belenky and Honnuth: Implications for transformative learning theory. In T. Fleming, A. Kokkos, & F. Finnegan (eds.), *European perspectives on transformation theory* (pp. 29–42). Cham: Palgrave Macmillan.

Fleming, T., Kokkos, A., & Finnegan, F. (eds.). (2019). *European perspectives on transformation theory.* London: Palgrave Macmillan.

Fløttum, K. (ed.). (2017). *The role of language in the climate change debate.* New York: Routledge.

Foster, E. (1997). Transformative learning in adult second language learning. *New Directions for Adult and Continuing Education, 74,* 33–40.

Freels, S., Kisselev, O., & Alsufieva, A. (2017). Adding breadth to the undergraduate curriculum: Flagship approaches to interdisciplinary language learning. In D.

Murphy & K. Evans-Romaine (eds.), *Exploring the US Language Flagship program: Professional competence in a second language by graduation* (pp. 51–69). Bristol: Multilingual Matters.

Freeman, D. (1989). Teacher training, development, and decision making: A model of teaching and related strategies for language teacher education. *TESOL Quarterly, 23*(1), 27–45.

Freeman, D. & Johnson, K. (1998). Reconceptualizing the knowledge base of language teacher education. *TESOL Quarterly, 32*(3), 397–417.

Freeman, Y., Freeman, D., & Mercuri, S. (2018). *Dual language essentials for teachers and administrators* (2nd ed.). Portsmouth: Heinemann.

Freire, P. (1970). *Pedagogy of the oppressed.* New York: Continuum.

Freire, P. (1975). *Conscientization.* Geneva: World Council of Churches.

Freire, P. (1993a). *Pedagogy of the city.* New York: Continuum.

Freire, P. (1993b). *Pedagogy of the oppressed* (2nd ed.). New York: Continuum.

Freire, P. (1998a). *Pedagogy of freedom: Ethics, democracy and civic courage.* Lanham: Rowman & Littlefield.

Freire, P. (1998b). *Teachers as cultural workers: Letters to those who dare teach.* Boulder: Westview Press.

Freire, P. (1998c). *The pedagogy of the oppressed.* Translated by M. Ramos. New York: Continuum.

Freire, P. (2018). *Pedagogy of the oppressed* (4th ed., 50th anniversary ed.). New York: Bloomsbury.

Freire, P. & Freire, A. (1994). *Pedagogy of hope: Reliving pedagogy of the oppressed.* New York: Continuum.

Freire, P. & Freire, A. (1997). *Pedagogy of the heart.* New York: Continuum.

Frye, R. & Garza, T. (1992). Authentic contact with native speech and culture at home and abroad. In W. Rivers (ed.), *Teaching languages in college: Curriculum and content.* Lincolnwood: National Textbook Co.

Fullerton, J. (2010). *Transformative learning in college students: A mixed methods study.* University of Nebraska-Lincoln. Retrieved from http://digitalcommons.unl.edu/cgi/viewcontent.cgi?article=1064&context=cehsdiss.

Furco, A. (1996). Service-learning: A blended approach to experiential education. In *Expanding boundaries: Serving and learning* (pp. 2–6). Washington, DC: Corporation for National Service.

Furstenberg, G. & Levet, S. (2014). *Cultura: From then to now. Its origins, key features, methodology, and how it has evolved. Reflections on the past and musings on the future.* In D. Chun (ed.), *Cultura-inspired intercultural exchanges: Focus on Asian and Pacific languages* (pp. 1–31). Honolulu: National Foreign Language Resource Center.

Furstenberg, G., Levet, S., English, K., & Maillet, K. (2001). Giving a virtual voice to the silent language of culture: The *Cultura* project. *Language Learning and Technology, 5*(1), 55–102.

Galloway, V. (1998). Constructing cultural realities: "Facts" and frameworks of association. In J. Harper, M. Lively, & M. Williams (eds.), *The coming of age of the profession* (pp. 129–140). Boston: Heinle & Heinle.

Gao, Y. H. (2014). Faithful imitator, legitimate speaker, playful creator and dialogical communicator: Shift in English learners' identity prototypes. *Language and Intercultural Communication, 14*(1), 59–75.

García, D. & Wei, L. (2014). Translanguaging and education. In *Translanguaging: Language, bilingualism and education* (pp. 63–77). London: Palgrave Macmillan.

García, O. (2017). Problematizing linguistic integration of adult migrants: The role of translanguaging and language teachers. In J.-C. Beacco, H.-J. Krumm, D. Little, & P. Thalgott (eds.), *The linguistic integration of adult migrants/ L'intégration linguistique des migrants adultes. Some lessons from research/ Les enseignements de la recherche* (pp. 11–26). Berlin: de Gruyter.

Gardner, R. & Lambert, W. (1972). *Attitudes and motivation in second language learning*. Rowley: Newbury House Publishers.

Garza, T. J. (2017). Raise the flag(ship)! Creating hybrid language programs on the Flagship model. In D. Murphy & K. Evans-Romaine (eds.), *Exploring the US Language Flagship program: Professional competence in a second language by graduation* (pp. 224–243). Bristol: Multilingual Matters.

Garza, T. J. (2018). *Making Russian great again: Language, dissent, and critical pedagogy. SEEJ blog*. Retrieved from http://u.osu.edu/seej/2018/09/26/ making-russian-great-again-language-dissent-and-critical-pedagogy/.

Ghahari, S. & Farokhnia, F. (2017). Triangulation of learning assessment modes: Learning benefits and socio-cognitive prospects. *Pedagogies: An International Journal, 12*(3), 275–294. doi: 10.1080/1554480X.2017.1342540.

Gibbs, J. C. (2010). *Moral development and reality: Beyond the theories of Kohlberg and Hoffman* (2nd ed.). Boston: Allyn & Bacon.

Girod, M. & Wong, D. (2002). An aesthetic (Deweyan) perspective on science learning: Case studies of three fourth graders. *Elementary School Journal, 102*, 199–224.

Glanville, P. J. (2017). The road through superior: Building learner independence. In D. Murphy & K. Evans-Romaine (eds.), *Exploring the US Language Flagship program: Professional competence in a second language by graduation* (pp. 70–89). Bristol: Multilingual Matters.

Glisan, E. & Donato, R. (2017). *Enacting the work of language instruction: High-leverage teaching practices*. Alexandria: ACTFL.

Glynn, C., Wesely, P., & Wassell, B. (2018). *Words and actions: Teaching languages through the lens of social justice* (2nd ed.). Alexandria: ACTFL.

Goleman, D. (1995). *Emotional intelligence: Why it can matter more than IQ*. New York: Bantam Books.

Goodman, A. (2002). Transformative learning and cultures of peace. In E. O' Sullivan, A. Morrell, & M. A. O' Connor (eds.), *Expanding the boundaries of transformative learning* (pp. 185–198). New York: Palgrave.

Goodman, J. (2017). *Meet Sheldon, the robot student.* Retrieved from www.insidehighered.com/digital-learning/article/2017/04/26/robots-classrooms connect-distance-learners-classrooms.

Goulah, J. (2006). Transformative second and foreign language learning for the 21st century. *Critical Inquiry in Language Studies: An International Journal, 3*(4), 201–221.

Goulah, J. (2007). Village voices, global visions: Digital video as a transformative foreign language learning tool. *Foreign Language Annals, 40*(1), 62–78.

Goulah, J. (2011). Ecospirituality in public foreign language education: A critical discourse analysis of a transformative world language learning approach. *Critical Inquiry in Language Studies: An International Journal, 8*(1), 27–52.

Goulah, J. (2012). Environmental displacement, English learners, identity and value creation: Considering Daisaku Ikeda in the East–West ecology of education. In J. Lin & R. Oxford (eds.), *Transformative eco-education for human and planetary survival* (pp. 41–58). Charlotte: Information Age Publishing.

Goulah, J. (2017). Climate change and TESOL: Language, literacies, and the creation of eco-ethical consciousness. *TESOL Quarterly, 51*(1), 90–114. doi: 10.1002/tesq.277.

Goulah, J. & Katunich, J. (eds.). (2020). *TESOL and sustainability: English language teaching in the Anthropocene era.* London: Bloomsbury.

Greene, J. (2009). Dual-process morality and the personal/impersonal distinction: A reply to McGuire, Langdon, Coltheart, and MacKenzie. *Journal of Experimental Social Psychology, 45*, 581–584.

Grévisse, M. (1936). *Le bon usage.* Paris: De Boeck-Duculot.

Griffith, B. (2019). *Transforming the transformative learning experience through 360, virtual reality, and augmented reality.* Paper presented at the Transformative Learning Conference, Oklahoma City, OK.

Guce, I. (2017). Investigating college students' views on mathematics learning through reflective journal writing. *International Journal of Evaluation and Research in Education, 6*(1), 38–44.

Guo, N. S. & Feng, D. (2015). Infusing multiliteracies into English language curriculum: The visual construction of knowledge in English textbooks from an ontogenetic perspective. *Linguistics and Education, 31*, 115–129.

Habermas, J. (1962). *Strukturwandel der Öffentlichkeit. Untersuchungen zu einer Kategorie der bürgerlichen Gesellschaft.* Translated by T. Burger and F. Lawrence as *Structural Transformation of the Public Sphere: An Inquiry into a Category of Bourgeois Society.* Berlin, Germany.

Habermas, J. (1971). *Knowledge and human interests.* Translated by J. Shapiro. Boston: Beacon Press.

Habermas, J. (1989). *The structural transformation of the public sphere: An inquiry into a category of bourgeois society* (translation of the 1962 ed.). Cambridge: MIT Press.

Haidt, J. (2008). Morality. *Perspectives on Psychological Science, 3*, 65–72.

Hall, E. (1976). *Beyond culture*. New York: Random House.

Halliday, M. (1978). *Language as social semiotic*. London: Edward Arnold.

Hammer, M. (1998). A measure of intercultural sensitivity: *The Intercultural Development Inventory*. In S. Fowler & M. Fowler (eds.), *The intercultural source book: Volume 2*. Yarmouth: Intercultural Press.

Hammer, M. (2009). *The Intercultural Development Inventory*: An approach for assessing and building intercultural competence. In M. Moodian (ed.), *Contemporary leadership and intercultural competence: Exploring the cross-cultural dynamics within organizations* (pp. 203–218). Thousand Oaks: Sage.

Hammer, M. (2012). *The Intercultural Development Inventory*: A new frontier in assessment and development of intercultural competence. In M. Vande Berg, R. Paige, & K. Lou (eds.), *Student learning abroad* (pp. 115–136). Sterling: Stylus Publishing.

Hammerly, H. (1982). *Synthesis in second language teaching: An introduction to linguistics*. Wayne: Second Language Publications.

Harper, L. (1994). *Seeing things from different corners: A story of learning and culture*. Unpublished thesis for Master of Arts, University of British Columbia, Vancouver, Canada.

Hartmann, E. (1991). *Boundaries in the mind: A new psychology of personality*. New York: Basic Books.

Hartmann, H. (1944/1964). *Ego psychology and the problem of adaptation*. Madison: International Universities Press.

Hathaway, M. (2011). *Transformative learning and the ecological crisis: Insights from the tao of liberation*. Paper presented at Adult Education Research Conference, Toronto. Retrieved from http://newprairiepress.org/aerc/2011/papers/43.

Hathaway, M. & Boff, L. (2009). *The Tao of liberation: Exploring the ecology of transformation*. Maryknoll: Orbis Books.

Hatton, N. & Smith, D. (1995). Reflection in teacher education: Towards definition and implementation. *Teaching and Teacher Education, 11*(1), 33–49.

Heddy, B. C. & Sinatra, G. M. (2013). Transforming misconceptions: Using transformative experience to promote positive affect and conceptual change in students learning about biological evolution. *Science Education, 97*, 723–744.

Henry, A., Davydenko, S., & Dörnyei, Z. (2015). The anatomy of directed motivational currents: Exploring and enduring periods of L2 motivation. *The Modern Language Journal, 99*(2), 329–345.

Higgs, T. V. (ed.). (1984). *Teaching for proficiency, the organizing principle*. The ACTFL Foreign Language Education Series. Lincolnwood: National Textbook Company.

Hilburn, J. (2014). Challenges facing immigrant students beyond the linguistic domain in a new gateway state. *The Urban Review, 46*(4), 654–680.

Hinkel, E. (1999). *Culture in second language teaching and learning*. Cambridge: Cambridge University Press.

Hoggan, C., Mälkki, K., & Finnegan, F. (2017). Developing the theory of perspective transformation: Continuity, intersubjectivity, and emancipatory praxis. *Adult Education Quarterly, 67*(1), 48–64.

Holden, C. & Sykes, J. (2011). Leveraging mobile games for place-based language learning. *International Journal of Game-Based Learning, 1*(2), 1–18.

Holec, H. (1979). *Autonomy and foreign language learning.* Strasbourg: Council of Europe.

Holec, H. (1981 [1979]). *Autonomy and foreign language learning.* Oxford: Pergamon Press.

Holt, M. (1994). Retesting a learning theory to explain intercultural competency. In K. Obloj (ed.), *High speed competition in new Europe. Published in the proceedings of the 20th Annual Conference of the European International Business Association* (pp. 53–78). Warsaw: University of Warsaw International Management Center.

Huba, M. & Freed, J. (2000). *Learner-centered assessment on college campuses: Shifting the focus from teaching to learning.* Boston: Allyn & Bacon.

Hunt, V. (2009). *Transformative leadership: A comparative case study in three established dual language programs.* Dissertation, Teachers' College, Columbia University.

Hwang, W. & Ting, J. (2008). Disaggregating the effects of acculturation and acculturative stress on the mental health of Asian Americans. *Cultural Diversity and Ethnic Minority Psychology, 14*, 147–154.

Ikeda, D. (1991–2011). *Ikeda Daisaku zenshu [The complete works of Ikeda Daisaku].* 150 Vols. Tokyo: Seikyo Shimbunsha.

Ikeda, D. (2003). *A global ethic of coexistence: Toward a "life-sized" paradigm for our age.* Tokyo: Soka Gakkai. Retrieved from www.daisakuikeda.org/assets/files/peace2003.pdf.

Ikeda, D. (2007). *Lectures on attaining Buddhahood in this lifetime.* Kuala Lumpur: Soka Gakkai Malaysia.

Ikeda, D. (2010a). *A new humanism: The university addresses of Daisaku Ikeda.* New York: I. B. Tauris.

Ikeda, D. (2010b). *Soka education: For the happiness of the individual.* Santa Monica: Middleway Press.

Ikeda, D. (2019). *Toward a new era of peace and disarmament: A people-centered approach.* Tokyo: Soka Gakkai. https://www.daisakuikeda.org/assets/files/peaceproposal2019.pdf.

ILR (Interagency Language Roundtable). (2012). *Interagency Language Roundtable skill level descriptions for competence in intercultural communication.* www.govtilr.org/Skills/Competence.htm.

Imel, S. (1998). *Transformative learning in adulthood.* ERIC Document Reproduction Service No. ED423426.

Ingold, C. & Hart, E. (2010). Taking the "L" out of LCTLS: The STARTALK experience. *Russian Language Journal, 60: Divergent Thinking Perspectives on the Language Enterprise in the 21st Century*, 183–198.

Inspection: United States Department of State and the Broadcasting Board of Governors, Office of the Inspector General. (2013). *Inspection of the Foreign Service Institute.* www.stateoig.gov/system/files/209366.pdf.

Institute of International Education. (2018). *Open doors: Report on international educational exchange.* Retrieved from www.iie.org/Research-and-Insights/Open-Doors.

Ismail, N. & Yusof, M. (2012). Using language learning contracts as a strategy to promote learner autonomy among ESL learners. *Procedia – Social and Behavioral Sciences, 66,* 472–480.

Jacobs, G. & Farrell, T. (2003). Understanding and implementing the CLT (communicative language teaching) paradigm. *RELC Journal, 34*(1), 5–30.

Jacoby, B. (1996). *Service-learning in higher education: Concepts and practices.* San Francisco: Jossey-Bass.

Janik, D. (2005). *Unlock the genius within: Neurobiological trauma, teaching, and transformative learning.* Lanham: Rowman & Littlefield.

Janne, H. (1977). *Organisation, content and methods of adult education.* Strasbourg: Council of Europe.

Johnson, K. (1996). The vision versus the reality: The tensions of the TESOL practicum. In D. Freeman & J. Richards (eds.), *Teacher learning in language teaching* (pp. 30–49). Cambridge: Cambridge University Press.

Johnson, S. M. (2015). *Adult learning in the language classroom.* Bristol: Multilingual Matters.

Johnson, S. M. & Mullins Nelson, B. (2010). Above and beyond the syllabus: Transformation in an adult, foreign language classroom. *Language Awareness, 19*(1), 35–50.

Johnson, W. (2010) *A simulation-based approach to training operational cultural competence.* Retrieved from https://ntrs.nasa.gov/search.jsp?R=20100012877.

Johnson-Laird, P. (2010). Mental models and human reasoning. *Proceedings of the National Academy of Sciences, 107*(43), 18243–18250.

Johnstone, B. (2012). Language and place. In W. Wolfram & R. Mesthrie (eds.), *Cambridge handbook of sociolinguistics* (pp. 203–217). Cambridge: Cambridge University Press.

Jones, P. (2010). Responding to the ecological crisis: Transformative pathways for social work education. *Journal of Social Work Education, 46*(1), 67–84.

Jorden, E. & Walton, R. (1987). Truly foreign languages: Instructional challenges. *The Annals of the American Academy of Political and Social Science, 490,* 110–124.

Jung, C. (1921). *Psychologischen typen.* Zurich: Rascher Verlag.

Jung, C. (1964). *Man and his symbols.* New York: Anchor Books.

Jung, C. (1969). *Archetypes and the collective unconscious.* Princeton: Princeton University Press.

Kamin, C., O'Sullivan, P., & Deterding, R. (2002). *Does project L.I.V.E. case modality impact critical thinking in PBL groups?* Paper presented at the annual meeting of the American Educational Research Association, New Orleans, LA (ERIC Document Reproduction Service No. ED464921).

Kamisky, A. (1997). *Individual–community tensions in collaborative inquiry: Voice, action, and empowerment in context.* Unpublished doctoral dissertation, Cornell University, NY.

Kant, I. (1781). *Kritik der reinen Vernunft [Critique of pure reason].* Riga, Latvia: Johann Friedrich Hartknoch.

Kasworm, C. & Bowles, T. (2012). Fostering transformative learning in higher education settings. In E. Taylor and P. Cranton (eds.). *The handbook of transformative learning. Theory, research, and practice* (pp. 388–407). San Francisco: Jossey-Bass.

Katunich, J., Goulah, J., Badenhorst, P., & Smoicic, E. (2017). *Considering the role of applied linguistics in the sustainability crisis.* Symposium session at the Annual Conference of the American Association of Applied Linguistics, Portland, OR.

Kearney, E. (2008a). Culture learning in a changed world: Student perspectives. *Journal of Language and Literacy Education, 4*(1), 62–82.

Kearney, E. (2008b). *Developing worldview(s): An ethnography of culture learning in a foreign language classroom.* Unpublished doctoral dissertation, University of Pennsylvania, Philadelphia. Available from ProQuest Dissertations and Theses database (UMI No. 3328597).

Kearney, E. (2012). Perspective-taking and meaning-making through engagement with cultural narratives: Bringing history to life in a foreign language classroom. *L2 Journal, 4*(1), 58–82.

Kearney, E. (2016). *Intercultural learning in modern language education: Expanding meaning-making potentials.* Clevedon: Multilingual Matters.

Kearney, E. (2019). *Developing interculturality in modern language education: A professional vision perspective on current practices and future directions.* Paper presented at the annual meeting of the Modern Language Association, Chicago, IL.

Kearney, E. & Ahn, S. (2014). Preschool world language learners' engagement with language: What are the possibilities? *Language Awareness, 23*(4), 319–333.

Kearney, E. & Barbour, A. (2015). Embracing, contesting and negotiating new languages: Young children's early socialization into foreign language learning. *Linguistics and Education, 31,* 159–173.

Keefe, M. (2012). The American pipedream. Cartoon, *Herald Times,* April 13. www.intoon.com.

Keeling, R. (ed.). (2004). *Learning reconsidered: A campus-wide focus on the student experience.* Washington, DC: NASPA: Student Affairs Administrators in Higher Education and American College Personnel Association.

Keeling, R. (ed.). (2006). *Learning reconsidered 2: Implementing a campus-wide focus on the student experience.* Washington, DC: American College Personnel Association; Association of College and University Housing Officers–International; Association of College Unions International; National Association for Campus Activities; NACADA: The Global Community for Academic Advising; National Association of Student Personnel Administrators; NIRSA: Leaders in Collegiate Recreation.

Keirsey, D. & Bates, M. (1987). *Please understand me.* Del Mar: Prometheus Books.

Kelly, U. (2009). *Migration and education in a multicultural world: Culture, loss, and identity.* New York: Palgrave.

Kember, D., Wong, A., & Leung, D. (1999). Reconsidering the dimensions of approaches to learning. *British Journal of Educational Psychology, 69*(3), 323–343.

Kern, R. & Develotte, C. (eds.). (2018). *Screens and scenes: Multimodal communication in online intercultural encounters.* London: Routledge.

Khanna, T. (2014). Contextual Intelligence. *Harvard Business Review, 92*(9), 58–68.

Kiely, R. (2005). A transformative learning model for service-learning: A longitudinal case study. *Michigan Journal of Community Service Learning, 12*(1), 5–22.

King, J. (2017). Operationalizing a process for co-curricular learning: A case study. *Leadership Exchange, 15*(1), 16–17. Retrieved from www.naspa.org/publications/leadership-e.

King, K. (2000). The adult ESL experience: Facilitating perspective transformation in the classroom. *Adult Basic Education, 10*(2), 69–89.

King, K. (2004). Both sides now: Examining transformative learning and professional development of educators. *Innovative Higher Education, 29*(2), 155–174.

Kitchenham, A. (2006). Teachers and technology: A transformative journey. *Journal of Transformative Education, 4,* 202–225.

Kitchenham, A. (2008). The evolution of John Mezirow's transformative learning theory. *Journal of Transformative Education, 6*(2), 104–123.

Kitchenham, A. (2015). Transformative learning in the academy: Good aspects and missing elements. *Journal of Transformative Learning, 3*(1), 13–17.

Knowles, M. (1986). *Using learning contracts.* San Francisco: Jossey-Bass.

Korzybski, A. (1995). *Science and sanity. An introduction to non-Aristotelian systems and general semantics.* Hillview: Institute of General Semantics.

Kovan, J. & Dirkx, J. (2003). "Being called awake": The role of transformative learning in the lives of environmental activists. *Adult Education Quarterly, 53*(2), 99–118.

Kramsch, C. (1993). *Context and culture in language teaching.* Oxford: Oxford University Press.

Kramsch, C. (2002). Language and culture: A social semiotic perspective. *ADFL Bulletin, 33*(2), 8–15.

Kramsch, C. (2006). From communicative competence to symbolic competence. *Modern Language Journal, 90*(2), 249–252.

Kramsch, C. (2009). *The multilingual subject: What language learners say about their experiences and why it matters.* Oxford: Oxford University Press.

Kramsch, C. (2014). Teaching foreign languages in an era of globalization: An introduction. *The Modern Language Journal, 98*(1), 296–311.

Kramsch, C. & Thorne, S. (2002). Foreign language learning as global communicative practice. In D. Block & D. Cameron (eds.), *Language learning and teaching in the age of globalization* (pp. 83–100). London: Routledge.

Kramsch, C. & Zhang, L. (2018). *The multilingual instructor.* Oxford: Oxford University Press.

Krasner, I. (2018). Open architecture approach to teaching Russian as a foreign language. *Newsletter of the American Council of Teachers of Russian, 45*(2), 1–5.

Kristjánsson, C. (2015). Earl W. Stevick: Keeping the faith in theory and practice. *International Journal of Christianity and English Language Teaching, 2*, 62–66. ISSN 2334-1866 (online).

Kroth, M. & Cranton, P. (2014). Transformative learning and social change. In M. Kroth & P. Cranton (eds.), *Stories of transformative learning* (pp. 67–76). Rotterdam: Sense.

Kubler, C. (2001). Some thoughts on the relationship between spoken Chinese and written Chinese and implications for teaching basic-level Chinese to non-native learners. *Linguistics Study,* (Supplement for 2001), Hubei University, 12–14.

Kubler, C. (2006). *NFLC guide for basic Chinese language programs* (2nd ed.). Edited by Task Force Chair C. Kubler with Y. Biq, G. Henrichson, A. Walton, M. Wong, W. Wu, & C. Yu. Columbus: Ohio State University, National East Asian Languages Resource Center.

Kubler, C. (2017). A new perspective on the Chinese writing system and implications for teaching Chinese. In Y. Jia, C. Li, & W. Wu (eds.), *Linguistics and Chinese as a second language: Curriculum development and testing* (pp. 118–131). Hong Kong: Commercial Press.

Küchler, U. (2017). Signs, images, and narratives: Climate change across languages and cultures. In S. Siperstein, S. Hall, & S. LeMenager (eds.), *Teaching climate change in the humanities* (pp. 153–160). London: Routledge.

Kuhn, T. S. (1962). *The structure of scientific revolutions.* Chicago: University of Chicago Press.

Kukulska-Hulme, A. (2012). Language learning defined by time and place: A framework for next generation designs. In J. Diaz-Vera (ed.), *Left to my own devices: Learner autonomy and mobile-assisted language learning: Innovation and leadership in English language teaching, 6* (pp. 1–13). Bingley: Emerald Publishing.

Kumaravadivelu, B. (2003). *Beyond methods: Macrostrategies for language teaching.* New Haven: Yale University Press. www.jstor.org/stable/j.ctt1np6r2.

Labaree, D. F. (2004). *The trouble with ed schools.* New Haven: Yale University Press.

Lane, J. (2015). Expanding access to study abroad for disadvantaged students. *APCA College Student Education International*. Retrieved from www.myacpa.org/article/expanding-access-study-abroad-disadvantaged-students-0.

Lange, E. (2004). Transformative and restorative learning: A vital dialectic for sustainable societies. *Adult Education Quarterly*, *54*, 121–139.

Lawrence, R. & Cranton, P. (2009). What you see depends on how you look: A photographic journey of transformative learning. *Journal of Transformative Education*, *7*, 312–331.

Leaver, B. L. (1989). Dismantling classroom walls for increased foreign language proficiency. *Foreign Language Annals*, *22*(1), 67–74.

Leaver, B. L. (2018). Front page dialogue: Transforming Russian classrooms through transformative education. *Newsletter of the American Council of Teachers of Russian*, *30*(1), 2–6.

Leaver, B. L. & Bilstein, P. (2000). Content, language, and task in content-based instruction. In R. Kecht & K. von Hammerstein (eds.), *Languages across the curriculum: Interdisciplinary structures, intersections of knowledge, and internationalized education*. Columbus: Ohio State University Press.

Leaver, B. L. & Campbell, C. (2015). Experience with higher levels of proficiency. In T. Brown & J. Bown (eds.), *To advanced proficiency and beyond: Theory and methods for developing superior second-language ability* (pp. 3–22). Washington, DC: Georgetown University Press.

Leaver, B. L. & Campbell, C. (2020). The shifting paradigm in Russian language programs from communicative language teaching to transformative language learning and teaching. In E. Dengub, I. Dubinina, & J. Merrill (eds.), *Art of teaching Russian*. Washington, DC: Georgetown University Press.

Leaver, B. L. & Cleret, E. (2018). Developing intercultural competence and idiocultural transformation in foreign language programs. In M. Welsch, V. Marsick, & D. Holt (eds.), *Building transformative community: Exacting possibility in today's times. Proceedings of the xiii biennial transformative learning conference* (pp. 405–411). New York: Teachers College, Columbia University.

Leaver, B. L. & Granoien, N. (2000). Философия образования: Почему мы преподаем определенными путями. [Philosophy of education: Why we teach the way we do]. *Философия Образования* [*Philosophy of Education*], *1*(1), 3–9.

Leaver, B. L., Campbell, C. M., Nyikos, M., & Oxford, R. L. (2019). *Transforming the transformers: Breaking through philosophical, cognitive, and emotional barriers*. Paper presented at the Society, Identity, and Transformation in Language Teacher Education Conference, University of Minnesota.

Le Doux, J. (1998). *The emotional brain: The mysterious underpinnings of emotional life*. New York: Simon & Schuster.

Lee, C., Curtis, J., & Curran, M. (2018). Shaping the vision for service-learning in language education. *Foreign Language Annals, 51,* 169–184. doi: 10.1111/flan.12329.

Lee, L. (1997). Using portfolios to develop L2 cultural knowledge and awareness of students in intermediate Spanish. *Hispania, 80,* 355–367.

Lee, N., Mikesell, L., Joaquin, A., Mates, A., & Schumann, J. (2009). *The interactional instinct: The evolution and acquisition of language.* New York: Oxford University Press.

Leeman, J., Rabin, L., & Román-Mendoza, E. (2011). Critical pedagogy beyond the classroom walls: Community service-learning and Spanish heritage language education. *Heritage Language Journal, 8*(3), 293–314.

Lefebvre, H. (1991). *The production of space.* Oxford: Blackwell.

Lewis, M. (2005). Bridging emotion theory and neurobiology through dynamic systems modeling. *Behavior and Brain Science, 28*(2), 169–245.

Liddicott, A. & Scarino, A. (2013). *Intercultural language teaching and learning.* Chichester: Wiley-Blackwell.

Little, D., Dam, L., & Legenhausen, L. (2017). *Language learner autonomy: Theory, practice and research.* Bristol: Multilingual Matters.

Little, D. & Kirwan, D. (2018a). Translanguaging as a key to educational success. In P. Van Avermaet, S. Slembrouk, K. Van Gorp, S. Sierens, & K. Maryns (eds.), *The multilingual edge of education* (pp. 313–339). London: Palgrave Macmillan.

Little, D. & Kirwan, D. (2018b). From plurilingual repertoires to language awareness: Developing primary pupils' proficiency in the language of schooling. In C. Frijns, K. Van Gorp, C. Hélot, & S. Sierens (eds.), *Language awareness in multilingual classrooms in Europe* (pp. 169–205). Berlin: Mouton de Gruyter.

Little, D. & Kirwan, D. (2019). *Engaging with linguistic diversity: A study of educational inclusion in an Irish primary school.* London: Bloomsbury Academic.

Lortie, D. (1975). *Schoolteacher: A sociological study.* Chicago: University of Chicago Press.

Lyu, H. (2018). Learning through discussion in a high-level language course. *Dialog on Language Instruction, 28*(1), 65–72.

MacIntyre, P. (2002). Motivation, anxiety, and emotion in second language acquisition. In P. Robinson (ed.), *Individual differences and instructed language learning* (pp. 45–68). Amsterdam: John Benjamins.

MacPherson, S. (2003). TESOL for biolinguistic sustainability: The ecology of English as a lingua mundi. *TESL Canada Journal, 20*(2), 1–22.

MacPherson, S. (2010). *Education and sustainability: Learning across the diaspora, indigenous, and minority divide.* London: Routledge.

Maffi, L. (ed.). (2001). *On biocultural diversity: Linking language, knowledge, and the environment.* Washington, DC: Smithsonian Institute Press.

Mahatmya, D., Brown, R., & Johnson, A. (2014). Student-as-client. *Phi Delta Kappan*, *95*(6), 30–34.

Maki, P. (2010). *Assessing for learning: Building a sustainable commitment across the institution*. Sterling: Stylus Publishing.

Makiguchi, T. (1981–1988). *Makiguchi Tsunesaburo zenshu [The complete works of Tsunesaburo Makiguchi]*. 10 Vols. Tokyo: Daisan Bunmeisha.

Markos, L. & McWhinney, W. (2004). Editors' perspectives: Building on and toward a shared vision. *Journal of Transformative Education*, *2*(2), 75–78.

Martin, K. (2016). *TEDx talks. Teachers create what they experience*. May 10. YouTube.

Martínez, J. (2017). *Realization of a language-as-resource orientation in language immersion mathematics classrooms*. North American Chapter of the International Group for the Psychology of Mathematics Education.

Martusewicz, R., Edmundson, J., & Lupinacci, J. (2011). *Ecojustice education: Toward diverse, democratic, and sustainable communities*. New York: Routledge.

Maslow, A. (1970). *Motivation and personality* (rev. ed.). New York: Harper & Row.

Maslow, A. (1971). *The farther reaches of human nature*. New York: Penguin Compass.

Matthiesson, C. (2009). Meaning in the making: Meaning potential emerging from acts of meaning. *Language Learning*, *59*(1), 206–229.

May, S. (2014). Introducing the multilingual turn. In S. May (ed.), *The multilingual turn: Implications for SLA, TESOL, and bilingual education* (pp. 1–6). New York: Routledge.

McBrien, J. (2005). Educational needs and barriers for refugee students in the United States: A review of the literature. *Review of Educational Research*, *75*(3), 329–364.

McClinton, J. (2005). Transformative learning: The English as a second language teacher's experience. *The CATESOL Journal*, *17*(1), 156–163.

McGuire, S. (2015). *Teach students how to learn: Strategies you can incorporate into any course to improve student metacognition, study skills, and motivation*. Sterling: Stylus Publishing.

McInerney, P., Smyth, J., & Down, B. (2011). "Coming to a place near you?" The politics and possibilities of a critical pedagogy of place-based education. *Asia-Pacific Journal of Teacher Education*, *39*(1), 3–16.

McTighe, J. & Wiggins, G. (2013). *Essential questions: Opening doors to student understanding*. Alexandria: Association for Supervision and Curriculum Development.

Mead, M. (2008). Margaret Mead. www.brainyquote.com/quotes/margaret_mead_100502Mead.

Menke, M. R. & Paesani, K. (2019). Analysing foreign language instructional materials through the lens of the multiliteracies framework. *Language, Culture, and Curriculum*, *32*(1), 34–39.

Merriam, S. & Bierema, L. (2014). *Adult learning: Linking theory with practice.* San Francisco: Jossey-Bass.

Mezirow, J. (1978a). *Education for perspective transformation: Women's re-entry programs in community colleges.* New York: Center for Adult Education, Teachers College, Columbia University.

Mezirow, J. (1978b). Perspective transformation. *Adult Education Quarterly, 28*(2), 100–110.

Mezirow, J. (1981). A critical theory of adult learning and education. *Adult Education Quarterly, 32*(1), 3–24.

Mezirow, J. (1990a). *Fostering critical reflection in adulthood: A guide to transformative and emancipatory learning.* San Francisco: Jossey-Bass.

Mezirow, J. (1990b). How critical reflection triggers transformative learning. In J. Mezirow (ed.). *Fostering critical reflection in adulthood: A guide to transformative and emancipatory learning* (pp. 1–20). San Francisco: Jossey-Bass.

Mezirow, J. (1991). *Transformative dimensions of adult learning.* San Francisco: Jossey-Bass.

Mezirow, J. (1994). Understanding transformation theory. *Adult Education Quarterly, 44*(4), 222–240.

Mezirow, J. (1995). Transformation theory of adult learning. In M. Welton (ed.), *In defense of the lifeworld: Critical perspectives on adult learning* (pp. 39–70). New York: SUNY Press.

Mezirow, J. (1996). Contemporary paradigms of learning. *Adult Education Quarterly, 46*(3), 158–172.

Mezirow, J. (1997). Transformative learning: Theory to practice. *New Directions for Adult and Continuing Education, 74,* 5–12.

Mezirow, J. (1998). On critical reflection. *Adult Education Quarterly, 48*(3), 185–198.

Mezirow, J. (2000). Learning to think like an adult: Core concepts of transformation theory. In J. Mezirow & Associates (eds.), *Learning as transformation: Critical perspectives on a theory in progress* (pp. 3–33). San Francisco: Jossey-Bass.

Mezirow, J. (2003a). Transformative learning as discourse. *Journal of Transformative Education, 1*(1), 58–63.

Mezirow, J. (2003b). *The ten phases of transformational learning.* https://sites .google.com/site/transformativelearning/elements-of-the-theory-1.

Mezirow, J. (2006). An overview of transformative learning. In P. Sutherland & J. Crowther (eds.), *Lifelong learning: Concepts and contexts* (pp. 24–38). New York: Routledge.

Mezirow, J. (2012). Learning to think like an adult: Core concepts of transformation theory. In E. Taylor and P. Cranton (eds.), *The handbook of transformative learning. Theory, research, and practice* (pp. 73–95). San Francisco: Jossey-Bass.

Mezirow, J. & Taylor, E. (eds.). (2009). *Transformative learning in practice: Insights from community, workplace and higher education.* San Francisco: Jossey-Bass.

Mezirow, J. and Associates (2000). *Learning as transformation: Critical perspectives on a theory in progress.* San Francisco: Jossey-Bass.

Miller, J. P. & Seller, W. (1985). *Curriculum: Perspectives and practice.* Boston: Addison-Wesley.

Miller, T. (2017). *Storming the wall: Climate change, migration, and homeland security.* San Francisco: City Light Books.

Mitchell, R. & Myles, F. (2004). *Second language learning theories* (2nd ed.). London: Edward Arnold.

Moeller, A. & Nugent, K. (2014). Building intercultural competence in the language classroom. In S. Dhonau (ed.), *Unlock the gateway to communication. Central States language report* (pp. 1–18). Eau Claire: Crown Prints.

Monazamfar, G. (2017). *Culture and language understanding through movies.* Unpublished master's capstone project, School of Computing and Design, California State University at Monterey Bay, Seaside, CA.

Moon, J. (2006). *Learning journals. A handbook for reflective practice and professional development* (2nd ed.). New York: Routledge.

Muhammed, F. (2018). *Pashto cultural orientation.* Unpublished master's capstone project, School of Computing and Design, California State University at Monterey Bay, Seaside, California.

Murphy, D. & Evans-Romaine, K. (eds.). (2017). *Exploring the US Language Flagship program: Professional competence in a second language by graduation.* Bristol: Multilingual Matters.

Murphy, D., Evans-Romaine, K., & Zheltoukhova, S. (2012). Student and tutor perspectives of tutoring in a Russian Flagship program. *Russian Language Journal, 62,* 107–127.

Murphy, D., Evans-Romaine, K., Anishchenkova, V., & Jing-Schmidt, Zh. (2017). Laying the groundwork: Programmatic models in US Language Flagship programs. In D. Murphy & K. Evans-Romaine (eds.), *Exploring the US Language Flagship program: Professional competence in a second language by graduation* (pp. 29–50). Bristol: Multilingual Matters.

Murphy, M. & Fleming, T. (2012). *Habermas, critical theory and education.* London: Routledge.

Murphy-Judy, K. & Quinlan, J. (2018) Tech, media, & engaging learners in new learning outcomes. In *Distance learning SIG webinar 2028,* Wednesday December 12, 2018. Retrieved from https://community.actfl.org/viewdocument/re upcomingwebinar?CommunityKey=ff3b683b-1041-422a-862e-4c9f045134de&tabion=librarydocuments.

Myers, I. B. & Myers, P. B. (1995). *Gifts differing: Understanding personality type.* Palo Alto: Consulting Psychologists Press.

NAFSA (Association of International Educators). (2018). *Trends in U.S. study abroad.* Retrieved from www.nafsa.org/Policy_and_Advocacy/Policy_Resources/Policy Trends and Data/Trends in US Study Abroad/.

Nation, I. & Newton, J. (2009). *Teaching ESL/EFL listening and speaking.* New York: Routledge.

Nemtchinova, E. (2014). Developing information literacy skills in the beginning language classroom: A case for webquests. *Russian Language Journal, 64,* 83–109.

Nettle, D. & Romaine, S. (2000). *Vanishing voices: The extinction of the world's languages.* New York: Oxford University Press.

Nugent, M. & Slater, R. (2017). The Language Flagship: Creating expectations and opportunities for professional-level language learning in undergraduate education. In D. Murphy & K. Evans-Romaine (eds.), *Exploring the US Language Flagship program: Professional competence in a second language by graduation* (pp. 9–28). Bristol: Multilingual Matters.

Nunan, D. (1988). *The learner-centered curriculum: A study in second language teaching.* Cambridge: Cambridge University Press.

Nunan, D. (1997a). Designing and adapting materials to encourage learner autonomy. In P. Benson & P. Voller (eds.), *Autonomy and independence in language learning* (pp. 192–203). London: Longman.

Nunan, D. (1997b). Does learner strategy training make a difference? *Lenguas Modernas, 24,* 123–142.

Nunan, D. (2006a). *Go for it! Energizing your classes: A learner-centered approach.* Retrieved from www.david.nunan.com.

Nunan, D. (2006b). *Task-based language teaching.* Cambridge: Cambridge University Press.

Ohta, A. (2017). Sociocultural theory and second/foreign language education. In N. Van Deusen-Scholl & S. May (eds.), *The encyclopedia of language and education, Volume 4: Foreign and second language education* (pp. 57–68). Dordrecht: Springer.

Ortega, L. (2010). *The bilingual turn in SLA.* Plenary speech delivered at the American Association for Applied Linguistics Conference, Atlanta, GA.

Ortega, L. (2011). SLA after the social turn: Where cognitivism and its alternatives stand. In D. Atkinson (ed.), *Alternative approaches to second language acquisition* (pp. 167–180). New York: Routledge.

Osborn, T. (2006). *Teaching world languages for social justice: A sourcebook of principles and practices.* Mahwah: Lawrence Erlbaum Associates.

Osterling, J. & Webb, W. (2009). On becoming a bilingual teacher: A transformative process for preservice and novice teachers. *Journal of Transformative Education, 7*(4), 267–293.

O'Sullivan, E. (1999). *Transformative learning: Educational vision for the 21st century.* New York: Zed Books.

O'Sullivan, E. (2002). The project and vision of transformative education: Integral transformative learning. In A. Morrell, M. O'Connor, & E. O'Sullivan (eds.), *Expanding the boundaries of transformative learning* (pp. 1–12). New York: Palgrave Macmillan.

O'Sullivan, E. (2008). Finding our way in the great work. *Journal of Transformative Education, 6*(1), 27–32.

O'Sullivan, E. & Taylor, M. (eds.). (2004). *Learning toward an ecological consciousness: Selected transformative practices.* New York: Palgrave.

O'Sullivan, E., Morrell, A., & O'Connor, M. (eds). (2002). *Expanding the boundaries of transformative learning: Essays on theory and praxis.* New York: Palgrave.

Oxford, R. L. (n.d.) *An informal study of applications of Mezirow's and Dirkx's transformational learning processes to language teacher education.* Birmingham: University of Alabama at Birmingham.

Oxford, R. L. (1990). *Language learning strategies: What every teacher should know.* New York: Newbury House Publisher.

Oxford, R. L. (1996). When emotion meets (meta)cognition in language learning histories. In A. Moeller (ed.), *The teaching of culture and language in the second language classroom: Focus on the learner. International Journal of Educational Research, 23*(7, special issue), 581–594.

Oxford, R. L. (2015). Emotion as the amplifier and the primary motive: Some theories of emotion with relevance to language learning. In S. Ryan & S. Mercer (eds.), *Psychology and language learning. Studies in Second Language Learning and Teaching, 5*(3, special issue), 371–393. doi: 10.14746/ ssllt.2015.5.3.2.

Oxford, R. L. (2016a). Creation spirituality as a spiritual research paradigm drawing on many faiths. In J. Lin, R. L. Oxford, & T. Culham (eds.), *Toward a spiritual research paradigm: Exploring new ways of knowing, researching and being* (pp. 199–232). Charlotte: Information Age Publishing.

Oxford, R. L. (2016b). Toward a psychology of well-being for language learners: The "EMPATHICS" vision. In P. MacIntyre, T. Gregersen, & S. Mercer (eds.), *Positive psychology in second language acquisition* (pp. 10–87). Bristol: Multilingual Matters.

Oxford, R. L. (2017). *Teaching and researching language learning strategies: Self-regulation in context* (2nd ed.). London: Routledge.

Oxford, R. L. (2018). EMPATHICS: A complex dynamic systems (CDS) vision of language learner well-being. In J. Liontas (ed.), *The TESOL encyclopedia of English language teaching.* San Francisco: Wiley & Sons. doi: 10.1002/9781118784235.eelt0953.

Oxford, R. L. (in press). Teaching and researching listening skills: Theory and research-based practices. In N. Polat, T. Gregersen, & P. MacIntyre (eds.), *Research-driven pedagogy: Implications of L2 theory and research for the teaching of language skills.* New York: Routledge.

Paesani, K. W., Allen, H. W., Dupuy, B., Liskin-Gasparro, J. E., & Laconte, M. (2016). *A multiliteracies framework for collegiate foreign language teaching.* New York: Pearson.

Palmer, D. (2019). *Critical consciousness at the core: Addressing inequities in dual-language bilingual education.* Paper presented at the Expanding the Education Research Agenda for Multilingual Language Learners: An AERA-TESOL Collaborative Symposium (Symposium session: "Leveraging education research in a 'post-truth' era – Multimodal narratives to democratize evidence"), annual meeting of the American Educational Research Association, Toronto, Canada.

Paluck, E. & Green, D. (2008). Prejudice reduction: What works? A review and assessment of research and practice. *Annual Review of Psychology, 60,* 339–359.

Pellegrino-Aveni, V. (2005). *Study abroad and second language use: Constructing the self.* Cambridge: Cambridge University Press.

Pellettieri, J. (2011). Measuring language-related outcomes of community-based learning in intermediate Spanish courses. *Hispania, 94*(2), 285–302.

Pennycook, A. (2001). *Critical applied linguistics: A critical introduction.* Mahwah: Lawrence Erlbaum Associates.

Pennycook, A. (2004). Language policy and the ecological turn. *Language Policy, 3*(3), 213–239. doi: 10.1007/s10993-004-3533-x.

Pennycook, A. (2017). *Posthumanist applied linguistics.* London: Routledge.

Pérez, B. (2017). Literacy, diversity, and programmatic responses. In T. McCarty, L. Watahomigie, T. Dien, B. Perez, & M. Torres-Guzman (eds.), *Sociocultural contexts of language and literacy* (pp. 5–24). London: Routledge.

Perry, W. (1981). Cognitive and ethical growth: The making of meaning. In A. Chickering et al. (eds.), *The modern American college* (pp. 76–116). San Francisco: Jossey-Bass.

Pettigrew, T. F. & Tropp, L. R. (2008). How does intergroup contact reduce prejudice? Meta-analytic tests of three mediators. *European Journal of Social Psychology, 38*(6), 922–934.

Piaget, J. (1981). *Intelligence and affectivity: Their relationship during child development.* Palo Alto: Annual Reviews.

Pierce, G. (2013). Transformative learning theory and spirituality. *Journal of Instructional Research, 2,* 30–42.

Platero, R. & Drager, E. (2015). Two trans* teachers in Madrid: Interrogating trans*formative pedagogies. *TSQ, 2*(3), 447–463.

Polinsky, M. & Kagan, O. (2007). Heritage languages: In the "wild" and in the classroom. *Language and Linguistics Compass, 1*(5), 368–395.

Popham, W. (2008). *Transformative assessment.* Alexandria: Association for Supervision and Curriculum Development.

Pugh, K. J., Linnenbrink-Garcia, L., Koskey, K. L. K., Stewart, V. C., & Manzey, C. (2010). Motivation, learning, and transformative experience: A study of deep engagement in science. *Science Education, 94,* 1–28.

Randolph, L. & Johnson, S. (2017). Social justice in the language classroom: A call to action. *Dimension,* 9–31.

Reagan, T. & Osborn, T. (eds.). (2012). *The foreign language educator in society: Toward a critical pedagogy.* Mahwah: Lawrence Erlbaum Associates.

Rhodes, T. (2010). *Assessing outcomes and improving achievement: Tips and tools for using rubrics.* Washington, DC: Association of American Colleges and Universities.

Richards, J. (2015). The changing face of language learning: Learning beyond the classroom. *RELC Journal, 46*(1), 5–22.

Rivers, W. M. (1973). From linguistic competence to communicative competence. *TESOL Quarterly, 7*(1), 25–34.

Rogers, C. (1969/1986). *Freedom to learn: A view of what education might become* (2nd ed.). Indianapolis: Merrill Publishing Company.

Rogers, C. (1978). The formative tendency. *Journal of Humanistic Psychology, 18*(1), 23–26.

Rogers, C. (1995). *A way of being.* Boston: Houghton-Mifflin.

Rosa, J. & Flores, N. (2017). Unsettling race and language: Toward a raciolinguistic perspective. *Language in Society, 46*(5), 621–647.

Rundle, N. (2016). *Guidelines for good assessment practice* (3rd ed.). Hobart, Tasmania: Tasmanian Institute of Learning and Teaching, University of Tasmania. www.teaching-learning.utas.edu.au/__data/assets/pdf_file/0004/158674/Guidelines-for-Good-Assessment_3rd-ed.pdf.

Rymes, B. (2014). *Communicating beyond language: Everyday encounters with diversity.* New York: Routledge.

Saavedra, E. (1995). *Teacher transformation: Creating text and contexts in study groups.* Unpublished doctoral dissertation, University of Arizona, Tucson.

Sacco, S. J. (2014). Integrating foreign languages and cultures into U.S. international business programs: Best practices and future considerations. *Journal of Teaching in International Business, 25*, 235–249.

Savicki, V., Binder, F., & Heller, L. (2008). Contrasts and changes in potential and actual psychological intercultural adjustment. In V. Slavicki (ed.), *Developing intercultural competence and transformation* (pp. 111–127). New York: Wiley.

Saydee, F. (2016). Less commonly taught languages: Factors that shape teachers' beliefs and guide their practices. *Journal of the National Council of Less Commonly Taught Languages.* Retrieved from www.ncolctl.org/jncolctl/jncolctl-editions.

Scherer, K. (1999). Appraisal theory. In T. Dalgleish & M. Power (eds.), *Handbook of cognition and emotion* (pp. 637–663). New York: John Wiley & Sons.

Schumann, J. (1997). *The neurobiology of affect in language.* Malden: Blackwell.

Seals, C. (2018). Positive and negative identity practices in heritage language education. *International Journal of Multilingualism, 15*(4), 329–348.

Shekhtman, B. S. (2003). *How to improve your foreign language immediately.* Hollister: MSI Press.

Shekhtman, B. S. (2013). *How to improve your foreign language immediately.* Virginia Beach: Villa Magna.

Shekhtman, B. S. & Leaver, B. L., with Lord, N., Kuznetsova, E., & Ovtcharenko, E. (2002). Developing profession-level oral proficiency: The Shekhtman method of communicative teaching. In B. L. Leaver & B. S. Shekhtman (eds.), *Developing professional-level foreign language proficiency* (pp. 1–10). Cambridge: Cambridge University Press.

Shrum, J. & Glisan, E. (2015). *Teachers handbook: Contextualized language instruction* (World languages; 5th ed.). Boston: Cengage.

Siemens, G. (2005). Connectivism: A learning theory for the digital age. *International Journal of Instructional Technology & Distance Learning 2*(1). www.edtechpolicy.org/AAASGW/Session2/siemens_article.pdf.

Sifakis, N. C. & Kordia, S. (2019). Promoting transformative learning through English as a *lingua franca*: An empirical study. In T. Fleming, A. Kokkos, & F. Finnegan (eds.), *European perspectives on transformation theory* (pp. 177–192). Cham: Palgrave Macmillan.

Sifuentes, E. (2008). Proposition 227: Ten years later. *The San Diego Union-Tribune.* Retrieved from www.sandiegouniontribune.com/sdut-education-proposition-227-10-years-later-2008nov08-story.html.

Sigelman, C. K. & Rider, E. A. (2012). *Life-span human development* (7th ed.). Belmont: Wadsworth.

Sigmon, R. (1979). Service learning: Three principles. *Action, 8*(1), 9–11.

Sigmon, R. (1994). *Serving to learn, learning to serve. Linking service with learning.* Report of Council for Independent Colleges.

Slavich, G. & Zimbardo, P. (2012). Transformational teaching: Theoretical underpinnings, basic principles, and core methods. *Educational Psychology Review, 24*(4), 569–608.

Smagulova, J. (2017). Ideologies of language revival: Kazakh as school talk. *International Journal of Bilingualism 2019, 23*(3), 740–756.

Smailova, A. (ed.). (2011). *Itogi natsional'noi perepisi naseleniia Respubliki Kazakhstan 2009 goda. Analiticheskii otchet.* Astana: Statistics Committee of the Kazakhstan Ministry of the National Economy.

Smith, D. & Osborn, T. (eds.). (2007). *Spirituality, social justice, and language learning.* Charlotte: Information Age.

Snyder, C. (2008). Grabbing hold of a moving target: Identifying and measuring the transformative learning process. *Journal of Transformative Education, 6*(3), 159–181.

Snyder-Renfro, C. (2019). *Leaving the cave: Transformative learning for Generation Z with social emotional learning.* Paper presented at the Transformative Learning Conference, Oklahoma City, OK.

Sobel, D. (2004). *Place-based education: Connecting classrooms & communities.* Great Barrington: The Orion Society.

Soja, E. (2003). Writing the city spatially. *City, 7*(3), 269–280.

Sosulski, M. (2013). From Broadway to Berlin: Transformative learning through German hip-hop. *Die Unterrichtspraxis/Teaching German, 46*(1), 91–105.

Spring, M. (2012). Language for specific purposes curriculum in the context of Chinese Language Flagship programs. *Modern Language Journal, 96*(1), 140–157.

Spring, M. (2015). The monolingual international: Support of language learning through national initiatives. *ADFL Bulletin, 43*(2), 19–25.

Stansberry, S. & Kymes, A. (2007). Transformative learning through "teaching with technology" electronic portfolios. *Journal of Adolescent and Adult Literacy, 50*(6), 488–496.

Stearns, P. (ed.). (2018). *Peacebuilding through dialogue: Education, human transformation, and conflict resolution.* Fairfax: George Mason University Press.

Stein-Smith, K. (2016). The role of multilingualism in effectively addressing global issues: The sustainable development goals and beyond. *Theory and Practice in Language Studies, 6*(12): 2254–2259.

Sternberg, R. & Grigorenko, E. (2002). *Dynamic testing: The nature and measurement of learning potential.* Cambridge: Cambridge University Press.

Stevick, E. (1990). *Humanism in language teaching.* New York: Oxford University Press.

Stibbe, A. (2015). *Ecolinguistics: Language, ecology and the stories we live by.* New York: Routledge.

Stryker, S. & Leaver, B. L. (eds.). (1997). *Content-based instruction in foreign language education: Models and methods.* Washington, DC: Georgetown University Press.

Sun, Q. (2013). Learning for transformation in a changing landscape. *Adult Learning, 24*(3), 131–136.

Swartz, A. & Sprow, K. (2010). *Is complexity science embedded in transformative learning?* Paper presented at the Adult Education Research Conference, Sacramento, CA. Retrieved from http://newprairiepress.org/aerc/2010/papers/73.

Tadayon, F. & Khodi, A. (2016). Empowerment of refugees by language: Can ESL learners affect the target culture? *TESL Canada Journal, 33*, 129–137.

Taketa, K. (2018) Chula Vista Elementary getting state, national recognition for equity work, high performance. *San Diego Union-Tribune*, November 27. Retrieved from https://www.sandiegouniontribune.com/news/education/sd-me-chula-vista-elementary-20181121-story.html.

Taloyan, M., Johansson, L., Saleh-Stattin, N., & Al-Windi, A. (2011). Acculturation strategies in migration stress among Kurdish men in Sweden: A narrative approach. *American Journal of Men's Health, 5*(3), 198–207.

Tankersley, D. (2001). Bombs or bilingual programmes? Dual-language immersion, transformative education, and community building in Macedonia. *International Journal of Bilingual Education and Bilingualism, 4*(2), 107–124.

Tarone, E. (2017). *Exploring learner language in language teacher education.* Paper presented at the pre-conference workshop at the Tenth International Conference on Language Teacher Education, University of California, Los Angeles, CA.

Tavares, J. & Potter, L. (2018). *Project-based learning applied to the language classroom*. São Paulo: Teach-In Education.

Taylor, E. (1993) *A learning model of becoming interculturally competent: A transformative process*. Unpublished doctoral dissertation, University of Georgia, Athens.

Taylor, E. (1998). *The theory and practice of transformative learning: A critical review*. ERIC Clearinghouse on Adult, Career, and Vocational Education (Information Series No. 374). Center on Education and Training for Employment. Columbus: The Ohio State University.

Taylor, E. (2008). Transformative learning theory. In S. Merriam (ed.), *Third update of adult learning. New directions for adult and continuing education, No. 119* (pp. 5–15). San Francisco: Jossey-Bass.

Taylor, E. (2009). Fostering transformative learning. In J. Mezirow and E. Taylor (eds.), *Transformative learning in practice: Insights from community, workplace, and higher education* (pp. 3–17). New York: Jossey Bass.

Taylor, E. (2017). Critical reflection and transformative learning: A critical review. *PAACE Journal of Lifelong Learning, 26*, 77–95.

Taylor, E. & Cranton, P. (eds.). (2012). *The handbook of transformative learning: Theory, research, and practice*. San Francisco: Jossey-Bass.

The National Clearinghouse for English Language Acquisition. (2012). *Promising practices in instruction: Sherman Academy, California: Where parents and teachers work together*. Washington, DC. Retrieved from www.ncela.gwu.edu/files/uploads/promising_EL/sherman.pdf.

The National Standards Collaborative Board. (2019). *World-Readiness standards for learning languages* (4th ed.). Alexandria: Author. www.actfl.org/sites/default/files/publications/standards/World-ReadinessStandardsforLearningLanguages.pdf.

The New London Group. (1996). A pedagogy of multiliteracies: Designing social futures. *Harvard Educational Review, 66*(1), 60–93.

Thomas, B. (2012). Meaning on the brain: How your mind organizes reality. *Scientific American Blog*. Retrieved from https://blogs.scientificamerican.com/guest-blog/meaning-on-the-brain-how-your-mind-organizes-reality/.

Thomas, I. (2009). Critical thinking, transformative learning, sustainable education, and problem-based learning in universities. *Journal of Transformative Education, 7*(3), 245–264.

Thorne, S., Black, R., & Sykes, J. (2009). Second language use, socialization, and learning in internet interest communities and online gaming. *The Modern Language Journal, 98*(1), 802–821.

Tillich, P. (1948). *The shaking of the foundations*. New York: Scribner.

Tillich, P. (2012). *The shaking of the foundations* (rev. ed.). Eugene: Wipf & Stock.

Torres-Guzman, M. (2002). *Dual language programs: Key features and results*. National Clearinghouse for English Language Acquisition. Retrieved from https://ncela.ed.gov/rcd/bibliography/BE021969.

United Nations. (2015). *Sustainable Development Goals*. Retrieved from https://sustainabledevelopment.un.org/sdgs.

United Nations High Commission on Refugees. (2018). *What is a refugee?* UNHCR. Retrieved from www.unrefugees.org/refugee-facts/what-is-a-refugee/.

Urbain, O. (2010). *Daisaku Ikeda's philosophy of peace: Dialogue, transformation and global citizenship*. New York: I. B. Tauris.

USGCRP (US Global Change Research Program). (2018). *Impacts, risks, and adaptation in the United States: Fourth national climate assessment, Volume II. Report-in-brief* (D. Reidmiller, C. Avery, D. Easterling, K. Kunkel, K. Lewis, T. Maycock, & B. Stewart [eds.]). Washington, DC: US Government Printing Office.

Van Lier, L. (1996). *Interaction in the language curriculum: Awareness, autonomy and authenticity*. Milton Park: Taylor & Francis.

Van Lier, L. (2004). *The ecology and semiotics of language learning: A sociocultural perspective*. Boston: Springer.

Vidal, E. & Tjaden, J. (2018). *Global migration indicators: Insights from the global migration data portal*. Retrieved from http://publications.iom.int/system/files/pdf/global_migration_indicators_2018.pdf.

Von Vacano, M. et al. (1992). *Two-way partial immersion program*. F. S. Key Elementary School. Arlington Public Schools, VA. Washington, DC: Center for Applied Linguistics.

Vygotsky, L. (1930). *Mind and society: The development of higher psychological processes*. Cambridge: Harvard University Press.

Vygotsky, L. (1930/1997). On psychological systems. In R. Rieber & J. Wollock (eds.), *The collected works of L. S. Vygotsky* (Vol. *3: Problems of the theory and history of psychology*, pp. 91–108). New York: Plenum Press.

Vygotsky, L. (1934/1986). *Thought and language*. Revised and edited by A. Kozulin. Cambridge: MIT Press.

Vygotsky, L. (1978/2013). Interaction between learning and development. In M. Cole, V. John-Steiner, S. Scribner, & E. Souberman (eds.), *Mind in society: The development of higher psychological processes*. Cambridge: Harvard University Press.

Vygotsky, L. (1987). Thinking and speech. In R. Rieber & A. Chickering (eds.), *The collected works of L. S. Vygotsky (Vol. 1: Problems of general psychology)*. New York: Plenum.

Vygotsky, L. (1997). *Thought and language* (rev. ed.). Cambridge: MIT Press.

Walker, A., Shafer, J., & Iiams, M. (2004). Not in my classroom: Teacher attitudes towards English language learners in the mainstream classroom. *NABE Journal of Research and Practice*, 2(1), 130–160.

Walker, G. & McGinnis, S. (1995). *Learning less commonly taught languages: An agreement on the bases for the training of teachers*. Columbus: The Ohio State University.

Wang, Y. (2018). *A study on transformative learning of UK students in China and Chinese students in the UK.* Unpublished Doctor of Philosophy dissertation, University of Edinburgh, UK.

Ward, C. (2008). Thinking outside the berry boxes: New perspectives on identity, acculturation, and intercultural relations. *International Journal of Intercultural Relations, 23*(2), 105–114.

Warner, C. & Dupuy, B. (2018), Moving toward multiliteracies in foreign language teaching: Past and present perspectives ... and beyond. *Foreign Language Annals, 51*(1), 116–128.

Watts, A. (1999). *The way of Zen.* New York: Vintage.

Weimer, M. (2002). *Learner-centered teaching: Five key changes to practice.* New York: John Wiley & Sons.

Wenden, A. (1991). *Learner strategies for learner autonomy.* Upper Saddle River: Prentice Hall.

World Bank. (2015). *World development report 2015: Mind, society, and behavior.* Washington, DC: World Bank. Retrieved from www.worldbank.org/content/dam/Worldbank/Publications/WDR/WDR%202015/.

Yorks, L. & Kasl, E. (2006). I know more than I can say: A taxonomy for using expressive ways of knowing to foster transformative learning. *Journal of Transformative Education, 4*(1), 43–64.

Zajonc, A. (2006). Love and knowledge: Recovering the heart of learning through contemplation. *Teachers College Record, 108*(9), 1742–1759.

Zapata, G. (2018). L2 Spanish university students' perceptions of the pedagogical benefits of culture portfolios. In *Language, culture, and curriculum* (Vol. 31). London: Taylor & Francis Group.

Zheng, X. & Gao, Y. (2017). Facilitating transformative learning toward productive bilingualism: Innovations in teaching English for intercultural communication in China. In H. Reinders, D. Nunan, & B. Zou (eds.), *Innovation in language learning and teaching: New language learning and teaching environments* (pp. 261–287). London: Palgrave Macmillan.

Index

Printed in the USA
CPSIA information can be obtained
at www.ICGtesting.com
LVHW020318010224
770514LV00003B/337